M000236123

Rebound

Rebound

The Dennis Rodman Story

Dennis Rodman, Pat Rich, and Alan Steinberg

Crown Publishers, Inc.
New York

Published by Crown Publishers, Inc., 201 East 50th Street, New York, New York 10022. Member of the Crown Publishing Group.

Random House, Inc. New York, Toronto, London, Sydney, Auckland

CROWN is a trademark of Crown Publishers, Inc.

Manufactured in the United States of America

Library of Congress Cataloging-in-Publication Data
Rodman, Dennis, 1961–
Rebound : the Dennis Rodman story
/ by Dennis Rodman, Pat Rich, and Alan Steinberg.—1st ed.
p.   cm.
1. Rodman, Dennis, 1961– . 2. Rich, Bryne. 3. Basketball players—United States—Biography. 4. Friendship—United States—Case studies. I. Rich, Pat, 1942– . II. Steinberg, Alan, 1945–
III. Title.
GV884.R618A3   1994
796.323'092—dc20
[B]   93–14373
                                                                        CIP

ISBN 0–517–59294–0

10   9   8   7   6   5   4   3   2   1

First Edition

This book is dedicated to the memory of
Bradley Thomas Robinson
whose vivacious spirit, love of life
and sports, and grace of character
still inspires us all.

—Pat, James, and Bryne Rich

Contents

Rebound

Bokchito

Change comes hard in Bokchito, "The Biggest Little Town in Oklahoma," population 607.

Like dozens of other four-corner towns dotting the fertile southeastern plains, Bokchito (Choctaw for "Big Creek") crouches obscurely around a water tower, city hall, post office, bank, and a handful of homey shops on Main Street: Easter's Cafe—Lil's Hobby and Craft—McCann's Feed Store—Marvin & Don's Carpet—Kimberley's Dress Shop ("Tax Forms, Typing, Copying") . . . The town's speed limit is thirty-five and so is its pulse—and people like it that way. In warm weather, the only spots more populated than the cemetery are the adjoining baseball park and catfish pond in the dense, secluded brush. Even at summer's height, businesses languish like the pensive old farmers on benches out front. In winter, the town seems as bare as the vast surrounding tracts of fallow fields.

Farming and ranching have always been "the whole thing" here, so everyday life can be harsh and routine. Predictably, gossip is a major—often intrusive—pastime. While everyone feels "practically related" to everyone else—as a local adage goes, "You can't talk about nobody 'cause you might be talkin' about your own cousin"—this doesn't deter idle chatter. Thus, the "female gossip" at Leota's Beauty Shop invariably spins around the next homecoming or class reunion, and who's sick in hospital. "Male gossip" at McCann's Feed Store typically covers the weather, the worth of this year's peanuts and hay, the price of cattle, and the latest wreck out at the "Y" in the road to Bennington. Not long ago, even the consolidation of area high schools raised a stir. Many still can't accept the nickname change from the traditional Bokchito Roughriders to the "new-sounding" Rock Creek Mustangs.

Largely white, Bible Belt Baptists, Bokchitans faithfully attend their seven local churches, which outnumber restaurants and gas stations combined; address each other warmly as "y'all"; call anything fancy "high dollar"; and relish old country maxims like, "Don't put *that* horse on my back" and "We're gonna go do it, even if it harelips the governor." Like their neighbors in nearby Bennington, Caddo, and Durant, they are simple, insular folk, as straightforward as the EAT sign over Frank's Cafe. Honor and trust are implicit; residents leave their homes unlocked and vehicles open, billfolds on the seat. And while some still cling to provincial prejudices, Bokchitans can't be beat for banding together to help someone in need. If a house burns or resident dies, everyone contributes food and clothes, which the churches team up to distribute. If someone falls ill, neighbors phone daily and send greeting cards: "Hurry up and get well. We're all thinking about you." If they could wave a single moral message as their standard, it would most likely be: "Love Your Fellow Man."

"God Works in Mysterious Ways, His Wonders to Perform"

That's how it was in Bokchito on sunny Halloween Day, 1982, when thirteen-year-old Bryne Rich and best friend Brad Robinson emerged together from Sunday school at the Church of Christ.

As usual, they were excited to go quail hunting in the woods behind the Riches' six-hundred-acre farm. Hunting here is custom; kids learn to shoot when they're big enough to hold a gun. Buddies since kindergarten, having schooled and worshipped together, traded weekend sleepovers, hung with the same friends, competed in the same sports, and most especially shared their obsessive love of basketball, Bryne and Brad viewed today's outing as their next adventure together in life. They had no idea it would be their last.

After eating dinner at Easter's with their other close pals Bill and Jeff Penz, they all returned to the Riches' to prepare for the hunt. As they checked their gear outside, Brad paced eagerly with the hammer cocked on his shotgun. Bryne's eyes went wide. "Don't ever walk with a loaded gun like that," he warned. "All you gotta do is touch the hammer and it's gonna go off." Chastened, Brad complied. Meantime, Bryne checked out his own gun, a 20-gauge he used only when one of his brothers borrowed his favorite. But he was comfortable with it; he'd test-shot it earlier and it worked fine.

The foursome ambled past the wheat fields and hay bales some two hundred yards behind the house to the edge of the woods. Here, as always, they gathered big green horse apples from the bois d'arc tree for practice shots. This was the fun part; they were eager just to fire their guns. While the others stood safely behind the shooter, one of them tossed the target apples toward the top of the tree. Bryne shot last, getting the feel of his unfamiliar gun. When he finished, Bill and Jeff turned and started walking toward the woods. As Brad came out from behind a tree, Bryne braced his gun against his hip to reload. But when he slipped a shell into the chamber and slammed the bolt shut ... "Boom!" ... the gun fired. Amazed, he thought: "How'd the gun go off? I ain't even got my finger on the trigger."

When Bryne looked up, he was startled to find Brad facing him fifteen feet away, clutching his vest. It didn't register—they all thought Brad was joking. Until he groaned, and they rushed over and saw he'd been hit. Carefully, Bryne unzipped Brad's vest and found the wound. Jeff said, "We're goin' for help," and he and Bill dropped their guns and bolted for the house.

Bryne eased Brad to the ground and cradled him in his arms. "God!" he shrieked at the sky. "This can't be true! Please let this not be real!" Then he started to cry. "Don't die on me, Brad," he pleaded through tears. "You're gonna be okay." He knew not to move Brad or cover his wound; he would just hold him quietly until help arrived. But Brad turned pale and kept closing his eyes. Bryne tried frantically to keep him awake: "Talk to me, Brad. Stay with me. You're gonna be all right." Brad opened his eyes again and said, "Just let me rest a minute. Let me sleep."

"No!" Bryne shook him gently. He was afraid if Brad closed his eyes, he might never open them again. "Hang tough, man. Talk to me." But Brad couldn't keep awake. So all Bryne could do was agonize silently: "God, where *are* they? What's *takin'* so long?" He felt like hours had passed. Then, suddenly, he noticed the commotion: am-

bulance siren; flashing lights; dirt and dust flying; motorbikes screaming across the field. Relieved, yet filled with dread, Bryne clutched
Brad closer and whispered desperately through tears, "I didn't mean
it. It was an accident."

Brad whispered back, "I know."

"I love you, Brad."

"I love you, too," were Brad's last words.

People converged in a blur: Bill and Jeff Penz; Bryne's brothers,
Barry and Mike, and their dad, James; Brad's father; policemen; med-
ics. Someone touched Bryne on the shoulder. "We got him, we got
him now." Finally, reluctantly, still disbelieving, he released his hold
on Brad. It was the most wrenching moment of his life; he sensed he
would never see his best friend again.

In shock, Bryne slipped off alone through the field.

Bill Penz yelled from behind, "Bryne! C'mere!" but Bryne didn't hear.
Finally, Bill caught up with him halfway across the field, and they
embraced and cried in despair. "Why, why, why?" Bryne pleaded in
pain. "Why me? This has gotta be a dream. It can't be real. Let me
wake up, please let me wake up." They looked at each other, per-
plexed. "God," cried Bill, "what's happened? What the hell's happened?"

Bryne entered his house alone, slumped onto the couch in the
TV room, and cried fiercely. He felt he might never be able to stop.
Shortly, James found him and sat him up and held him close. "Every-
thing's gonna be all right, son," he assured in his calm, soothing drawl.
"It wasn't your fault. Everybody knows that. It could've happened to
anyone." Though Bryne knew this was true, it didn't quell his grief.
"But, Daddy," he sobbed, "why did it happen to *me?*"

They hugged a long time before Bryne's mom, Pat, arrived home.
She'd been at a beauty pageant meeting in town when her son, Mike,
had phoned with the news, which had literally buckled her knees.
She'd needed help to get to her feet and regain herself before driving

home. Now, the three of them hugged and cried. Afterward, James took Bryne to talk with the police, while Pat drove to the hospital in Durant to try to see Brad. But, since only family was allowed in, she paid her respects and hurried back home.

The next few days were hell for the Riches, particularly Bryne. He fell into a deep depression. When neighbors and friends came by to sympathize, he could barely mutter a thanks before retreating to his room. He didn't know how to act or what to say. Even when Jeff and Bill Penz came over, the three could only sit and stare at each other in shocked disbelief. Bryne told his parents, "I just don't feel like bein' around people now. If any more show up, just say I can't see 'em." If not for his little pal, Russell Adamson, who came every day anyway to play games and build model cars, Bryne might've stayed, mortified, in bed. Even so, he couldn't eat or sleep, and would often burst out crying. He mostly stayed inside so no one else would see him like this. Of course, going to the hospital was out of the question; he was terrified Brad wouldn't make it.

The Riches closed ranks. Older brothers Barry and Mike provided constant support. Both James, a rural mail carrier, and Pat, a housewife and now home beautician, stayed round the clock with their son. James, a shy, temperate man of few words but staunchly decent values, was blessed with a farmer's adaptable soul. Patient, practical, disarmingly direct, he was a pillar of strength at home—advisor to all and manly model. Pat was more complex, though equally strong, in ways soon to be tested. An archetypal nurturer, she tended to family, God and church, then herself, last but not least. A dedicated talker, and possessed of an independent streak, she took pride in creating—anything from a special recipe to the beauty shop she'd devised at home for extra income. Though not a town gossip, a part of her delighted in stirring up still waters. Yet, another part recoiled at making too many waves. As outgoing as James was subdued, Pat nearly always followed her heart. To Bryne, she was more than just Mom; she was his biggest supporter and fan, and spiritual best friend.

In those first rough days, Bryne paced the house—"like a cat prowling around, searching for somethin'," Pat would say later. Or else he watched TV and played distractedly with Russell. At night, he torturously reviewed the tragedy in his mind, vaguely hoping something might change. He didn't feel guilty; he felt responsible that it had been his gun that had hurt his friend. So he prayed incessantly: "I don't know how it happened. I didn't mean to do it. Please let Brad be all right again." Pat and James counseled him day and night, helping him cope: "Bryne, everyone knows it was an accident, and you know it was, and Brad's parents know it was; they told us there wasn't a doubt in their minds. Everyone they talked to said the same thing. Bill and Jeff verified that your gun just discharged automatically. You can't blame yourself. You gotta be strong."

Pat phoned the hospital constantly, awaiting good news. But none came: "Critical condition, no change." Late that first night, after retiring, Pat arose to find Bryne awake in his bed, crying. So she went to the den and turned on the TV, and in he came to sit on her lap in the rocking chair. Finally, he asked the question he would repeat for months, "Why did this have to happen to me?" Then Pat rocked him for hours, sedating his soul. "I don't know why, Bryne. But God knows, so we just have to trust in Him. Scripture says He will not put anything on you that you will not be able to bear. This is too big for us to handle, so let's just turn it over to Him and let Him work it out." They cried and prayed in their hearts: "Dear God, please let Brad live. And help us all get through this all right." She wiped away his tears. "Remember, Bryne," she added, offering her deepest conviction in life: "*God works in mysterious ways, His wonders to perform.*"

Shortly after Pat returned to bed, Bryne dragged in and said, "I wanna sleep with y'all." He climbed between his parents, and Pat draped him in her arms. "You don't know how it feels," he moaned. "You can't know what I'm goin' through." And though he still couldn't sleep, he felt safer here, shielded from thought.

■   ■   ■

The tormenting wait stretched two more days.

Bryne asked for updates and Pat phoned the hospital every few hours and fed him reports. November 1: "Brad's' hanging in there, Bryne. They said he's got a chance." November 2: "He's still fighting." Since Brad was holding his own, Bryne convinced himself his pal would be coming home for sure. "When's he gettin' out?" he asked Pat hopefully. "You think it'll be soon?" She replied cautiously, "Well, it might be a few weeks," though she'd perked up a little herself. Each day, Bryne lay in bed imagining Brad's return to school. He pictured himself helping Brad to recover his strength and to play again. He couldn't wait to do everything for Brad, and see him every day . . . if only he'd hurry and get well so they could be together again.

Pat also suffered. Consumed with worry about Brad, and now her own declining son, she, too, could barely eat or sleep. Memories of Brad and Bryne playing together racked her. And always the haunting, cruel irony of teaching Sunday school the day of the incident as a last-minute substitute—the only time Pat ever taught Bryne and Brad in their teen class. She remembered asking questions on scripture, each one answered earnestly by Brad. The last question was: "Why did Jesus die on the cross?" To which Brad had replied, "For the forgiveness of sin." Pat had said, "Yes, that is correct, Brad. Jesus' suffering made it possible for all people to have forgiveness, *if they ask and are willing to try to live better lives in the future.*" She couldn't know then how the last part of this creed would resonate in her own life, further down the road.

Despite her own private pain, Pat trained a vigilant eye on Bryne, checking him constantly, reassuring all day, rocking and praying at night. He was so exhausted, she thought he might need a doctor. But then, mercifully, after only a few fitful hours of rest over three full days, a depleted Bryne finally cried himself to sleep. Next morning when he awoke around ten, Pat was sitting beside him. "How's Brad?" he automatically asked. Pat sat silent a moment, then grasped his hand.

"He didn't make it, Bryne," she said softly, in tears. "Brad is gone."

In a gesture of Christian grace, Billie and Morley Robinson stopped by to reassure Bryne that they still loved him and understood it was an accident, and that he shouldn't blame himself. They hugged him and left. It had helped, but Bryne still couldn't bring himself to attend Brad's funeral. Bewildered, overwhelmed, he was afraid to face anyone yet. Besides, he imagined that if he had to walk past the casket, he'd've grabbed hold of Brad and never let go. So, instead, Pat drove Bryne and Russell Adamson to the Collinville Mall in Plano, Texas, to spend the day shopping for whatever they liked. She hoped it would take Bryne's mind off the funeral. It worked—until the drive home. When they hit the outskirts of Bokchito, familiar sites pierced him; he was surprised how it hurt. He thought he was prepared, knowing all along there was a good chance of losing Brad; in fact, out in the field when it had happened, he could hardly believe Brad hadn't died on the spot. Still, the impact of Brad being gone struck him for the first time *now*, like a hammer to the heart.

James and Pat spent day after day consoling their son. They tried to convey that: no one blamed him; God took Brad because it was his time; he was in good hands now; and, most importantly, Brad would want him to be strong now. Although this sunk in, Bryne's gut still throbbed. Unlike the sports he and Brad had played, there was no training for this, no drills to practice, no clock on his hurt, no end in sight to the pain.

Bryne tried to be strong but only grew more miserable. He was still unable to sleep in his own bed, or eat more than scraps, or enjoy his favorite sports. He told James, "I don't ever wanna touch a gun again. I ain't never huntin' again, either." Pat read him letters every day from people claiming they'd experienced a similar loss, and advising him how to deal with it. Nevertheless, he missed school for at least two months, mostly watching TV and feeling sick and morose. Teachers brought his lessons to the house, abridged and with extended dead-lines. Once, when Pat announced, "Bryne, your friends are here to see you," he was amazed to learn it was his whole class of thirty-five. But he couldn't face them yet. He was afraid he'd cry and make everyone sad, and embarrass himself. Also, something inside him still gnawed: *he* knew it was an accident, but what did *other* people think? Right now, he couldn't bear to find out.

Bedtime was always the worst. That's when the incident would flood back to his mind in brutal detail. Forlornly, he'd beseech God, "Please let this all be a big dream and let me wake up one day and have everything be back the same again. Please bring Brad back." But he knew Brad would not be back. There were also the weird dreams. Whenever he dozed off, he would see himself and Brad playing bas-ketball, sometimes here at the house, sometimes in what he believed was heaven. They'd be carrying on like nothing had happened, and it was as though Brad were his guardian angel, assuring, "Put it out of your mind. I'm still here by you." These dreams were so vivid, Bryne would awaken with a start, thinking Brad was right there in the room. That scared him, made him petrified of sleep. Pat would explain sin-cerely, "You don't have to be afraid of those dreams, Bryne. It's just Brad comin' to see you to say hi, and make sure you're okay." Still, he hated to dream because it wasn't real; and he hated waking up . . . because that didn't seem real either. And the whole next day, he'd suffer a fresh, deep wound of loss.

Many other nights when he couldn't sleep at all, he would lay on his bed reminiscing about Brad: how funny he was when he carried on with their friends . . .

. . . how he always flirted with the girls . . .

. . . the times he'd acted rough and tough—"Mr. Macho Man" . . .

. . . how he had everything going: good-looking; good grades; tall and strong; a natural athlete, especially in their favorite sport, basketball . . .

. . . the way he teased Bryne, good-naturedly, about being two inches shorter and less agile than him, which they always contended in their fiercely competitive games . . .

. . . how great it was going to basketball camps together every summer all around the state, growing closer and sharing their biggest dream: making the NBA.

One special memory recurred: the time Barry drove Bryne and Brad to one of their first camps in Tulsa, when Bryne was clumsy and small and Brad had the "Most Valuable Player" trophy sewed up, and they had to play each other in the final one-on-one tournament, and Brad wanted Bryne to get a trophy, too, so he let Bryne beat him in their game. Bryne lost in the next round, but won the "Best Defensive Player" trophy instead. He cherished that trophy now; it reminded him of that princely gesture from his best friend for life.

Thus, grieving late many nights, he would realize in despair: "God, I'll never go to another basketball camp. I can't anymore . . . without Brad."

Months later, although Bryne had returned to school and occasionally played outside, he remained despondent and remote. Even the sight of Brad's empty seat in class would make him cringe. He continued sleeping in his parents' bed, scared of bad dreams, and prayed every night for strength. And he still shrank from schoolmates, uncertain of how they viewed the accident. His Christmas was dreary; he felt no sense of cheer. Pat and James kept encouraging him to get back on his feet and go on with his life, but he couldn't shake the grip of sadness. Every hour, every day, he felt lost and alone.

The spring thaw seemed to brighten Bryne a little. He saw more of Bill and Jeff Penz, played some basketball, threw himself vigorously into his chores on the farm. Then, late in May, he became possessed of a peculiar idea that would not leave his mind. He thought about how his brothers had always had him to play with and to teach things to, because they were older and above him; but he had no one. And he was tired of feeling so lonely. So one day he approached Pat and asked her straight out, "Mom, would you adopt me a little brother so I can teach him how to play basketball?"

That floored her. "What do you mean?"

"Well, do you think Daddy would let us adopt a little brother?"

"Now, why in the world do you want a little brother, Bryne? You already have Barry and Mike."

"I know, but it ain't the same thing. They're much older than me. If I had a little brother, I could play with him and teach him basketball, and look after him and stuff. It would be different."

She realized he was serious. "Well, I don't know," she said, serious too. "I guess I can ask Dad and see what he says."

When she asked James, he looked at her sideways. "Hell," he chuckled, "I'd do good just to raise the three I got." Pat pressed more, but James was firm. Yes, he felt for Bryne, but no, this was flat impossible. "We can't afford any more kids in this house. I got all I can take care of right now. And that's it."

Pat eventually told Bryne, "Well, Dad said we can't have a little brother"—and it deflated him badly. "I tell you what, though," she added, thinking fast. "God hears prayers and He knows what you're goin' through, and if He thinks that you should have a little brother, then He'll send you one. He will, He'll send you one." She took his hand and said a little prayer: "Dear God, if it's meant for Bryne to have a little brother, if you think it would be good for him, then please send him a little brother." Bryne looked skeptical; maybe this wasn't the fastest way to go . . .

Pat looked reassuring. "You never know about life, Bryne. Have you ever heard of the stork flyin' over and leavin' a baby on your doorstep? Well, maybe God will hear our prayer and send a stork over, and you might just wake up some morning and check the doorstep and find out you got a little baby brother!"

To Pat, this was just like any other mother telling her child a fantasy story. Besides, she'd say almost anything to help Bryne cope. So she gave a little laugh—unaware that God apparently had a sense of humor, too—and that the *last* laugh would soon be on them.

2

The Hard

Way

Shirley Rodman is fifty-three now, but she never thought she'd make fifty.

Sometimes, she feels her entire adult life was, like meeting her first husband—who literally bowled her over at a skating rink—a series of disabling bumps. In 1960, as a sheltered, devout, naive college student who had never dated, she knew little of men and nothing of sex or love. Unexpectedly, the crash at the rink led to a whirlwind affair, ending three months later in a foolhardy marriage.

Philander Rodman Jr., U.S. Air Force, was stationed in Texas and then New Jersey, so that's where she moved. During Shirley's pregnancy with their first child, Dennis, in New Jersey, Philander started living up to his name with local ladies who hung around the base. When strange women started calling her house, Shirley was appalled. Philander's indiscretions continued for a few years, through the births of daughters Debra and Kim. Twice Shirley retreated home to Texas, but both times he persuaded her back. Then one day, with Philander in the field on maneuvers, Shirley stole back to Dallas with the kids to save herself and provide a permanent home for them. So, after years of what she would later term the "emotional abuse of a man who was obviously never taught any morals in life"—and, even then, only after they'd separated and he'd taken up with a white woman whom he would also eventually marry—Shirley agreed to divorce. Though she'd been faithful to him through it all, she nevertheless crucified herself over the breakup, wondering, "Why does he prefer this white girl to me? What did I do wrong?" She never found out.

One thing she knows she did wrong was hide the truth about Philander from her kids. She told them only the good things. But because she blamed herself for depriving them of a father, she admittedly overprotected "like a mother tiger guarding her cubs"—which cost her, too. For, although she had three marriage proposals after her divorce, and had desired companionship, she always declined. She says now that because of the emotional bruises on her heart from their father, she could not risk exposing the children to a possibly abusive stepfather.

At just twenty-five, throwing off years of self-pity and toughened by what she still calls "my rude awakening," Shirley resolved that her children would not just survive but would be self-sufficient, at whatever cost to herself. Thus, over the next eighteen years she put her own needs on hold. Despite never having worked a job, she held as many as four at once—assembly-line worker; school bus driver; English teacher; and on Sundays, organ player and choir director at church— to provide not merely bare necessities, but quality food and clothes, decent places to live, and, most importantly, free time for the kids to enjoy their youth without taking jobs. She regretted not having much free time for hugging and petting the kids, and having to harden herself to bring them up alone ("I never let them see me desperate or unhappy. Even when I felt like crying and giving up, I always put on a happy face for them."). And she was always concerned that because they didn't often see her love, they might view her more as a disciplinarian than as the vulnerable, loving mom she'd wanted to be. There were plenty of "soft moments" to remember, she insists today—especially when the kids would climb onto the piano and imitate the way

Shirley sang in church, and whenever the four of them took fun va-
cations together—but she worried it wouldn't be enough.

Nevertheless, Shirley took fierce pride in the fact that she instilled the right values: cleanliness, honesty, pride, and independence;
no cursing, drinking, smoking, or drugs. "We survived," she later
surmised, "because even though I didn't know a thing about raising
children, I kept my faith in God and my morals intact. And I knew
these three children did not ask to come here and were entitled to
have supportive parents, like normal children had. So I kept my children babies a long time because I didn't want them jumping out there,
like me, having to be grown before their time."

Since her most sensitive baby, Dennis, was a "soft, painfully shy,
passive child who listened to what anyone said and went along with
the program," Shirley kept closest watch on him. She felt he needed
more attention. As a four-year-old, he was so attached to her that
when she arranged to send him to a day nursery, he wedged himself
in the doorway of the bus and wouldn't budge. But most worrisome
was his reluctance to accept the fact that his father was gone, constantly insisting, "My daddy is coming back." She believed that his
constant allergy attacks and facial sores, which embarrassed him un-
bearably, were stress disorders from keeping things in, especially the
longing for his dad. "What I should have done with Dennis," she now
admits, "was when he got to the point where I thought he could understand it, I should have told him point-blank, 'Your father was a
dog.'" But she didn't and Dennis idealized him, and he never returned.
As a result, Dennis grew angry, confused, and even more withdrawn.

Debra, strong and independent, together with calm, reliable Kim,
watched and played with Dennis daily. For a while, that was easy; as
the girls grew deft at sports, particularly basketball at the rec center
next door, he idolized and clung to them. But once in their teens,
Debra and Kim became a two-sided sword for Dennis. First: when the
girls suddenly sprouted taller than him, it hurt him to watch them
zoom past. Second: while they loved each other, and though Dennis

prized playing basketball with them, he envied their natural athletic grace, feeling ashamed of his own bewildering gawkishness.

Ungainly and frail, lacking self-esteem, he didn't handle adversity well. When money kept disappearing from Shirley's purse—and she knew she'd given each child their share for the week—she deliberately laid out some cash where Dennis would find it. Next day, the cash had vanished. She knew it was Dennis, but couldn't understand why he would rob from his mom. When confronted, he broke down in tears, only then complaining that kids were beating him up at school and taking his lunch money—and that they swore to hurt him worse if he told. Why didn't he defend himself, Shirley asked. "I don't know," was his answer. "I just don't like to fight." Though it took Shirley only a few days to end the terrorization, she quickly transferred Dennis to another school. She was afraid he wouldn't survive where he was.

One of his biggest challenges came in tenth grade. Perhaps trying to prove he was better than his sisters in something, he showed up—for the first time on his own—to try out for the South Oak Cliff High School football team. He didn't tell anyone, but Shirley found out and watched from the stands. When Dennis won his sprinting trial and the coach picked his opponent anyway, Dennis was openly crushed. So was Shirley; she knew how much it meant to him. So she cornered the coach and demanded to know why he hadn't selected her son; everyone saw he was faster! The coach agreed. "I know, he's faster," he said. "And he deserves a spot on the team. But the boy's too small, he's too thin. I need a stronger kid." Later, she tried to explain this to Dennis, but, as always, he shut himself off like a light bulb. He knew he was small, but so what? Hell, he played football all the time around the apartment complex: reckless damn bandit, hit somebody, *kill!* Any position: blocker, halfback, quarterback—ten on a team; tackle; no pads. "Damn," he cursed bitterly in his room, "I can *play* football."

He hurt so badly, Shirley went back to the coach a second time, with Dennis in tow. Ultimately, she got what she wanted: a private meeting between the coach and Dennis, who, by this time, was wishing he were anywhere else. Afterward, though Dennis said he understood the reasons, he never accepted the rejection.

Making the basketball team didn't help. He was still only 5–9—all gangly arms and legs, a hyper bundle of nerves unable to make a simple, poised lay-up. Predictably, after riding the bench for half a season, he quit. Then Shirley introduced him to music—her passion—and, surprisingly, he took to the bass viola. He practiced at home and played solos with "feel." Shirley was thrilled. She thought: "Good. My son has the talent, he is going to follow in my footsteps with music." She was wrong. He quickly grew bored with his small success, quit playing, and started withdrawing again. When he announced, "Momma, I don't wanna be around people no more," and started spending all his free time playing computer video games in his room, Shirley decided he needed a father figure to draw him out of his shell. So she contacted the Big Brother Association and signed him up. The guidelines were strict: single parents weren't allowed much interaction; they were introduced to the big brother and he took it from there.

Dennis's big brother was a Mr. Haynes—a professional man, married to a teacher with whom he had two daughters but always wanted a son. A seemingly compatible match. And they *were* compatible—too much so. Ironically, Mr. Haynes was almost as quiet and shy as Dennis. While he always brought gifts and took Dennis to Dallas Cowboys games, they spent little time communicating. But when Shirley called the association to complain, "I don't think this will work. Neither of them *talk!*" the response was, "Well, give it a chance. There's such a rarity of black men in the program." She hadn't thought about that, so she backed off. Eventually, as with music, Dennis lost interest and quit.

All through high school he would lag behind, emotionally. Protected and domineered by the females in his life, playing sports and hanging with Debra and Kim, taunted as "momma's boy" and having no close male friends, Dennis once even wondered, naively, if he wouldn't end up gay from following his sisters around so much. So at sixteen, seventeen, eighteen, when others were planning their futures, he had no sense of himself or his goals in life, beyond: "Finish high school and maybe get a regular nine-to-five job and my own car, and take it from there."

Curiously, though, he started feeling comfortable with himself and his undirected life. It felt good to just "hang out" in his own little world: video arcade, McDonald's parking lot, pool hall, rec center gym, skating rink, bowling alley . . . In fact, it was considered cool to bum around the complex, looking for trouble. Dennis's favorite times in high school, for instance, occurred after it closed. He and his crafty pals would jump the fence, sneak inside, and skateboard the halls, ducking the oblivious janitor as part of the prank. They'd even haul their bicycles in and skid the hallways on them. Another weird, fun thing: trekking and even crawling at night through the putrid drainage tunnel in the complex, exiting through a hole by the state fairgrounds, where they would hop a fence and romp around the rides.

Dennis still wondered about his dad—he'd seen him twice since the divorce, though it never felt like father and son—but he reasoned coolly now: "I never knew my dad after I was three, so why should I miss him? Can't really miss what you never had." Unwilling to explore, let alone share, his deepest feelings about this, he remained a detached, pliable, yes-no kid, convinced it hurt too much to care. Deliberately, almost defiantly, he sent the classic loner's message: Don't try to know me.

Yet, he was making friends more easily. Although still a follower, he seemed tougher, no longer the frightened, gawky young kid. And, for the first time, more confident in himself as an entity apart from Momma and the girls. It was nothing for him now to lift a five or a ten from Shirley's purse, or cop her car keys for nighttime joyrides, telling himself: "She'll never miss it." But she *would* miss it; and she'd warn him angrily, "If you're going to keep stealing from me, you don't need to be here." But she didn't have the heart to follow through on her threats.

Maybe Dennis's new boldness derived from his friendships—especially with Terry, Claude, and Robert, neighborhood boys he joined mainly for pinball, cruising, even some serious hoops at the gym. Maybe it came from checking out the ladies and finally having his first date. Or from the esteem and freedom of driving Shirley's Monte Carlo. What could be sharper than joining the exclusive Monte Carlo Club, slicking up your (or your mother's) big Monte every week with the latest ultra-glide trash—auxiliary antennas, curb-finders, fog lights, outrageous hubs, you name it—then cruising the nearby towns, en masse, cool as poolroom-cool?

Bumming and fun became all that mattered. Even Dennis's jobs were only a means to prolonging that fun. One of Shirley's strongest objections back then was that Dennis never strived, like his sisters, to get ahead; he just strived to get gas money for his car. Admittedly, responsibility was not a priority; it wasn't even in his vocabulary. Like the time Dennis worked as a car valet at a local dealership, and drove a client to work in his flashy DeLorean, and then, instead of driving it right back to the dealership for servicing, "borrowed" it for an afternoon jaunt. Unencumbered by any sense of impropriety or even liability, Dennis swung through his neighborhood, cruising by the boys like some black Great Gatsby, "sporting" the fabulous car. Once back at the dealership, of course, he was instantly canned— they just checked the odometer. No sweat, though; he just finished the day there and had Claude get him a job in the body shop—learn as you go.

"Free and just hangin' loose at eighteen," he thought at the time. "Man, how you gonna top *that* for a life?"

In 1979, happy as hell to be out, Dennis Rodman bid good-bye to high school by calling his mom and proclaiming, "Well, I graduated. You can go pick up the diploma." Although Debra and Kim were still in high school, their immediate futures were set. As highly recruited basketball stars, they had their choice of big-time college scholarships. Ultimately, 6-2 Debra chose soon-to-be national champion Louisiana Tech and 6-0 Kim picked prominent Stephen F. Austin. Meantime,

Dennis loitered around Dallas with vagrant pals whom Shirley called "hoodlums" to his face. In fact, she suspected them of stealing from her—with Dennis's knowledge. He denied it; all his friends worked decent-paying jobs, he claimed, so they didn't need to steal. But she believed they did, and that Dennis let them roll over him so he wouldn't lose their friendship.

Things had grown tense between Dennis and Shirley. She disapproved a lot and pushed him to toe the line. He largely ignored her now, reassuring himself: "Nobody tells me what to do." When she decided to marry a man Dennis disliked, he went roller-skating instead of attending the wedding. She was hurt but undeterred; neither Shirley, who cherished her son, nor anyone else could fathom his peculiar perspective on things.

As it turned out, Dennis was relieved when, six months later, the marriage collapsed. But unfortunately, so did Shirley's health. She started missing work, vomiting and losing weight. At first her doctors thought cancer, but they eventually diagnosed gallstones, allergies, and stress. Between physical problems, emotional stress over Dennis, and addictive tranquilizers for tension, Shirley was falling apart in bits and pieces. "You're doing a hundred in a thirty zone," one doctor told her. Finally, in the midst of what would eventually be five surgeries, she quit her teaching job with the district and stayed home for six months, counting on unemployment. But the first three months were denied as the district, to which she'd devoted herself the past ten years, challenged her claim in court, insisting she'd left due to stress. Which, of course, heaped more stress onto her life. Unexpectedly, she came into another job more to her liking—as a credit analyst—that would last the next twenty years. But meantime, while she won the court case, her apartment was burglarized, so she was forced to put her belongings in storage and squeeze into her niece's place until she could find another, smaller place of her own.

And all through these ordeals, her overriding concern remained Dennis, who, now nineteen, was still headed nowhere. He worked menial day jobs, hung with the boys, and pulled night shifts at the

Dallas–Fort Worth Airport as a custodian: sweeping, mopping, cleaning up. Then one night, spurred by a dare from two coworkers, twins who'd already done it themselves, Dennis maneuvered his broom handle through a gift shop gate and fished watches off a display case. Some were worth up to $50. To him, it was nothing more than a kick—just like the time he'd copped a cheap billfold from the 7-Eleven store where he worked as a cashier. Both times he told himself: "I shouldn't have done that," but then: "Aw, forget it. I did it, so what the hell."

Aside from the violations of trust, he didn't *need* these things; he just decided he *wanted* them. He felt this strange, persistent compulsion to always have something more than the next guy, to be one up on somebody else. Yet, while he kept the billfold (as a sentimental reminder of what he might've been), he gave away all fifteen watches, first to his unsuspecting sisters and mother, then to friends. But even calling them friends, he knew in his heart, was a lie; while doling out the watches, he realized: "Yeah, who *wouldn't* be friends with someone who just gave you a new watch?"

Paranoia had set in immediately after he'd brought the booty home; something told him he'd get caught. But when two weeks passed uneventfully, he thought he was in the clear. Until he showed up for work one night at the airport, and got fired instead. When he asked why, his supervisor hedged, "Because you're not doing the job." No mention of watches, no accusation. Next day, Dennis heard that the twins who'd started the stealing had also been canned. When a neighbor informed him the cops were now looking for him, his paranoia returned with a vengeance. Yet, he didn't hide out. He went about his usual routine—which happened to include staying away from home a lot.

Nevertheless, days later, the inevitable knock came at Shirley Rodman's door. She opened it to find two grim-looking white men in suits—not her everyday Oak Cliff callers. "Is your son Dennis Rodman?" one of them asked.

"Yes," she said warily. "Who are you?"

They flashed badges and a document. "We have a warrant for Dennis Rodman's arrest."

"Why? What is the charge?"

"Stealing watches from the Dallas–Fort Worth Airport."

They showed her some watches identical to one Dennis had given her. Shirley was flabbergasted; Dennis had been in trouble before, but police had never come to her home, let alone with warrant and evidence in hand. "I have failed this boy," was her first disgusted thought. "I have let him down."

But she hadn't; Dennis had failed himself. And he was about to find that out.

The hard way.

"Dennis, why did you do this?" Shirley pressed, as her son cried loud and hard. Simultaneously, the men in suits—airport security who'd reviewed the theft on videotape—started escorting Dennis outside in his undershirt and shorts. Shirley protested, insisting he be allowed to put on his shirt, pants, and shoes. They assented grudgingly; they thought he might try to escape. She thought: typical white cop attitude.

Once they were gone, Shirley agonized over the idea of her helpless son being locked in jail. But she'd been frustrated with him for so long, and felt so furious now—over his hanging around, his so-called friends, and for *this*. When she calmed down, it crossed her mind that maybe sometimes you have to hit bottom before you can find your way back up. So after debating for hours, rebuking herself for even considering it, she finally decided to leave Dennis in jail. She hadn't even called a lawyer yet; she just figured they could only hold Dennis for seventy-two hours, and that might be a good lesson for him.

Good thing no one asked Dennis. Because this, he would later claim, was one of the few times he'd ever been "totally scared shitless." He felt trapped in the cell—with another man arrested for flying without paying—because he could only move two ways: back and forth.

Petrified, he thought: "What the hell's goin' on? Why am I *here?*" Somehow, though he knew he'd tempted fate for years, Dennis never imagined he would end up in jail. That was one reason he hadn't hid from police. Another reason was that he didn't regard this as stealing; he called it "takin'"—as in: "I was just takin' things." Plus: nobody saw, so how would they find him?

If not exactly sensible, this logic was not surprising coming from Dennis at the time. Having *felt* invisible most of his life, and having gotten away with so much "takin'" till now, it was easy to assume he *was* sort of invisible. Plus, throw in some pure naïveté. "Even if they find me," he'd actually figured, "what can they do? Probably just say, 'Give the watches back.' "

Nobody had said that yet, as he cried through the night. Enveloped in darkness, ashamed, and as lonely and scared as he'd ever felt, Dennis seriously reflected on his life for the first time. He knew he was messed up; he could see his life heading straight to hell. Suddenly, he found prayer: "Please, Lord, let me out of this place. Why is this happening to me? Don't leave me here. I will never take another thing. Never again. Just let me out, Lord. Please let me out."

Maybe God heard, because back at her apartment Shirley thought *she* did. Feeling guilty beyond description, and discovering that Dennis wasn't in the local county lockup but rather the Dallas–Fort Worth Jail, her resolve melted away. She was still determined that he stay in jail, but only, say, *overnight.* That should do the trick.

He ended up staying longer—it took her most of the next day to raise bond. When they finally returned home together that evening, they cried some more—he still scared, she still pissed. Finally, she screamed at the top of her lungs, "Why in the world did you steal those watches? What were you thinking?" He got very shook up. "I never stole the watches," he chafed. "A couple friends stole 'em and gave me some to sell. I just took 'em and gave 'em away." And that's what he told the cops, he said. So they were only calling him an accessory.

Shirley looked skeptical. Too much history.

"Momma," he quickly switched tracks, "do you have any idea what it's like to be in jail? It was the scariest night I ever spent!" He told about not eating or sleeping, and the walls closing in. And then he offered a police interrogation scene out of a bad "B" movie: "They asked me all these questions," he said, still stressed-out. "About: 'Did you steal any watches?' I kept saying, 'No, no, no! I didn't steal any watches. Someone else did. They just gave me some to sell.' Then all of a sudden they started drillin' and drillin', and they said, 'We know you took the watches. And we're gonna let you go. But you can rest assured that your ass is gonna land right back here in jail. And then we're gonna let these guys in here kick your ass. And then you're gonna do three or four years.' And they was sayin' . . . well, you know what cops can say to people to get information from 'em. And that's exactly what they did."

Shirley didn't buy it. And even though ill, she could be tougher on him than any police interrogation. "Dennis," she bored in, "don't you scam me, son. Did you or did you not steal those watches? Tell me the truth, you hear?"

He said, "Momma, I sat in there sweatin' and sweatin', and all of a sudden I just broke down and said, 'Okay, okay, okay!' They said, 'If you tell us, we'll make sure you won't have a record. We just wanna know what you did with those watches.' And I started tellin' 'em where the watches were: 'All my friends got 'em.' And they said, 'Did you actually sell the watches?' And I said, 'No, I never sold any, I just gave 'em to people.' One of 'em said, 'Okay, because if you sold 'em, that's a felony and they can put you away a few years for that.' Then they took me back to the cell and then you came, and that was it."

Armed with Dennis's information, police had gone to his high school searching for the kids with the stolen goods. One kid led to another until all fifteen watches turned up. Interestingly, unlike in the movies, none of these kids sought revenge against Dennis for ratting them out. In fact, they met with him later and laughed it off: "Man, these cops came up here and asked me if I had a watch, and they

looked at it and looked at it, and it was so weird I finally gave it back."
No big deal.

But it *was* a big deal for Dennis; he was still sweating a trial. At
first, his lawyer had said he would probably get a light sentence because
he didn't sell the watches and had helped the police recover them all.
Maybe six months and probation. Dennis would have been happy to
get only that. Fortunately, his good luck held out. As he and Shirley
ascended the courthouse steps for his trial, they bumped into their
lawyer on his way down. He told them, "Good news. There's no trial.
They were satisfied to just get the watches back, so they dropped the
case. Your record's clean. You can go on home." Dennis whooped,
"Oh man!" and "Thank you, Lord!" and ran up and down the steps
in ecstatic relief.

And all the way home he reminded himself: "That was my lucky
break. I *gotta* change things around. I ain't ever gonna do that again.
Man, I never wanna go to jail as long as I live."

3

Bottom

A year later, at twenty, essentially he *was* back in jail.

While bumming around Dallas, Dennis Rodman's hormones con-vulsed. Suddenly he'd exploded from what, to him, was a puny 5–9 to an unimaginable 6–8. "Skinny" was now an understatement; he thought he'd turned into a *stick*. No laughing matter for an already mercurial kid, this eruption took a toll. Feeling he looked like a geek, Dennis burrowed in at home again. He was too embarrassed to go out, except to his part-time job cleaning used cars at an Olds dealership for $3.50 an hour. Since none of his clothes fit anymore, when he did venture out at night once in a while—to play pinball or video games—he wore the only thing that *did* fit: his oversized work coveralls.

The only plus to this spurt was that Dennis started really loving basketball. He picked it up like *that*, as though a spell had been cast with a wand. Where he used to blunder, he now glided and soared. Moves came as natural to him now as they'd felt clumsy before. He finally had his basketball "Jones"—a full-fledged addiction—just like Debra and Kim.

But he still lacked the self-confidence to make something out of it. So his sisters, as usual looking out for him, acted on his behalf. A girlfriend of theirs who'd seen Dennis play, and who herself played at Cooke County Junior College in Gainesville, Texas, arranged a tryout for him at the tiny school, only an hour away. He went because he'd promised to change, and he wanted to make his mom as proud of him as she was of his sisters, and make *them* proud, too. Leaving Dallas, he figured, might be a start. On the other hand, he knew that school would probably be a waste of time. For one thing, he had no interest in that kind of learning anymore; anything was better than wasting time on things you didn't care about. In other words, anything was better than failure. More importantly, he only knew rec center ball; he'd never played in an *organized* basketball game.

Didn't matter. Cooke County drooled at first sight: big-city black kid; huge hands; roadrunner legs with high-tension springs . . . Lord! Two-year scholarship for '83–'84 and '84–'85, full boat, sign here. Dennis was flattered, but bewildered by how easily they were fooled. He thought he didn't have it; he joked that he still couldn't whip his sisters in a game. "These people must be crazy," he thought. "But if they want to pay for me to play . . . "

As a starting center, at first he was nervous and scared: "I don't know about this. I don't wanna look like a fool." But gradually he settled in and just played. Shot fair, rebounded okay . . . he thought. In actuality, he played much better, especially with his double-figure rebounding. One impressed observer, Lonn Reisman, noted to himself: *Remember this kid.* Assistant basketball coach at Southeastern Oklahoma State, Reisman was actually visiting Cooke County JC as a tennis coach, an extra responsibility that came with his job. But every time he coached a tennis match against a junior college, he would also watch basketball practices to search for possible recruits. That day, he was checking out Cooke County's talent when Dennis Rodman caught his eye. He didn't see a great basketball player in Rodman, "just a long, lanky ole kid with tremendous raw ability: speed, timing, intensity, stamina." His first impression was: "Great diamond in the rough."

Reisman took mental notes, his eyes never leaving Rodman. Boy, he wished he could recruit a player of Rodman's calibre at the National Association of Intercollegiate Athletics level. At 6–8, with that much talent, there was no one else like him in the NAIA. Reisman knew he was looking at the kind of dominant player small-college coaches dream about: a kid who could lead a team to the national championship tournament in Kansas City, the small-college equivalent of the NCAA's annual "March Madness"—the ultimate goal of every NAIA coach. And not just lead the team there, but give it a realistic chance to *win*.

Halfway through the practice, Reisman came back to reality. He knew that in his business you might want a player but you can't spend all your time on any specific one, especially if your chances of getting him are practically nil. So he reminded himself, "Don't be spittin' in the wind here. He'll probably be an NCAA Division One player. Somebody's gonna come and get him." So he started observing other players. But his thoughts kept drifting back to Rodman. He reminded himself, too, that as a recruiter you have to always keep a great prospect in the back of your mind, even if he *does* go to a Division I school. Because once he's there he could become disenchanted . . . and you might pick him up on a rebound.

Next day, Reisman reported back to Southeastern head coach Jack Hedden. "Hey, there's a great prospect at Cooke," he said, excited. "He's a freshman, so we can't touch him now. But I think we should keep him in mind for later and look at him again. The kid's six-eight and he's got as much athletic ability as anybody I've seen all year. Maybe more. I think he's a real diamond in the rough." As Reisman chronicled Rodman's skills, Hedden listened attentively. But all he really had to hear was "six-eight." "Watch him close," he ordered.

Even the tiny Cooke County campus was an unexpected balm now for Dennis: peaceful and friendly; only about a thousand students; and he'd already bumped into some homeboys he knew from the complex. Only one major problem: while the potential was there on the court, it wasn't in class. Probably because, even though he'd enrolled for only ten hours—just enough to be eligible—he rarely *made* a class. Especially English. Thus, after only one semester and fourteen tantalizing games, Dennis flunked out. Curiously, he could have salvaged everything with some makeup work over Christmas, but instead he thought: "The hell with it. I ain't gonna make it. What do I want this for?"—and, almost willfully, gave up.

He was flunking in life, too; returning to Dallas, drifting back to the streets. This time, he ran with a much tougher crowd—unsavory older guys looking for trouble, not kicks. He liked it a while; it was a distraction from thought. But realizing he was headed for prison or death, or both, he grew withdrawn and depressed. He hated that old feeling, but couldn't assert himself over it. "The hell with it" was so much easier. And: "Can't really miss what you never had." So, just four months after leaving college in December '82, Dennis was back at home with his mom, stalled in neutral again. Same outlaw friends, same empty drift. Losing patience, Shirley would give him money to search for a decent job, but he'd drop it all indifferently at the video arcade.

Even though she'd perfected the survivor's knack of pushing unpleasant problems out of her mind, Shirley couldn't budge this one. Ill and stressed, she repeatedly scolded Dennis about his friends, insisting adamantly, "I can't live like this every day, worried about you being with those hoodlums. You are never to see them again!" But he always ignored her. His only appeasement was to clean the apartment while she was away, making it as spotless as the cars he shined at work. But she couldn't be assuaged; she kept urging him to do more with his life than just hang around home and clean.

Shirley resisted mentioning his sisters' successes at school—they'd both made All-American in basketball—because she knew how sensitive he was about being compared to them. But the contrast bedeviled her. "What's wrong with this boy?" she tormented herself. "He's brighter than he shows, he's talented, he could make something out of himself if he tried. Why won't he try?" Then, in a moment of disgust and regret, came clarity of purpose wrapped in a familiar thought: *"Maybe sometimes you have to hit bottom before you can find your way back up."* And, suddenly, she knew what to do.

In a grim conference that surprised them both, Shirley laid it on the line: "Dennis, I am your mother and I love you dearly. But I am not going to stand by any longer and watch you waste your life the way you have done. I just can't do it anymore. So you have three choices. You can either get back in school someplace and earn a degree, or you can get a serious job, or you can go into the service. You are going to do one of those three," she concluded gravely, "or you will no longer be welcome in my home." She was amazed she could've said that. Dennis was, too. But he knew she meant every word.

Only days later, when she discovered Dennis hanging around with the people she abhorred, Shirley exploded in rage. "Get out!" she ordered, packing his clothes herself. "You want to be with your friends, go live with your friends! I want you to go live with your friends starting right now!" And she literally shoved him out the door. And then cried hysterically, wondering how she could've done such a thing: taken the terrible chance of losing her son to the streets. "How many mothers," she berated herself, "could throw their own children out?"

She cried every day he was gone. He shed tears, too. But things remained a standoff. He didn't think he had any real options. Forget school—though basketball proved to him he was better than he thought, and he liked that kind of competition, that was out because he could never get through college. Finding a good job was probably out, too. What did Shirley expect, that a big, important job was gonna jump up at him from behind his Armor All and car wax rag? That left, what . . . the army? Marines? "Uh-uh. No, Lord, not me. Better off here in the streets."

So, while Shirley recuperated from her maladies, he roamed around for months, perfecting his hanging out and sleeping who knows where. Even when she did know, she refused to call, reasoning: "This is Dennis's crash course in reality. If he is going to survive in this world, he will have to grow up." She was adamant that he find out the life he'd lived with her was a luxury compared to the way his friends lived with their parents. Most of those parents, she felt, let their children get away with anything. They could live like animals and do what they wanted and the parents put up with it. But she would not. In fact, as far as she was concerned, even though they were both suffering over this, Dennis would have to call her first and say, "I am ready to accept responsibility for my life and do what is necessary." If not, her door would stay closed.

Finally he called, but, as usual, with little to say. Least of all, "I'm ready." Yet, over the next few weeks he called often, each time less tentative, more conciliatory. Occasionally, he blurted he'd like to come home. But that wasn't enough for Shirley; not without a convincing commitment to change. After similar calls—especially when Dennis implored, "Momma, I'm goin' hungry out here!"—Shirley softened under the guilt and was ready to bring him in. But somehow she held the line.

Around this time, Lonn Reisman returned to Cooke County JC to look at two prospects. But he was most eagerly anticipating the chance to watch Dennis Rodman play in a game. Shocked to discover he was gone, Reisman asked coach Jim Voight, "What happened to that Rodman kid?"

"Oh, he flunked an English class," replied the coach.

"Well, what's goin' on with him?"

"I imagine every junior college in the world's tryin' to pick him up and get him back in school."

"Yeah, well I know *one* that's gonna be."

Reisman knew now that he had to try to find Rodman. Thus, the day Southeastern's season ended in mid-April, Rodman popped back in his mind: "I wonder where he's at." So Reisman called the Registrar's Office at Cooke County College: "You had a player there last semester, Dennis Rodman. I'd like to have his home phone number." But the clerk replied, "I'm sorry. I cannot give that to you, sir. That's private information." That wouldn't sit; if he lost this kid to another school, fine; at least he'd have tried. But to have no chance at all just because he couldn't get a phone number? No way.

Phoning back the next day Reisman got lucky: this time a student-employee handled the call. "Look," Reisman implored the overmatched novice, "this is an emergency. I am a relative of Dennis Rodman's and we have a serious emergency and I need his home phone number."

And, boy, she whipped that phone number right out to him.

One day in early May the phone rang and Shirley Rodman hoped it was Dennis, because she was ready to fold and let him come home. Instead, it was Lonn Reisman. He explained who he was and that he'd scouted her son at Cooke County and was real impressed. Then he dropped a familiar name: "I have a young man that plays for me up here by the name of Emery Aaron and I believe he and Dennis know each other." He hoped that his personal familiarity with another kid from the area, with whom Dennis had attended high school, would help convince her that he was on the up-and-up. It did: "How is Emery doing?" . . . "Hey, he's doin' well"—and that broke the ice. Then Reisman said he was interested in recruiting Dennis for Southeastern, and did she know where they could reach him? Shirley said he was in and out.

Reisman explained that they hoped to recruit him for the coming fall, and that he and head coach Jack Hedden would like to meet with Dennis and talk it over because they felt Dennis needed to get back in school. And she agreed wholeheartedly with that. "I just wanna come up and visit with him and bring him back to the school. We're only two hours away. If he doesn't like it, I'll bring him home. But we gotta get him back in school. What do you think?"

Shirley didn't know what to think. "Well, I don't know," she hedged, ever-protective. "I will have to get ahold of my son and ask him."

Reisman called a second time to follow up, but Shirley hadn't heard from her son recently. When Dennis finally called, she was shocked to get her profoundest wish. "Momma," he sobbed, distraught, "can I please come home? I'm tired of livin' out here; please let me come home. I'll do whatever you want."

"You will do whatever is necessary?" she had to confirm.

"I promise, Momma. I'll do whatever you want me to do. Just let me come home." She had him; he sounded just like he had in jail.

"All right, then. But remember what you said."

"I will."

"Okay. Come on home."

Predictably unpredictable, he didn't show up as planned. Meantime, Reisman phoned again: full-court press. Sensing the urgency of seizing this opportunity, Shirley committed Dennis to a meeting the following week. "I promise you that I will have him here at the apartment for you," she said, and she gave her niece's address. When Dennis next phoned to say when he'd *really* be home, she informed him of his new obligation. "By the way," she said, matter-of-factly, "you've had several calls from a coach at this school, Southeastern-something in Oklahoma. They want to recruit you for their team and they've asked to meet with you. Since you did not come home when you were expected to, I went ahead and scheduled a meeting for you on Saturday. Do you hear, Dennis? You need to be here."

A little leery, he promised he would be.

When Lonn Reisman next phoned Shirley Rodman's, Dennis answered the phone and they talked for the first time. Dennis was reticent, at first, mumbling or grunting responses to the coach's cordial overtures. But when Reisman mentioned Emery Aaron, that seemed to score with him as it had with Shirley: "Oh, I know Emery! How's he doin'?" Then Reisman explained about Southeastern's basketball program, covering mostly "the little things," and pressed like a good salesman: "I'd like to come down and visit with you and bring you back to the school for a day and let you get the feel of the place." Though Dennis was still skeptical, he finally agreed and they confirmed a meeting for the coming Saturday morning. Reisman figured

Dennis was probably thinking: "If I don't wanna be there, I don't have to," but he and Jack Hedden were prepared to make the effort anyway.

Early that Saturday morning, Shirley answered the door in her robe, still foggy with sleep. Jack Hedden and Lonn Reisman introduced themselves and she said, "Hold on a minute," then shut the door to go tell Dennis. She thought it was interesting they'd come earlier than planned. Apparently, they knew enough about Dennis to guess he might skip.

Shirley awakened Dennis to tell him they were here. His response was typical: "No, I don't wanna talk to nobody. I don't wanna go. Tell 'em I ain't here." She pressed it lightly, then returned to the front door and opened it partway again. "You will have to excuse me," she said firmly but politely. "You're a little early and I am not dressed and Dennis is still asleep." She asked them to wait until she could get things squared away. Mainly, she meant Dennis's attitude.

So Shirley went back to his bedroom to make her point more forcefully: "Listen, young man, you made me a promise. You gave me your word that you would do whatever was necessary to come back home." Dennis grunted, "I know, I know," but she barreled right through: "You gave me your word and you will not break it." But he still wouldn't come out. So she returned to the front door a third time—she felt like a yo-yo going back and forth—and said, "I don't think he wants to talk to you. I can't get him up." Unruffled, they asked to come in.

Since Debra and Kim were there also, Shirley introduced them, and the four sat and talked. For twenty minutes, the sisters discussed their basketball careers. When Debra mentioned Louisiana Tech, one of the top programs in the nation, Hedden thought something like: "The genes are here. If *she's* that good, what'll *he* be like?" Also, Hedden and Reisman had worked together at Arkansas State in the same conference as Louisiana Tech, so here was common ground. They were aware that since brothers and sisters are usually close, if the girls thought they were okay, likely Dennis would think so, too.

But as time passed and Dennis didn't appear, they wondered

where he was. Finally, Shirley went back for one last try: "Dennis, please," she appealed to his conscience. "These gentlemen drove two hours to talk to you about your future, so I think you owe it to them to at least give them a chance. You don't have to commit yourself to anything. Just listen to what they have to say. You have nothing to lose." He thought he did; he wasn't too eager to fail again. But he agreed to at least listen, if he didn't have to come out of the room. So, though certainly strange, Hedden and Reisman started their pitch . . . to Dennis's *door*.

Eventually Dennis emerged in underwear and shorts, smiling bashfully but in a pretty good mood. Hedden was surprised at how uncomfortable he looked—he seemed almost afraid. Then, when he sat down with them, he had nothing to say. They'd explain their program and he'd chuckle and grin nervously, eyes cast down, and still say nothing. Finally, Reisman said, "Let's load up and go to Durant and let's look around and I'll bring you back." Dennis didn't say yes or no; he just sat silently, thinking it over. Since Shirley had to do most of the talking for him, the coaches finally realized they had to convince *her* that Dennis needed to be at Southeastern and that they were the right people to look after him there.

She was pleasant but skeptical. She'd never heard of Southeastern or been in Durant, but she knew Oklahoma and how most people there felt about blacks, especially in rural areas. To Shirley, it was "redneck country"—not on any black person's list of places to live. Hedden sensed her concern. He was used to it, especially in black athletes' homes where the families openly expressed their distrust of white recruiters pitching them about all the good things a white school in a white town could do for them. What helped, however, was that Hedden and Reisman addressed Dennis's needs as a person, not just as a basketball player: the school was only ninety miles from home, so the family could visit often and see him play; there would be other blacks on the team; the place was quiet and friendly, and the school academically sound; this would get Dennis out of the streets, where there was no telling what might happen to him. They also knew that in order to get a good prospect at a small school like Southeastern, they would probably have to deal with other concerns, like trouble with grades or even behavioral problems. Their whole program, they tried to assure her, was geared to that: discipline; responsibility; intensely personal attention both on and off the court. In the end, what Shirley heard was: *We can make Dennis a man.* Nobody knew what Dennis heard.

When they were done, Dennis retreated to his room to make the most momentous decision of his life. Not surprisingly, it only took minutes: "I'm gonna go." Meaning he would drive back with them and check out the place for himself, and then decide. So he packed some basketball clothes in a small black bag and off they headed for Durant. On the way, Dennis talked about some of the kids he knew in Dallas and the parks where he'd played ball; and Reisman told him how he'd seen him play the first time at Cooke County JC. Reisman had a really good feeling about Dennis now; he felt that he and Dennis had "jelled."

If Bokchito, about fourteen miles away, was a one-horse town, then Durant was a mini-metropolis: a variety of shops; theaters; gyms; library; bars—all the trappings of urban life. The university served some 4,500 students, mostly instate, and like Durant, virtually all white. Apocrypha had it that Durant was one of those towns trains flew through with shades pulled down to shield the blacks inside; and that there used to be a sign at a fork in the road outside town that read something like: "DON'T LET THE SUN SET ON YOU, NIGGER!" The 1982 version of Durant, however, was rimmed by several towns with sizable black populations. So, while Durant remained provincial and to a degree "redneck," it wasn't so thick that you could not breathe. No mob mentality; no midnight rides down backwoods roads. In fact it really seemed, for the most part, as Hedden and Reisman had said—a quiet, friendly place.

They drove Dennis around campus, pointing out how attractive and convenient everything was. Dennis remained mostly silent but was obviously interested. When they took him to the gym, they gave Dennis a basketball and let him shoot alone at the NBA-type baskets with the orange rings of the hoops; the thick twine nets that "swished" the ball through like wind; the clear glass backboards that "squeaked" when leather bounced off . . . Dennis was openly impressed. So was Hedden. Though he'd never seen Dennis play, he especially liked his "basketball-looking body," his quickness, and his jumping ability—even just shooting around by himself.

When he'd seen enough, Hedden withdrew to his office to let Reisman do what he did best: put on the "sell." So Reisman, a blunt, no-nonsense guy who had already begun to like Dennis a lot, said, "C'mon, I'll whip your butt in HORSE." Standard childhood shoot-around game: take a shot of your choice and if you make it, your opponent has to shoot the identical shot. If he misses, he gets a letter. First one to reach H-O-R-S-E loses. Inspired idea; just the way to get to know someone like Dennis: compete against him in a friendly, familiar, down-to-earth game while chewing the fat as you play. No room for phoniness or recruiting hype; just two guys cutting up at the "playground" on Saturday afternoon.

Meantime, while playing the game, Reisman told Dennis what his great basketball assets were. At one point, he took the ball from Dennis and dribbled the length of the floor as hard as he could, and laid the ball off the glass, and it dropped cleanly through the net. "You go hard like that all the time," he hollered back. "You got great speed, Dennis." Dribbling back, he continued his appraisal: "And you rebound the ball so doggone good. And you seem like you have a lot of stamina. I watched you during your practice at Cooke when the coach sat you down on the bench a minute, and then when he called your name again, you ran onto the court so *quick*, like you were ready to go in and play hard again. That's a *player*."

Dennis's eyes sparkled with pride; he listened intently now, like it really mattered. Then Reisman surprised himself with an uncharacteristic prediction: "You know what, Dennis? You're gonna be a *pro* someday." And he meant it. Dennis looked shocked, almost embarrassed; he gave Reisman a big, shy grin. It was obvious that all he'd ever heard before was how good his sisters were; and now, finally, here was somebody telling him how good *he* was. Somebody he liked, somebody who knew.

Afterward, Reisman exposed Dennis to a piece of the school's basketball tradition. Encased on the wall were the retired jerseys of two Southeastern Athletic Hall of Famers: three-time All-American Jim Spivey, who led the Savages in the mid-fifties to four straight trips to the NAIA nationals; and two-time conference scoring leader and later captain of the 1964 Olympic team, Jerry Shipp. "These guys were two of the greatest players you ever saw. And they went on to be real successful in life after leavin' here."

Dennis pondered that a moment. Then Reisman said with sincerity, "Someday, your jersey could be right up here with theirs, Dennis. What do you think?"

Awestruck, Dennis said, "Coach, I'm comin' here."

Reisman was stunned; he'd never expected a commitment so fast. Hell, they'd barely looked at the *campus* yet. "You sure?" he had to confirm.

"Yeah, I'm sure. I wanna come here."

Swept up in the emotion, Reisman made a promise he intended to keep: "If you do, Dennis, I promise you we're gonna make you the best damn basketball player you ever could become. It's gonna be hard, we're gonna work you hard, but you're gonna be around people that really care about you. We need to get you ready to go to summer school and get you set to play next fall. You're gonna have three great years." Dennis liked that; he looked as though he could hardly wait.

Reisman had rarely felt so excited about a recruit; it was obvious he'd developed a special bond with Dennis already. If he could have articulated it to someone just then, he would've said this: "I liked his heart, his emotion. He didn't have a big ego. Stars have big egos, they're hard to talk to: 'I'm damn good. I want this, I want that.'

Dennis didn't ask for things. He didn't *know* he was good. He didn't *have* an ego. He was a great young kid with great talent just waitin' to happen."

He accompanied Dennis in to see Hedden and they talked it through again together. Then they phoned Harold Harmon, the sports information director and also sports editor of the *Durant Daily Democrat*, who came over to snap photographs and take notes for a story. Finally, Dennis sat down and officially signed on.

When they got back to Shirley's, Reisman reminded Dennis that they'd be back in one week to pick him up. He knew they were taking a chance, but they had no choice because Dennis had loose ends to tie up first. So Reisman called him several times that week and kept talking to Shirley to make sure everyone was still on the same page. They were; in fact, Dennis couldn't stop talking about it and Shirley thought it was a dream come true.

When the day finally came, Reisman drove down and Dennis was there like he'd promised, and they drove straight back and signed him right into his dorm. Left alone there for a while, he thought about the guys back in Dallas who'd said, "You ain't goin' nowhere, man. Just like us"—and how he'd always believed them. But now he didn't want to anymore. So he told himself: "Damn. I am not goin' back home until I *make* something outta myself." He knew he'd made a similar vow in jail, but somehow this felt different. This wasn't a prayer to God, this was a promise to himself. Which he intended to keep.

The coaches started greasing the path right away. First, they got him a spending-money job for the fall, mowing the lawn and cleaning up at a local radio station. Then Hedden had a better offer for right now: since Dennis would have to make up credits in summer session to assure eligibility, how would he like to work the basketball camp in June? He could teach shooting and ball-handling drills to the youngsters as part of the staff: himself, Coach Reisman, local high school and junior college coaches. Basketball every day; have some fun teaching; get acquainted with campus before the students arrive; earn $100 a week easy extra cash.

Sounded great to Dennis. And though he was nervous and scared and still unsure of himself, as far as living up there and playing on a "big-time" college team, he really felt good about one thing: he was resolved that this time, no matter what, one way or another, he would do something *good* with his life.

4

Worm for Dinner

It was headline news, with photos, in Durant: Dennis "The Snake" Rodman, 6–8 out of Cook County JC, to play for Southeastern Savages in '83–'84.

Mike Rich had already read about it. He didn't know yet, however, that the nickname "The Snake" had been erroneously attributed to Rodman—it really belonged to a teammate. Rodman's nickname was "Worm."

Mike had been eating in the Durant Dairy Queen behind Coach Hedden and Coach Reisman, who were talking about their newest recruit. "Boy," he heard Reisman say, "I think this kid is really gonna be good. I think he'll help us a lot." Mike thought it was cool to hear about "The Snake" straight from the coach's mouth. When he finished eating, he went out to his truck to head back to work. That's when he noticed passengers stepping off the Greyhound at the station across the street—especially this tall, thin, black kid. One look at his "city-slicker clothes" and suede derby cap, and Mike chuckled to himself: "Boy, is he weird-lookin'. This guy's gotta be from Dallas." Then it hit him: "Hey, that's gotta be 'The Snake!' "

His suspicion was confirmed when Hedden and Reisman crossed to the station to greet the black kid. "Boy, this guy's gonna be interesting," giggled Mike, driving away.

As May stretched over Bokchito, Bryne Rich tended cattle and fences in the brown, dewy fields. He had been feeling better every day, eating more regularly and doing his schoolwork while staying pretty much to himself. He still slept in his parents' bed and felt the constant dull ache of his loss. Often, when the weather turned rainy, his spirit dampened, too. That's when he brooded, feeling sorry for himself and missing Brad keenly. Particularly now, with June approaching, he couldn't help thinking about the basketball camp at Southeastern that he and Brad used to attend every summer. They had planned to go this year, too.

James and Pat Rich knew that. So they each sat down with Bryne and tried to motivate him. James said simply, "You can't stay like this forever. You need to get yourself together." Pat went further; she said, "You can sit around here and be thinking about, 'Well, this happened to me and now what do I do?' But that won't get you anywhere. This happened for a reason, Bryne, and we might never find out what it is. So, you know what I think? I think if Brad was right here today, he wouldn't want you to keep mopin' around. He would want you to be tough and strong and just go on about your life."

"I want to," he replied, a little confused. "I just don't know how." Then Pat found the key.

"Why don't you go to that basketball camp in Durant. It might be good for you."

"I can't go to that camp," he balked. "I just can't go without Brad."

"I think Brad would want you to. You know why? Because of all the fun you had there together. I think Brad would want you to go there and enjoy yourself and play twice as hard, *for him*." This struck a chord: play for Brad; go *for him*. And a memory popped into his mind: the one-on-one game that Brad let him win at that first Tulsa camp.

So—more for Brad than himself—he decided to go.

Southeastern had no trouble filling its camp with the usual fifty to sixty teenagers. Each day of the five-day session, from 8:00 A.M. to noon, they followed the same routine: warm-up shooting; station drills; scrimmage games between teams coached by camp personnel. Bryne Rich found himself on the "Sixers," coached by the talk of the town: Dennis Rodman, aka "The Worm," formerly aka "The Snake." When Bryne first saw him, Dennis was shooting around in the gym . . . with quarters in his ears because he had no pockets on his sweats. Bryne chuckled, thinking exactly what his brother Mike had thought: "Boy, is he weird-lookin'.'' But he was also intrigued at how self-contained Dennis seemed. He could be shooting alone with dozens of kids watching—lots of them snickering at the goofy quarters—yet he looked totally oblivious, as if he didn't care or wasn't really there. Bryne liked that. Along with the fact that he was an actual player on the Southeastern team; Bryne automatically looked up to him for that.

Dennis noticed the scrawny little kid on his team with the wristbands, the high-tops, and the hungry expression. Man, he just *looked* like a player. And so eager to learn. Dennis took to him immediately, metal to magnet. During the first station drills, he slapped Bryne on the rear and said, "Are you ready to play?" and kept pumping him up. Later, during the Sixers' scrimmage, Dennis pulled Bryne aside several times to encourage or advise: "I want you to *hustle*. I want you to dive on the floor for that ball"; "You got a good shot. Whenever you get the ball, take it in and shoot it. Go to the hole *strong*"; "When you play defense, you gotta be *tough*. Go stand in there and take a charge"; "You can *beat* this guy. You're quicker than he is and you got a better shot"; "Okay, you be the point guard. I want you to take control of the game." Anxious to impress his new mentor, Bryne would do everything he said and run right back and ask, "What can I do now?" It was obvious that Dennis approved; he instructed the other kids only in groups.

After camp ended that day, some kids stayed to swim in the pool, most went home, and a few came to the rec center to shoot more baskets. That's where Bryne went. He hadn't had this much fun in almost eight months, and wasn't ready to stop. When he phoned home, he surprised a worried Pat when he said, "Take your time pickin' me up today. I'm gonna hang around a little bit. I'll probably be in the rec center when you come over." It was as though something had steered his mind back into the groove, back to how he used to feel. Plus, he was still basking in the thrill of all that special attention from a big-time college player like Dennis Rodman. Wait till he told his parents about *that*.

When Bryne entered the gym, some of the new recruits were playing a pickup game, checking out each other's moves. He noticed Coach Rodman, so he watched in awe, like a fan backstage. Bryne loved watching his coach pull the same moves he'd just learned from him at camp. But as the game wore on, Bryne felt the itch himself. So he dribbled a ball over to a side basket and started shooting alone.

About twenty minutes later, the weirdest thing:

Dennis Rodman wanders over and says, "Lemme shoot with you," and starts rebounding for him, and then teasing him with two-handed dunks that Bryne can only make in his dreams. Or so he thinks; because all of a sudden, Dennis lifts him up to the hoop and lets him "stuff" for himself, to see how it feels. Finally, Dennis asks his name and when Bryne tells him, he goes, "Okay, Bryne, let's see what you got," and starts playing him one-on-one. Bryne is amazed and excited—he has his own personal star to play with! So he tries too hard to "swish" every shot. Dennis sees he's still awkward, so he starts bolstering and offering tips. "You're good," he says, "you got quickness and speed"—and he teaches Bryne some useful fakes. "Dribble with your *left!*" he commands, forcing him left, again and again. "Most kids only wanna dribble and shoot with their right. But if you can go left, you can really put the hurt on someone."

By the time this improbable session had ended, Bryne felt attached to his new coach. Strangely, Dennis felt the same way and wondered why. It wasn't every day he went over to a little kid and said, "Lemme shoot with you." And he didn't really want to mess with a little white kid in someplace like Durant where people could raise holy hell. It was just that something was drawing him to this kid, almost like he was a younger brother. He'd always wanted a brother. And he really loved the way the kid looked up to him and did everything he told him.

Second day at drills, Coach Rodman cheered Bryne on and gave him more approving nods and more special attention. In turn, Bryne tried harder to please and impress him. During the scrimmage game, Dennis pushed Bryne constantly: "Shoot it!"; "Go to the hole!"; "Take him *left!*" All the stuff they'd worked on yesterday. Later, in the rec center gym, Bryne shot by himself until Dennis joined him again, and they had another great time. Afterward, they went to Dennis's dorm room, where he showed Bryne his summer league jerseys: "NC-UCLA"; "PRO-AM"; "CONVERSE ALL-STARS"—really cool stuff. Then he grabbed some money and they walked across campus to the bookstore snack shop, laughing and talking basketball.

They kept on laughing and talking over burgers and Cokes: where they each were from; what their families were like; life on a farm versus life in the city; how much they loved basketball; even Bryne's dream of playing pro. "If you wanna make pro," Dennis urged seriously, "you might be able to do it. But you got to work hard and push yourself all the time." And Bryne absorbed it as gospel. They spent the rest of the afternoon playing pinball and video games. Bryne couldn't believe it; here was this 6–8 college basketball star paying him so much attention, treating him so nice, buying him food, playing ball with him, and talking with him like they were both the same age. Almost like best friends. Even . . . brothers.

As they returned to campus together, a white man driving past yelled at Dennis, "Go back to Africa! We don't want your kind around here!" Dennis didn't flinch because, he said, it had happened before. But Bryne was infuriated; uncharacteristically, he cursed the driver, who sped away. Walking now in silence, Bryne was surprised at how fiercely protective he'd felt toward his new friend.

■   ■   ■

Shortly after Dennis left for his dorm, Pat arrived at the rec center to drive Bryne home. First in the car and later at home, Bryne
talked excitedly about his camp counselor: what a nice guy he was;
which new basketball moves he'd taught him today; the bookstore
talk; the pinball and video games . . . nonstop "My New Friend" reports. Then he casually dropped in, "I'm gonna ask him to dinner
sometime." That would be fine with Pat—if it ever happened, which
it probably wouldn't. She figured it was a passing thing: he had this
older guy he admired because he was a basketball player, and he'd
look up to him for a while and then it would fade away. But she was
delighted to hear him talk this way; she hadn't seen him so animated
since the accident.

Wednesday, before going to the bookstore to eat, Dennis gave
Bryne two of his basketball jerseys as a gift. Bryne was thrilled; he
didn't know what to say. So he said what he'd been contemplating
since yesterday: "Why don't you come home with me tonight and have
dinner with us. Meet my mom and dad. I been talkin' all about you."
Caught off-guard, Dennis stammered, "No, no, no, I can't do it," and
invented an excuse. He couldn't understand why Bryne would ask.
Dennis considered it too chancey: little white kid; nine years
younger—it wouldn't be right. Every rationalization in the book. But
Bryne looked dejected, so Dennis tried smoothing it over. "Don't
worry," he hedged, "maybe one day I'll come eat dinner with you."
Knowing he never would.

Early that evening, Bryne tacked the jerseys proudly on his wall.
Pat and James wondered where they came from, so he raved again, in
adoring terms, about his friend, the counselor at camp. They were so
happy to see Bryne this way, they didn't press for details. Later, while
Pat was cooking—with three boys she was *always* cooking—Bryne
raised the dinner issue again, approaching it, as he always did when
he wanted his way, through the back door. "You know, I really like
my counselor at camp. He's doin' a lot of great things for me." Only

half-listening, Pat responded, "Well, that's nice, Bryne. I'm glad. I'm real happy about that." And she was.

Then Step No. 2: *Make It Personal:* "Mom, *you'll* like him, too. So will Dad and Barry and Mike."

"Well, I'm sure we will, Bryne."

"I might have him down for dinner. Real soon."

Kid-talk; in one ear, out the other: "Well, you can do that. That would be nice." But Bryne meant business.

"He don't drink or smoke, or nothin'. And I think he's kinda lonesome. Would it be all right if I invited him, you know . . . like this week?"

"Well, of course. Tell him to come ahead. I think we could do it on Friday." Swish! Three-pointer at the buzzer to win.

Elated, Bryne went back to his room. Shortly, though, something occurred to him that he hadn't considered before, and he wanted to make absolutely sure. So he returned to the kitchen, sat on his usual bar stool, and said flatly, "There's one thing I forgot to tell you, Mom." She asked what, and he replied, almost offhandedly, "He's *black.*"

Pat was surprised; it took a second to register. Naturally, she'd assumed he was white. If circumstances had been normal, she might have questioned it more. After all, it was just a fact of life around here that blacks and whites did not interact, and everyone had always known their own place. Nobody considered it racism; it was just the way they'd all been taught. Personally, Pat was not concerned. She'd been raised around black people and never had problems with that. She did think this would be strange, however, or at least "different." How could it *not* be? Bryne had never had a black friend; and she had never had a black person over to her house. Normally, though, her house was like a busy concourse with all kinds of people shuffling in and out, no ID required. Everyone knew that Pat Rich would open her door to a *tramp,* if he was hungry. In fact, because both she and James had soft spots for orphaned kids, they'd taken a few in—even a young American Indian boy—for weeks at a time. Besides, she felt good for Bryne because he really liked this guy and seemed much more adjusted since they'd met. She wanted that to go on; she was thrilled her son was coming back to life.

Since Pat always consulted with James, she mentioned the idea to him. They both agreed it was no big deal for Bryne to have a friend over to eat, no matter who he was. Especially since it was for only one night.

Again on Thursday Dennis and Bryne spent the whole day together. People who knew them from camp had noticed their bond—they were sort of a "Mutt and Jeff" duo on campus now. As they bummed around, Bryne pressed the dinner invitation, but Dennis still declined. Last place he wanted to be. But Bryne pressured him mercilessly, until finally—though reluctantly—Dennis said yes. However, later that day, he phoned Bryne at home to say he couldn't come tomorrow night for dinner because he had no way to get there. So Bryne told his mom that his friend was so shy, he didn't want to come, and his latest excuse was that he didn't have a ride. As Bryne had planned, Pat said, "Then we'll pick him up ourselves." Major relief for Bryne: now Dennis had no way out.

Suddenly curious, Pat asked Bryne, "What is your friend's name?" Now he realized he'd only referred to Dennis as "my friend."

"Oh," he grinned mischievously. "His name is Worm."

Pat thought: "Well, that's kind of a funny name: Worm." But she didn't want to put Bryne on the spot about it, so she didn't follow up.

Shirley Rodman didn't hear regularly from Dennis once he'd left Dallas for Durant. In one sense she had wanted it that way. She'd come to the difficult conclusion when he left that if she ran to see him at school too often, he might end up depending on her the rest of his life. So she wrote him a little note, stating simply, "I am here if you need me," and stayed in touch, but left the rest up to him.

The first time he called her was the day after he met Bryne in basketball camp. "Momma, I met this little white kid," he'd raved, "and he's really nice. I liked him the first time I saw him." He rambled on in fragments about coaching Bryne; and that Bryne had two older brothers and lived on a farm; and that he seemed to need a friend. Finally, Shirley cut him off: "Slow down, Dennis. What are we talking about? Is this really important?" To him it was, so he tried to explain more clearly what he didn't understand himself: his attachment to a twelve-year-old white kid. Shirley was skeptical but accepting; this was the first time in years that he'd sounded excited and animated about anything, so she was happy about that. And it didn't bother her, either, that Bryne was white and only twelve, because she perceived Dennis now as "basically this thirteen-year-old kid inside that lost his father and needs a companion."

In his next call that week, Dennis chattered on about his budding camaraderie with Bryne, about their jaunts around Durant, and things Bryne told him about his parents. But when he mentioned the racial slurs in town, it rankled Shirley no end; she took this intolerance personally and started to fear for her son's safety. Thus, the night before camp ended, when Dennis called her again to announce, all geared up, "Momma, Bryne invited me to come eat dinner at his house!" Shirley tried to discourage him from going. "That's fine, Dennis," she said in a reticent tone. "But what is so great about that?" Her fears had kicked in full-force; aware that Durant had virtually no black families, and that Dennis hadn't made any black friends yet, she didn't want him walking blindly into any potential "racial situations." She felt compelled to keep warning him not to do anything rash: "You must be very careful, Dennis, about how you handle yourself with white people up there." He conceded, "Okay, I will be"—but he wasn't concerned.

The next day, at camp's close, Bryne was noticeably subdued. Something was obviously on his mind. After their final shoot-around together at the gym, he and Dennis sat down for Cokes, also apparently for the last time. Bryne said, a little sadly: "Well, I guess I'm never gonna see you anymore after tonight." He was already dreading the next day's void without Worm. Dennis just ate his burger quietly. He didn't let on, but he'd been dreading the end of camp almost as much as Bryne. The afternoon closed in silence, and Bryne went home to prepare for the dinner. At least he still had that to look forward to.

At seven-fifteen, James drove his excited son back to Durant in the little red Subaru that he used to deliver the mail. They found Dennis shooting baskets at the rec center. Bryne hurried him up until Dennis finally said, "All right, all right, I'm ready," and put on his derby cap and sauntered outside. But then he hung back, nervously. So Bryne summoned his dad out to meet him. James was startled when he saw Dennis; his first thought was: "He's *tall*." And when they shook hands, he sensed how shy Dennis was—a lot like himself.

When James said, "Well, let's get goin'" and started for the car, Worm didn't budge. "Small town . . . white family's house . . . God!" went through his mind, so he decided he had no reason to go through with this. But with Bryne urging him on, and James waiting patiently, he felt he was on the spot. "Damn!" he thought, caving in. "I guess I'll just go and get it over with." So they piled in the car and drove, mostly in silence, out to the family farm.

Mike and Barry Rich were gassing up at the service station in Bokchito when they spotted their dad's little Subaru chugging home. They'd been invited to the house for dinner to meet Bryne's new celebrity friend, so they were tickled to see them all in the car. But what really caught their eyes was Dennis's huge bulk totally obliterating the backseat. Barry, who always had a hard time keeping a straight face anyway, remarked, "Man, it looks like he's *wearin'* the car, not ridin' in it!" Then, when Bryne recognized Mike's truck and waved, so did Dennis. Barry and Mike started laughing so hard, they couldn't catch a breath. Mike managed to snort, "God dog! I never *seen* such a big hand!" And the biggest hand in the world kept waving away as the little red car disappeared up the road.

Maybe that set the tone for the whole night: "Goofiness in Store." Starting with Pat, cooking the meal, awaiting her family's arrival. A little apprehensive, she was wondering: "What will this Worm guy be like?" when the phone interrupted her thought. It was a friend, who asked innocently enough, "What're you doing?" Suddenly, Pat felt playful. "Oh, nothin'," she replied, deliberately casual. "I'm just cookin' dinner for a worm." Suckered, her friend responded just as Pat had hoped: "You're doin' *what?*" Then Pat dropped the coup de grace: "You heard me. We're gonna have a *Worm* for dinner!" And they both cracked up like babies, while she finally explained.

When James pulled into the drive, Pat watched amazed from the porch as this enormously tall, incredibly thin black boy unfolded himself like a collapsible table out of the little red car. "Weird-lookin'," she thought—perhaps setting some psychic record for Same First Impression by Three Members of a Family About the Same Stranger. But Pat also thought: "Well, no wonder this guy didn't want to come. Why would a big, older black guy want to have dinner with a thirteen-year-old white boy and his family?" And as Dennis barely ducked under the ceiling fan on his way inside, he was wondering the same thing.

Bryne made introductions. Then he, his dad, and Dennis sat in the living room while Pat finished preparing the meal. James broke the ice: "So, where are you from, Dennis?"

"Dallas."

"Uh-huh. I suppose you played some pretty tough ball down there?"

"Oh yeah. Had a rec gym right next to my mom's place."

"Oh, uh-huh. Well, what about this deal . . . I mean, did I read that you played for that junior college over to Gainesville?"

"Cooke County. Yep. I played."

"What position?"

"Center."

"Uh-huh. Well, how 'bout Southeastern? I mean, man, I tell you, you play at Southeastern and you're gonna have to be pretty good."

"Oh yeah. Better be."

There were more casual questions about home and his studies in school . . . until Barry and Mike showed up. Still tickled by their earlier impressions, they started off giggling and kept it up. Everything about Worm was a crack-up to them: his nickname; how he dressed; how he talked; how he walked; his huge hands; those size-99 feet! Worm eventually got a kick out of them, too. But at the moment, he felt like the Richard Pryor character he'd seen in the movie *The Toy*, when Pryor auditioned for the job of Human Toy for a wealthy man's son. Only here, Dennis felt like he was auditioning for the job of Friend.

This, it turned out, was more overreaction than fact. The Riches were open, informal, sincere, while he had been defensive and scared coming in. Besides, as he well knew, it was much more like *Bryne* auditioning for *him*. In any case, Saved by Pat: "Dinner is served."

The Riches still joke about this today: "You'd've thought a *king* was comin' to dinner!" That's because Bryne had worked in a frenzy for hours cleaning and recleaning the house, and arranging the table as though it *were* for a king. He set out Pat's finest, seldom-used china, her sterling silverware, elegant crystal glasses, napkins folded in holders, and fine linen tablecloth. "Very richy-lookin'" is how Pat still thinks of it today—no pun intended. Later, she would blame this self-conscious display for Worm's mistaken notion that they were, in fact, rich.

Finally, Pat's bounty: thick country steaks as big as saddles, fist-sized baked potatoes, and fresh-picked salad galore. A feast fit for, if not a king, at least a king-sized Worm.

"Do you eat like this all the time?" Dennis asked, wondering what to try first. "I don't eat like this at home." He didn't mean his mother's; he meant more like his Bumming-Around-Town-Kentucky Fried Chicken-McDonald's-type home.

"Oh yeah," Bryne said to impress him, "we *always* eat like this." Which happened to be true.

Mike and Barry giggled.

Right away, Dennis had trouble with the tall, trim, crystal glasses Bryne had insisted on using for the iced tea. Every time he tried to drink, the tea spilled over the rim. He couldn't get more than drops. No one had noticed, and Dennis was too embarrassed, and polite, to say anything. Eventually, Bryne picked up on it and asked what was wrong.

"They're too small," Dennis almost whispered, looking away. He would rather have left than get into this.

"You mean you want more to drink?" offered Pat.

"No. I just can't drink out of it." Now everyone was stumped. Especially Pat.

"Why?" she pressed, concerned. "Is it broken?"

"No, it ain't broken. But do you have anything bigger than this?" Mike and Barry giggled.

Bigger? No problem. They handed him one of their tall jumbo mugs, filled with enough tea for three big glasses. Normally overkill; but, for him, just about capacity. And it worked; he could drink fine out of that. No one knew that the real problem wasn't the glass, it was Dennis's *lips*. They were simply too big for the narrow crystal rim.

If Mike and Barry had known, they surely would've giggled. Worm had little to say for a while after that, until James started talking basketball again, inquiring about his scholarship. The topic triggered Dennis's low self-esteem, and maybe some fears: "Oh, my mom wanted me to take it. I guess I'll just stick around long enough to flunk out, so she'll be satisfied."

Bryne wouldn't hear it. He said, "No, Worm. If you stay in college you're gonna make All-American and become a pro. I know you will."

"No way. I ain't good enough."

"You *will* be. You'll go pro, you wait and see if you don't."

"Dennis," Pat interrupted, "can I ask you something?"

"Yep."

"Why are you called 'Worm'?" She couldn't hold back a snicker.

Bryne answered for him: "'Cause he's so skinny and long, when he used to play pinball he wiggled around that machine so much they started callin' him Worm."

Then Worm explained 'Worm': "And whenever I played street ball, and I fell down—"

"Yeah," Bryne chimed in, "he'd be down on the ground just squirmin' all around like a big ole worm."

Everyone giggled at once for a change. Things loosened up.

After dinner, in the twilight, Bryne, James, and Worm shot free throws at the basketball hoop outside. Then, James watched as Bryne and Worm went one-on-one. A student of the game he'd loved since playing in high school, James couldn't resist a little coaching. "Don't forget rebounding," he kept reminding Worm, who concentrated mostly on scoring and fancy slam-dunks. "Your opponent shoots one up there, the ball goes in, there ain't nothin' you can do about that. But if he misses and you get up there and grab that ball, well, there's your chance." Worm gave no indication he was listening to this advice; but he was. He would admit years later, in fact, that this simple guidance helped inspire him to focus harder on rebounding than his other skills.

Shortly, James wandered back into the den, where he and Pat listened to the friendly, spirited basketball chatter outside as Bryne and Worm played through the last soft rays of light.

"I like him," Pat remarked.

"Bryne sure does," said James, taking her hand. "I was scared we'd never hear him talk excited like that again."

Afterward, Bryne led Worm to his room to proudly show him the jerseys he'd tacked on the wall. Barry and Mike joined them, and they all stayed in there for hours, jabbering and laughing like grade-school kids. Finally, Bryne emerged tugging Worm by the hand toward the den. They approached Pat and James, who were quietly watching TV. Dennis felt as uncomfortable as when Shirley had forced his football coach to tell him, face-to-face, why he wasn't good enough to make the team. But too late to back out now; they were on a mission.

"Momma, Daddy," Bryne began boldly, though crossing his fingers, too. "Can Worm stay overnight?"

Lightning bolt.

Dennis thought he saw shock in their eyes. Pat's fleeting thought—"Bryne, this is a colored boy you're talkin' about"—even caught *her* by surprise. She knew that wasn't really her; it was only her upbringing. Squirming, she looked at James, who was a little caught-short himself. Neither knew what to say. Bryne's disappointed look tipped the scale for Pat, who finally managed to blurt, "Well, yes. Sure he can stay."

Figuring: "Okay, he'll spend the night and the phase will pass and that'll be the end of it."

5

James

and Pat

JAMES RICH: My daddy's name was Therrell.

He went to war, probably in '41, and I don't think he ever come back to my mother. They just didn't get along, so they got a divorce. She never explained what happened, he was just gone when I was three. Once in a while I'd hear he was in Wyoming or Louisiana, or here or there. I don't guess you would call him, just exactly, a drifter. I think he was a welder, but I can't say for sure.

After he left, I only saw him twice that I can remember. The first time was around 1965, when I graduated from high school and was a daddy myself. He was in Dallas visiting his sister. So I went to Dallas with Pat and the kids, just to see what he looked like, I guess. I remember he didn't seem like he was my dad, more like just another person. Probably 'cause I didn't really know him, I more knew *of* him— that's what it amounted to. And he never did come up here to see me, so I never went back to see him. Until he died and I went to his funeral.

I felt I had to go to my own daddy's funeral, since he was my flesh and blood. But I didn't feel any emotion at all. I mainly went out of respect; we visited his sister after it was over, and we stayed with that whole side of the family and just really felt good about goin'. I haven't thought about my daddy since.

When I was about five, I started livin' with my uncle and aunt, Clarence and Odessa Gray, who actually raised me—in the same house where me and Pat live now. What happened was, Clarence got into it with my mother. This was their place and she wasn't doin' what they thought she should, so she bought her a place in Bokchito and moved over there. I went back and forth; spent the week down at Odessa's and then weekends with my mother. Eventually, I stayed full-time with Clarence and Des.

They give me most of my values. They were good, moral people; they instilled things like honesty, knowin' right from wrong, and, probably most of all, hard work. I remember I could go to town on a weekend night and come in at twelve or one, and they wouldn't say a word. But next mornin' at six I got up to go to work. One time when I was in seventh or eighth grade, I slipped off to town on my bike to play ball, without tellin' Clarence, and he come down there yellin', "You get to the house! You got chores!" And when I got back, he pulled out his belt and whipped my rear good. You had to take work serious, boy.

I played basketball and baseball as a kid—I was a real good athlete. Averaged 32 a game in basketball, pretty good for a southpaw. I always got to play after school, like everyone else, but then I'd have to go home and work the farm. Every day, I had to feed the hogs and gather the eggs from the chickens. Winter, there were cattle to feed. Summertime, I'd plant the peanuts and the corn, and if there was plowin' to do, I'd do the plowin' and Des would do the feedin'. Aunt Des was one heck of a workin' woman. I mean, she would go out there and work her tail off. She'd be out drivin' the tractor and feedin' the cattle and hoein' the peanuts, row by row. I'm talkin' about seven, eight hours a day in the burnin' hot sun, ninety, ninety-five degrees.

Uncle Clarence did most of the work till I was fifteen. Then he got real sick with lung cancer and had an operation, and it paralyzed him; when he tried to walk, he would stagger. When he got real bad,

I had to make a choice about my life. I remember I was playin' baseball one Sunday, and I went to the hospital in my baseball uniform and he was out of it. He said, "James, I don't think I'm gonna make it. You'll have to take care of Des." But it wasn't actually that I had to take care of her; she could've sold everything and lived off that. He just wanted to know she'd be looked after. He told me that on Sunday and then he died on Monday. He was only fifty-three. Probably would've lived another ten or fifteen years, and I could've worked into it slow; that would've been a whole lot better.

Thing about it was, I didn't have a chance to do what I wanted. I always wanted to be a major league baseball player—I was a pretty good left-handed pitcher and that was my dream. I could've went to Murray State Junior College on a scholarship. Des said, "If you want to go to college, you go ahead and we'll sell this place. But if you want to run it, we can run it together." I just said, "Let's run it, then." And I stuck with that. So here I am, steppin' outta high school when other kids was gettin' jobs and playin' ball, and I'm wantin' to do that, too, but I had so much stuff out there to do that I couldn't be like them anymore. I had to take on the responsibilities of a grown person.

As far as farming, we completely depended on nature for our living, so we always prayed for rain. We used to say, "If it don't rain, we're goin' hungry," and sometimes we did. But I learned something new every year. Like when I started irrigating my own peanuts out of the pond on our land. I rigged a motor by the pond and ran a sixteen-inch pipe into the fields to sprinklers on either side of the peanut rows, and I'd pump that pond near dry. It could go six weeks in July without rain sometimes, so you had to figure ways to make it. You couldn't just fall back and quit when it got tough; you had to hang on and be self-sufficient.

It got easier every year, because I learned my lessons. I remember the first year I planted peanuts, the first field we planted it rained two or three times and the crabgrass come up as big as the peanuts, so I only had about eight or ten acres growin' on the whole forty we planted. That was back in the days before you used chemicals to kill off the grass. I was out there tryin' to plant, and the grass was all grown up, and I had to start again. Boy, that was my first lesson. I said: "I won't do that anymore. It cost too much time and money." And I never did it again.

Then I had an older guy that helped me a lot, named Claude Edwards, and he told me, "James, it don't make any difference whatever you do, always put plenty of fertilizer down and plenty of seed." And that settled in my head, because I remember when I was plantin' peanuts before that, I'd be plantin' thirty or thirty-five pounds, which I thought was a whole lot. But after what Claude told me, I planted *fifty* pounds. My aunt said, "Boy, you are plantin' these peanuts way too thick. You're puttin' way too many seeds down." And I said, "Well, I would rather *have* a stand than *not* have a stand"—and they turned out to be the best damned peanut crop we ever made in our lives. Here I am, twenty-three years old and I'm makin' better crops than the people when they was fifty and sixty years old! My aunt furnished the money and I did most of the work, so we split what we made. I ended up makin' my aunt a living, and me, too.

For as long as I can remember, we always worked with the black people from around here. I never saw color myself; I could care less. A person's a person to me. I worked in the fields with black people every year, so I knew 'em just like I would know anyone else in town. I remember it took about twenty-five people to bring the peanuts to the thrasher. So we'd all go out and fill these five-gallon buckets with peanuts, and then dump 'em into tote sacks and sew the sacks up and leave 'em out there to dry for about two weeks. Then we'd go back and haul the sacks to the thrasher. They drove these wagons between the peanut rows, and two people would start loadin' the sacks onto the wagon. All of us workin' together all day long; white and black— didn't make no difference to the peanuts. And wherever you worked at, people helped each other and everybody fixed food for everybody.

Only thing was, the white people would eat first and then the black people would sit and eat—this was older-generation black people, back when they didn't *want* to eat with the whites. That was just the only way I had ever seen; I didn't know any different. I always wondered why, though. I thought: "Well, I don't see any reason for this." Because I grew up with 'em, there was probably ten or twelve black kids my age. And I worked the fields with 'em, and I wrestled 'em just like I would a white person, and I just as soon sit by one of them as have two white people on each side of me. I just didn't know any better 'cause nobody said too much about it, not even them.

We had this fella who used to work over to Riddle's Grocery, and he remembered that black folks used to come in the store through the back door. Because they wanted to, not because they had to. There wasn't any reason for it; we didn't have a racial problem here. It was just that they were more comfortable that way, so they kept on doin' it. And some of those same people raised their own peanuts, and I would work for *them*—we would trade off workin' each other's farms: "You help me and I'll help you." They earned their own land same as the white folks did. But it's a fact, you always knew there was a separation between you, even though you didn't know why. I guess you could say it was like the land we farmed: it was always just there.

PAT RICH: My dad was a farmer, and my mother, my brother and my three sisters all picked cotton on the farm back in the forties.

When I was a child, a black woman named Lucy Mars used to baby-set me at our house when everyone was out pickin' cotton. Momma said I was the cryin'-ist baby she ever had; she said I cried so much she would call Lucy over because she was the only one that could get me to stop. Lucy used to rock me on her knee and sing me this song:

> Hey! Hot Tod Lucy, Hot Tod Lucy,
> Ooo-weee, Ooo-weee.
> Hey! Hot Tod Lucy, Hot Tod Lucy,
> Luuuu-ceee! Hot Tod, Hot Tod Lucy.

The way she got her nickname was because when you got a cold back then, they would mix you a hot toddy. And we only had one doctor and he lived miles away, so whenever one of us kids got sick, if a hot toddy didn't cure us, they had to call these black people over because they had their own remedies. My mother would call Lucy, and she'd doctor us with her broomweed tea and herb-juice drinks. They worked as good as a hot toddy, too. So we called her "Hot Tod" Lucy.

All of my growin'-up days, my family lived in a small community called Beams, and what we used to call the "colored" section was just down the road. My dad hired a lot of black people and we never had any conflicts. But we didn't eat at the same table with them: you eat there and we eat over here. They had their community and we had ours, and we interacted, but it was a socially accepted fact that whites didn't get too involved with blacks. It was just understood.

Black people always fascinated me as a kid. I remember one day, a few of us snuck through the woods to the cemetery and decided to watch how they had their funerals. I was still really scared of 'em— maybe because they talked so different than us and were from this other community we didn't know much about. So we hid behind this big oak tree and I thought: "If they catch us, they will put me in that grave and cover me up." I really believed that. So we watched real quiet-like as they all circled around the grave, holdin' hands and cryin' and singin' gospel songs. It was a strange service to us, but yet I really enjoyed it. It surprised me they were such emotional people: mourning the dead by singin' and cryin'.

I guess they scared me a little because they seemed so different. A lot of that went back to my raising. I used to have to walk to school, and since we lived so nearby the black section, my mom and dad would always tell me, "Be careful of Chester and Reesa"—these two black guys in the community. It was like, "Don't talk to strangers." And they didn't know what Chester and Reesa would do with us girls. So they told us, "Don't talk to 'em. Go on about your business and don't mess with 'em."

So one day when I was about eight, I was walkin' to school and

Chester topped the hill behind me. I kept walkin' and lookin' back, and it looked like he was followin' me. So I went faster because I was scared of what my momma and daddy had said—beware, and be careful, and all this. But when we got to the crossroad, Chester just kept walkin' and I went on to school. He wasn't followin' me, he was just walkin' down the road.

We had all this fear from hearin' people talk about what black people did. But we never heard about what white people did; we were never taught to be afraid of a white person. There was nothin' wrong with Chester and Reesa; they became kinda casual friends of the family. But here is where the fear was: we had three girls, and Chester and Reesa would come over and visit with us. Reesa was just kinda there, but Chester interacted with us more. He liked to play guitar with my sister, so they would sit around pickin' together. Chester got to where he was over quite a bit, but my dad put a stop to it because he thought my sister was gonna start dating a black guy. We didn't understand all that. We were just kids havin' fun.

When I was in grade school, we moved into the house James Rich grew up in, which we're livin' in today. And James was livin' over in his aunt Des's house, practically right next door. I believe God has a plan for everyone, and that had to be a part of the plan for me. Actually, James and I barely knew each other then. I used to lay on my bed and watch him out my bedroom window, loading hay in his pickup. Every time he left, he'd peel out of there and throw gravel and dig a hole, and I thought: "What a smart aleck."

But then I saw him on the school bus and he looked like he just got out of a bathtub, and I thought: "There's the smart aleck. But he looks so neat and clean." His shirt was always ironed, and Des put creases in his pants, and he had this cowlick that wouldn't stay down so he combed his hair all neat with oil. And he always had this smile on his face, and I would think: "Hey, he's a neat guy." But I wasn't physically attracted to him then; and it wasn't time for me to fall in love.

In high school, I had a real good figure and I was kind of conceited; I thought: "Well, I can go with any boy I want to." I was always after a challenge. My junior year, I considered James as a challenge. I was dating this older guy, Ron, and my best girlfriend Donnella was dating a guy named Joe, and one day she said, "Pat, you need to get you a boyfriend in high school so we could have a lot more fun. James Rich is who you need to date. He is so cute; he's got the prettiest legs. Sometimes, you look at his legs when he puts on his basketball suit and comes out on the floor, and they're so smooth they look like *Marilyn Monroe's* legs!" I had never thought about it before, but she drilled it into my head: "He is so cute. You need to date him. I'll date Joe and you date James, and they are cousins and we can go on double dates." Finally, she got me intrigued, and I started seein' James.

He was real popular and always got good grades, except in English. So I decided to help him out with his book reports. Once, I read the same book he had to read and I got up and gave a report in front of my class. The teacher said, "Very good, Geraldine"—Geraldine was my middle name, which they called me in high school. Then I thought the teacher had forgot about my report, so I let James give the same one in his class, and she said, "James, you can sit down. Geraldine has already given that report once."

Another time, we were driving up this hill in James's '55 Chevy and this old guy my daddy knew, he was drinkin', and he would act crazy when he drank, and James kind of darted at him with the car, just jokin' with him. But that sucker turned his car around and pulled us over and told James to get out so he could whip him. James was gonna fight; he's a proud and stubborn man and he won't tolerate bein' bullied. But I was just as stubborn. He was a young boy and this guy was older and much bigger, and James had never had a real fight like that before. So I just backed James up against the car and I spread my arms out across him and I said to the guy, "If you whip him, you have to whip me, too! My daddy wouldn't like that, now would he? You just get your butt down the road, because you ain't gonna jump on James!" And he got back in his car and left. I had a lot of self-confidence when I was younger. I could be hardheaded if I had to, and pretty darn resourceful. Which came in handy later on.

I dated James through senior year, and he got to really liking me. But I wasn't ready for that so I kept seein' Ron also, and just playin' the field. I used to write on a piece of paper, "Which one will I marry, Ron or James?" And I'd think about that at school all day. Well, one night I went out with Ron and the next night I went to graduation with James, and next day I was the talk of the town: "Can you believe Geraldine done James so *dirty!*" But I never did tell James I would go steady, and I resented that small-town gossip. That's what really started my phobias about this town.

Like when I was fifteen and I went to Dallas in the summertime to hold down a job and earn my school clothes. The first summer, I worked in a cafeteria; the second in a hat factory; the third at Texas Instruments. I kept gettin' better jobs for more money, so every summer I would come back with all these lovely clothes, probably the prettiest in Bokchito. Well, one time these two little old ladies started a rumor on me. They said I was down in Dallas *prostitutin'* for money! They started gossipin' about me because I had nicer clothes than maybe their daughters, and I looked real good in those clothes.

I was very sensitive to what people said about me, and I had earned those clothes, so the gossip really hurt me. And the same thing happened to James. His uncle Clarence was on the school board, so the gossipers said: "James Rich gets by with plenty and he always comes up smellin' like roses." And it was common knowledge that James would inherit his aunt and uncle's estate someday, and that he had one of the best futures in town. So then we heard: "James Rich has got it made. He's gonna inherit his uncle's land." And when we got married: "She's marryin' him for his money."

They just always did gossip here, and I grew up with it and hated it and I still hate it because it's wrong to say slanderous things about people. That is the only thing I don't like about the town—the people are nice here but some of 'em always want to make everyone else's business their business. For example, out here in the country, you would think you had your privacy. You don't think anyone's watchin' you, but some people are. When I was fifteen, we didn't have city water at our house. I remember it was real hot one day, so I decided to go draw me a bucket of cool water from the well. I had on this flimsy ole crop-top, but I thought: "I can get this water drawed before anyone sees me." So I ran out there and drew my water and ran back inside. Darned if I didn't hear about it the very next day! Someone had seen me before I got back in the house, and now the whole town was gossipin': "Pat was caught outside, *plum-naked*, drawin' water!"

One time for Christmas, I had this Santa Claus, but I didn't have a clear bulb to put in it, so I put a red bulb in. Well, around here red signifies a whorehouse. And so a guy down the road went to town and told everyone, "Pat has a red light in her window. If you don't believe me, go out there and look!" And everybody laughed about it and hurried on out to see Pat's new red Santa. After I heard about that in town, I hurried home and changed the bulb.

James always says I think people are talkin' about me when they probably aren't. Or if they are, I pay 'em too much mind. But he don't like to face the fact that people do gossip, and that it can have a real serious effect on you. He has these two sayings: "People need to think before they talk," and "If they're talkin' about me, then they're lettin' someone else rest." And that's as far as he thinks about it; it just don't bother him. But he's a man, and gossip don't bother a man as much as a woman, especially in a little town like this where your reputation is everything. Men would never hear the things I have heard about myself. And I can tell you, I have just about heard it all.

6

Pretty Nice Life to Be Part of

Giggles and bursts of laughter issued from Bryne's room all night.

Past midnight, Barry and Mike were still in stitches on the floor, while Worm sat on the bed with Bryne, who started to doze. When he fell asleep, they pulled out the trundle bed and Pat brought sheets and a blanket for Worm, and everyone called it a night. Early next morning, Pat decided to look in on Bryne. When she opened the door, she was met with the comical sight on the trundle bed of two colossal black feet protruding from under the blanket, which Dennis had yanked up over his head. Chuckling to herself, she tiptoed out. On the way back to her bedroom, she realized this was the first time since the accident that Bryne had slept through the night in his own room.

James arose after dawn and left for the post office. The boys got up late and chattered about the fun they'd had last night, and it struck Pat how comfortable her sons were around their new guest. Dennis, though, still seemed tentative and a little uncomfortable. So Bryne took him along to help with some chores and then showed him around the farm, introducing him to plows, calves, and cattle. The farm was a revelation to Dennis; even the insects and frogs seemed to fascinate him. Then they grabbed the basketball to play their usual one-on-one.

Afterward, Bryne drove Worm into Bokchito, even though he didn't have his driver's license yet. There was just one cop in town, and since Bryne had snuck around in the car numerous times for fun, he knew where the cop would be. Dennis was impressed with Bryne's savvy and guts; plus, *he* thought it was fun, too. They stopped at Easter's Cafe for lunch, and of course when Dennis walked in the door, heads turned. He looked unnerved; he thought they were staring because he was black. Bryne said no, it was because he was so tall and they were all wondering: "Who's this guy with Bryne?" Dennis believed him, so they sat at the counter and ordered their staple: hamburgers and Cokes.

That evening, though no one broached the subject, Pat automatically set a place for Dennis at the dinner table. Like them, he felt more relaxed, though not entirely at ease. But later, when the four boys drifted again to Bryne's room, they carried the first night's gains further with more giggling, laughing, teasing. Later, Barry and Mike departed to cruise Durant for girls. Since Dennis loved to stay up late watching TV, he and Bryne ended up in the den watching MTV videos and sports reports into the night.

From her bed, Pat heard them return to Bryne's room to sleep. She and James were not only delighted at how well all the boys were getting along, they were ecstatic that Bryne had found himself again. They were still shaking their heads that he'd finally returned to his own bed, as though he'd never left it. And while last night had been mostly circumstance, tonight was different. Tonight, he *chose* to sleep in his room. Obviously, Pat told herself, Bryne was no longer scared of having bad dreams.

The third day unfolded like the second: farm chores, games of one-on-one, casual exploration. In the afternoon James said to Dennis, "Come on with me. I wanna take you back here to the pond and show you how we feed the catfish." As they started outside, Pat warned Dennis pointedly, "Better be careful, Worm. That pond's stocked with *alligators*, you know." Despite Bryne's assurances that she was pulling his chain, and that they stocked the pond themselves with only catfish,

Dennis still half-believed her. A farm was as foreign to him as Russia; he didn't know what to expect and he didn't speak the language. Damn; for all he knew, out here "catfish" might mean "Oklahoma alligator." "Worm, we ain't *got* no alligators around here," Bryne tried to reassure him. "Yeah," Dennis shot back, "but till now you didn't have no *black folks* here, neither." Apparently, he was loosening up.

Once at the pond, James reached his hand into a bucket of bait. "Watch this," he said, winking at Bryne. "When I throw this stuff out there, boy, you are gonna see all hell breakin' loose." As James heaved the bait, Dennis focused intently on the pond—and sure enough, when the bait broke water so did fish, in a splashing frenzy the likes of which Dennis had never seen. "Gawd!" he blurted in awe. Then they let *him* try it, and he was thrilled he could create the same commotion with the fish. "Damn!" he said. "Yeah," Bryne added, "all you gotta do is throw a *cork* in there and they start hittin' all around." So James suggested some fishing.

Dennis had no idea how to catch a fish from shore. Fact was, if he couldn't put a quarter, or a car key, or a basketball in it, he had no earthly use for it. That's why it took him a frustrating two hours to land what James and Bryne mockingly dubbed "the oldest, blindest, stupidest fish in the pond." However, Dennis had another quandary. Now that he had the poor fish hooked, how did he reel it in? So they showed him, and he pulled it up without using the net: a nice-sized bluegill—that ended up, ironically, their biggest catch of the day. But when Dennis pulled it in, the death rattle emitted by this fish—a spooky clicking of gills—got him unnerved. He was suddenly too squeamish to remove the hook or even handle the fish. "Get it away," he cringed. "It's too slimy to touch!"

Apparently not too slimy, though, to later wave like a trophy at a startled Pat in her kitchen. "Miss Rich," he bragged exuberantly then, "you know why I caught the biggest one?"

"No, why?" she blundered in.

"'Cause there ain't nothin' a fish likes better than a worm. And I'm the biggest Worm *he* ever seen!"

Also apparently not too slimy to devour at the backyard family fish fry, either, where—final wonder—Dennis couldn't get enough.

That evening, Bryne and Dennis watched a TV replay of a boxing match and started perfecting their special brand of "The Dozens"— the ancient, streetwise cut-upsmanship that always began with "Your momma" and, at least a dozen cuts later, finished there, too. Their version, of course, was softer, though no less ferociously felt:

Worm: "Oh, look at that chump. He punches like your momma."

Bryne: "No, he punches like you. And you punch like *your* momma."

Worm: "What you know 'bout fightin'? Most thing you ever fought was a cold with a aspirin! Gawd Awmighty! Look at that chump. He can't punch his shadow, just like you."

Bryne: "Well, if he can't punch, how come he's beatin' up on your homeboy? He's whuppin' your boy *big-time*, son."

Worm: "No, I told you, he's whippin' your momma. That's about all he *could* whip. 'Cept maybe your daddy."

And so on. Couched in mock-sarcasm and phony malice, the point was the bonding, not the banter. Although, overhearing bits and pieces from the living room, Pat and James weren't certain what to make of it; they just knew Dennis and Bryne were having fun.

Late that night, when Bryne and Dennis had returned to their room, and the talking and laughing and reliving of the day's events had ceased, Pat strolled over to tuck Bryne in, as usual, before retiring herself. Quietly opening the door, she was surprised to find Dennis's trundle bed empty, sheets uncreased. Then, in a glance, she was absolutely stunned. There was Bryne, dead to the world in his bed, all curled up . . . in Worm's entwining arms.

Dennis stayed with the Riches for nearly two weeks straight. He and Bryne continued sleeping in the same bed, like inverted bowling pins now: Worm's head by Bryne's feet to make more room. Bryne told his mom he felt safe with Worm, like he had with her and James. It was clear now: Bryne had found a true "soul brother" in Dennis, who'd started weaning him emotionally from Pat and James.

At the same time, because the Riches were such a close-knit family, it was only natural for Pat and James to participate in their son's bonding process with Dennis—even though, with Dennis along, they no longer resembled your ordinary Bokchito family. This was to be less an issue for James than for Pat. While he didn't consider Dennis a member of their family yet, James wouldn't have blinked if he was. If he drew any distinction at all just then, it was simply that Dennis had become more important to Bryne than anyone had anticipated. But heck, that was okay, too; go with the flow. In fact, as a man of inconspicuous emotions, James rarely foundered in his own speculations. More like a mariner's sextant, he fixed his place in the world by nature, not design. Thus, in these early stages, James silently delighted that Bryne enjoyed Dennis's company, and while that kept up it was fine with him.

Pat had no major problem yet, either; she just wasn't so sure the friendship would last. Experience had taught her that an obvious mismatch like this would only be temporary—but as long as Dennis was so nice to Bryne, it didn't seem like such a big deal. Besides, she and James liked to treat everyone like human beings, opening their home as they had countless times before to orphans and strays—particularly kids—and priding themselves on their neighborly hospitality. She just thought: "Well, this is Bryne. When he takes to somebody, he likes them and likes to spend time with them." And Worm was fitting in, she felt, "like a missing piece of a puzzle, like putting a puzzle together. He just blended right in."

So, despite her slight reservations, and letting motherly instincts guide her, she indulged Dennis's sudden zest for fish by orchestrating their first dinner out together at Wobble's Fin and Feather, by Lake Texhoma in Durant. Dennis loved it: the feast of different fish he'd never tasted; and especially, mused Pat, that James paid the bill. Not in the sense that Dennis didn't have to pay for himself, but more that he could eat in a great place like this as part of the family. In other words, she inferred for Dennis: *Pretty nice life to be part of.*

Little wonder, then, that Wobble's Fin and Feather became his favorite place to eat. Not to say it wasn't a little awkward, at least for Pat. Because, when they drove through Bokchito on their way to eat, she believed that people stared at them, and were probably thinking something like: "Well, there's Pat and James, and there's Bryne, and then there's this black boy—I don't know why *he's* there." In time, these suspected ruminations would get under her skin. But for now, adjusting to this odd disruption in their normal routine, both James and Pat did well playing it by ear. Their only rule was unspoken: eight months of habitual protectiveness dictated that they continue accommodating Bryne's needs.

In many ways, that increasingly included Dennis, almost de rigueur. For as he and Bryne connected like brothers, they grew fiercely loyal to one another, making it difficult, for example, to apply the usual discipline methods at home. Neither James, a reasonable but toe-the-line disciplinarian—he subscribed to the old dictum: "There's a time for fun and a time for work"—nor the more yielding Pat dared press Bryne yet; they still considered his psyche fragile. And if they disapproved openly of something Dennis did, they drew cannonode from Bryne, devoted comrade-in-arms.

So, for now, they treated them both with kid gloves. Pat's syllogism on Dennis was simple: A: He liked Bryne. B: Bryne liked him so much, he was returning to normal. Therefore C: Don't do anything to jeopardize that. So, even where the daily farm chores were concerned, while Mike and Barry worked their butts off all summer, Bryne sometimes got a pass he might never have had without Worm. For instance, they often stayed out late at the movies and go-cart races, and slept till noon the following day, right through morning chores. Neither Barry nor Mike complained—though, once, James dropped a hint. "Boys," he said, jostling them on his way to work, "y'all should be gettin' up and goin' to work." Bryne mumbled foggily, "Gosh, Daddy, feels like we just got in." It was left at that.

Next day, aware that James's patience was limited—even with them—they head-faked a concession. When they heard James rustle awake, they got up, too, and pretended to ready themselves for work in the fields. But once James left, they dropped the ruse and literally fell back to bed. Around lunchtime, though, at the sound of the Subaru crunching gravel in the drive, they jumped from bed, scampered to the kitchen, and start gorging food as if famished from ungodly toil. James never really bought it, though often he said nothing.

But when his impatience boiled over, he let them know. "Why don't you go out there and grab that mower," he suggested, "like you're goin' to the *video* arcade!" James liked the way that sounded, and how they jumped to when he said it, so he used it repeatedly throughout the summer. It became a sort of running joke, and a serious warning. Ultimately, however, it wasn't anything James said that caused them to obey; they did it out of respect. They knew he was as fair-minded as they come, and that taking advantage was risky. Besides, as Bryne had already informed Worm, "When my daddy asks you to do somethin', he expects you to do it." So at least for now, they invariably did.

In fact, once James showed Dennis how to drive the tractor, there weren't *enough* chores he could do with it. He loved just riding up in the seat, bumping over the fields, because it was new to him, like fishing in a pond. The only problem was his aversion to the sun: he was petrified of getting blacker. Bryne thought this was hilarious and teased him about it mercilessly. "I think y'all got about two shades darker out there today, son," he'd say, sending Worm scurrying for a mirror. Dennis told Bryne once, "My mother has this theory: white people lay out in the sun from noon to seven, and we lay out from seven-thirty to nine-thirty—at *night*. She's right. White people wanna get darker but we wanna get lighter. That's why you won't ever see black people on beaches—'cause they get too damn dark. And they know once they get that dark, there ain't no goin' back to their original color." And Dennis thought his "original color" was *already* too dark.

His solution when riding the tractor caused a stir. He took to wrapping a red towel around his head that Pat said made him look like "an Egyptian from Mars." Others didn't know what to think. For instance, Bryne's school bus would drive by in spring and there would be Dennis on the tractor, with the tail of what appeared to be a red turban flapping in the wind. At first the kids and even the driver stared in amazement. Then Dennis started waving, and Bryne waved back; and pretty soon all the kids—and the driver—were waving back, too. Then there were the local farmers who drove their own tractors past the farm and, spotting the tall black boy on James's tractor with something peculiar on his head, promptly ran themselves off the road for gawking.

Dennis couldn't wait to tell his mother about Bryne and the Riches. So when he finally spent a weekend with her in Dallas, he happily told her the whole first-dinner story, adding as much as he could about the following weeks he'd spent at their farm: riding the tractor, fishing in the pond, feeding an actual cow. Shirley liked his happy tone; it even occurred to her: "Maybe now he will forgive me for putting him out of the house." But this quickly dissolved when he revealed, "I think they really liked me, Momma." Because, instantly, resentment welled in her heart. "I doubt that very much," she snapped. But then, realizing she may have overreacted, she added sincerely, "But it's fine with me if it makes you happy." Actually, though jealousy brewed, she was still thrilled that her baby had found a friend.

These were touchy, complex issues for them. Dennis wasn't aware that Shirley had been feeling unjustly denied of his affection since before he left for college. And while still wrestling with her guilt from having left him in jail too long, she didn't want him to talk so much now about his new little friend. Why couldn't they talk about their own relationship? Why not try to get closer again, like when he was a child? The reason was because Dennis felt it was *his* time now and he wanted to indulge *his* needs, not hers. While he did feel awkward about his temporary estrangement from Shirley, he couldn't control it. So they sparred a little; while she sought forgiveness and loving reconciliation, Dennis seemed to have something else in mind. But what? Spite? Revenge? Or was he just struggling with the indignation he still harbored over the same incidents that were torturing her? She couldn't tell; emotionally, he was still a closed book.

Overall, however, Dennis seemed happier. So she concluded that being away from her had been good for him, and that maybe she should continue to keep a distance and not interfere. Given her own emotional needs and precarious condition—still recuperating from her physical ailments; adjusting to living alone; sending extra money to all three of her college kids, despite not having worked in a while—this was an especially unselfish gesture. However, Dennis was unable, or unwilling, to fully appreciate that yet. His mind was focused on one thing now: having a good time for *himself*.

Thus, upon his return to Oklahoma, and for the rest of the summer, Dennis and Bryne indulged in a sort of extended camp of their own on the farm. With school still out, as long as they pulled their minimum weight on the chores—disking and planting the fields, flattening hay, fixing fences where cows might get out—they were free to play as they liked. Their favorite fun, aside from basketball, was using the trampoline James had placed in the yard for his sons. As with fishing, Dennis was a novice at this. Bryne had to coax him gradually into taking baby jumps at first, then tentative three-footers, and finally some skyscraper leaps—though never a flip; no way. Bryne was fearless; he'd as soon flip every time as jump at all. So they invented creative new moves on trampoline, and crazy new games. Bryne had a cool idea: what if they moved the tramp over by the basketball goal? Then they could play one-on-one with a ball! Which led to Worm's bizarre invention: The One-on-One Leap-Over-Yo'-Face Slam-Dunk Games: "What you doin', boy? You can't dunk over me" . . . "Okay, big homeboy, let's see what you got" . . . "You know what I got? I got over yo' face!"

That's when the farmers driving by stopped to stare at something else they'd never seen: a weird-looking duo stuffing basketballs on trampoline, screaming like banshees:

"No, no, that don't count, uh-uh! Ball goes over."

"What you mean, son? That was good! One-zip."

"No, uh-uh. You fouled me, boy."

"Sheeeet! You got beat."

"*I* got beat? No, no, no. *You* the one got . . . "

Another deranged idea: the Firecracker House Jumping Games. Right: the old firecracker house Bryne used as a kid every Fourth of July to sell his little fireworks out of. Just a storage shed now, near . . . Oh yeah! . . . the trampoline. First goal: jump as high as the top of the door. Second goal: as high as the roof. Third goal: *higher* than the roof. Fourth goal: *onto* the roof, then back to the tramp. Fifth goal: onto the roof and check out the view: Hey, ain't that Bokchito over there? Oh yeah!

But sometimes: "Oh no!"—like when Bryne hit the roof so hard he crashed right through, luckily coming away unhurt; and when Worm missed the roof and landed on the trampoline edge, his feet slipping through the tie-loops, almost castrating himself in the process. Bryne never laughed so hard. Except for the *other* castration that was part of their fun. *That* was hysterical—as far as Bryne was concerned, probably the funniest thing he'd ever seen. That happened the day Worm was introduced to . . . castrating the calves.

Actually termed "cutting" the calves. The concept, James explained briefly beforehand, was simple. Male cows are classified as bulls or steers. You raise a limited number of bulls to reproduce, and you castrate the rest to steers so they can eventually end up on grocery shelves. The "raising" part wasn't so hard, but the castration part could be tricky. Especially for someone from, say . . . *way out of town*. Like Dennis, who'd never *seen* a live bull before, never mind assisted in— as they relished teasing him—"cuttin' off their nuts." That was okay, James said, amused. All they wanted Worm to do was help hold the calves down. "Oh," Worm thought, once he saw the things up close, "that's *all?*"

Because even though they were babies, these beasts weighed in at from one to two hundred pounds. And they had to be flipped on their backs and held spread-legged for access; and you couldn't explain that to them; and they didn't come to you in handy, flippable sacks, they came with rock-hard hooves that could crack human bone like a stick—or, as Bryne would warn Worm only afterward, "tear the hide right off you." "Boy," Bryne thought, noting Worm's almost nauseated expression, "if he can't even pull the hook out of a little bitty catfish, this oughta *really* be somethin' to see."

Oh, and it was. There were some forty-five little calves to be cut, and it would take all five people to do it right. First, you had to throw the calf. Then everyone would immobilize its legs. Next, the quick swath of the knife, and the hair-raising yelps and flailing for life, and finally the swift douse of alcohol to disinfect. If you didn't do it right every time, these calves would wear you out. Though Bryne was too small yet to throw a calf, he knew how to hold and restrain the legs. He picked that up by watching his dad and brothers, but perfected it in his Future Farmers of America class at school—bring your own coveralls and water boots and grovel in the pigpen after a kicking, squealing pig, and then do the deed to it. Pig and calf castrations were pretty similar, so he knew the technique firsthand.

Worm knew nothing; essence of greenhorn. They tried to explain how to throw the calf hard, before it could resist. But he kept finessing, afraid he might hurt it, which gave the calf time to tear up his shins with its hooves. In fact, "Shit!—Ow!—Damn!" was Worm's only defense against a calf throwing *him*:

"Throw him! Throw him down, Worm!"

"Grab him like this, Worm!"

"Put your knee into him, Worm!"

"Hold his legs open! Make sure he don't kick you, Worm!"

"Shit!—Ow!—Damn!"

Everyone laughed at Worm all day long. His main problem was that he was too long in the legs to leverage himself firmly for a good takedown and hold. Yet, by the end of the day, too embarrassed and stubborn to quit, he finally mastered the technique and earned some respect—along with two badly bruised legs. To climax the day, on the way back to the house Worm asked Bryne what they did with all the testicles. Bryne casually remarked, "People *eat* them suckers, Worm"— and Dennis almost lost lunch. "Yeah," Bryne continued totally serious, "they're called 'calf fries' or 'calf nuts.' I've sampled 'em. And the sad thing is they're really good. But I ain't one that's real crazy about 'em myself—know what I mean?"

Oh yeah. Make that *two*.

7

"The NBA Story"

As August waned, Southeastern's varsity players started trickling into the gym, so Dennis spent time over there.

Finally, on August 20, fall practice officially commenced with the usual pickup games. Coaches Hedden and Reisman merely observed at this point to see what they had. Their initial assessments of Dennis Rodman were mixed but auspicious. Hedden: "Not a great player. In fact, not a very good player yet. Doesn't know how to play the post in an organized team-play concept. But has great physical ability and instinct for the ball, especially rebounding." Reisman: "Great speed, great timing, plays hard constantly, incredible athlete. But doesn't know what to do with the ball when he gets it. Needs lots of work in the post." Hedden knew they had their work cut out for them, but wasn't overly concerned. He saw the diamond-in-the-rough quality that Reisman had first spotted at Cooke County JC: Rodman's quickness, aggressiveness, and leaping ability were raw materials for a potentially dominant star. But he would have to be drilled and trained and carefully honed.

This crafting began in earnest on September 1, when Hedden started working with Dennis, individually, at a side basket. The mission was to teach him the tools he would need to become a starting center in the NAIA conference. Hedden worked him slowly but surely on developing "post moves," the repertoire critical for success at the low-post position, a spot near the basket where a center posts himself firmly to give and receive passes on set offensive plays. Simply put, if you have a good-sized, capable center, the low post is the hub of your offensive wheel.

This was worlds away from the hotdoggin', jive-talkin', helicopter-dunkin', rec center ball of the neighborhood, where looking cool was as important as skill, and where you weren't burdened with coach-imposed, team-oriented offensive strategies. Your basic strategy was to take the ball to the hoop, however you could, and try to look good in the act. Thus, now, after a lifetime of "in yo' face" variations on essentially one playground move—"To the Hoop"—suddenly here was a new menu with an array of moves Dennis had never tried before: post shot; drop step; jump hook; forty-five-degree angle for getting the lob; protecting the ball in the "pocket."

To say the least, Dennis was raw; he was starting from scratch. Yet, he quickly began mastering everything. As Reisman would later explain to a reporter eager for material on the Savages' exciting new player: "He ate it up like a baby. He's like a baby when he takes that first step. Or a kindergartner when he's learning his ABC's: the more you teach him, the more he absorbs, the more he wants to know. Never questioning; just 'Give me more, give me more!' It was like taking a spoon and feeding him. The more you gave 'im, the more he absorbed, the more he produced."

Another quality Reisman liked was that while Dennis appeared to be shy enough to break on a whisper, he could actually "take a lickin' and keep on tickin'." Reisman found, in other words, that he could chew on Dennis as good as anybody he'd ever had in all his years of coaching, yet Dennis would never pout, never brood, never talk back. To trained observers like Reisman and Hedden, this was a promising sign of a deep inner will. They didn't know yet that it was also a sign of an inner chasm, which Dennis longed to fill with love, approval, praise. But once Reisman did pick that up, he discovered the key to motivating Dennis to greatness: "He needs to be pushed. You gotta push him hard so he knows you care. And then he goes and performs at another level—to prove to you he can do it, to make you *proud*. Man, he just *feeds* off that need to have you be proud of him; I can read that in him like a book."

Jack Hedden unknowingly read the same page on October 1, when they almost lost Dennis. This was the first of Hedden's infamous "14 Days of Hell"—fourteen consecutive intensely demanding, marine boot camp-type training sessions that would cull the boys from the men. Slacking off was not tolerated, even in routine drills, because they ran unconventional drills. Like putting a kid at half-court and having him dribble full speed to the basket, and then just before he gets there, having another kid step in his path and let himself get steamrolled to learn how to take a "charging" foul. No bucket, ball goes over. Or putting two guys on the "blocks"—one on one side of the free-throw line, one on the other—with Hedden rolling the ball out to the foul line, where the players have to dive and wrangle for it. That drill often produced bruises, burns, and bloody noses and teeth; but also, in Reisman's words, "the big guts to go after the ball."

And while some players in the program considered these work-outs extreme because they risked injury, Hedden and Reisman felt the benefits outweighed the risks. The drills, they believed, showed them "who would step up there and take a helluva lick." Special measures for special results. Just like their grueling conditioning sprints, which were also designed to expose mental weakness or strength. Crucial information for finding the true "heart" of the team: when you're down twelve points with four minutes to go, who will quit and who will be tough enough to help you win?

This day, Hedden and Reisman wanted especially to learn what Dennis Rodman was made of, and where they still had to take him. So, following the usual rigorous, two-and-a-half-hour workout, they watched him in the individual sprints and then the dreaded "Sui-cides": mad dashes from the baseline to the near free-throw line and

back; then to the half-court line and back; then to the far free-throw
line and back; and finally, to the far baseline and back. Hard enough
in itself—explosive starts, abrupt stops, explosive starts—and never
mind that you had to do it in thirty-two flat. Finish in thirty-three,
and you go all over again. Which often left even the best-conditioned
athletes hacking by a wall, winded, nauseated, drained. Forget about
the half-hearted kids who'd never extended to the limit before—or as
Reisman liked to describe it emphatically to the rookies: "You push
yourself to a *Pain Threshold*. You get to the point where you say, 'I
can't do this anymore, I can't do it, I'm dyin'!' But you get up on that
line again and you push yourself *through* that threshold, you get *over*
that point of hurt. Or you don't, and you find *that* out, too."

Since one of Hedden's unwritten rules was "Always be ready to
give more of yourself," following the first "Suicide" round he directed,
"Okay, back on the line. Let's go again." Everyone stepped up—except
Dennis Rodman, who had never been to that "point of hurt" before.
Bent over his knees, sucking air, he complained, "I can't go." But
Hedden wouldn't hear it. "Yeah, you *can* go," he insisted impatiently.
"And you're *gonna* go." So Dennis dragged back to the line and "Sui-
cided" again.

One condition of these murderous sprints: give a hundred percent. Anyone dogs it, everyone runs again. Peer pressure psychology;
Anti-Shirking Insurance. So, next round, when Dennis openly dragged
as if he was miffed he had to run at all, Hedden—a man who valued
the team over any individual, regardless of how gifted or promising
that player could be for the program—drew attention to Dennis and
angrily ordered, "Everybody goes again." Dennis refused: "I can't do
it, I can't go no more." But Hedden barked back, "Yeah, Dennis, you
can go some more, and you're gonna go some more. Now get up on
the line, or get your ass *outta* here." Dennis returned to the line and
not only ran again, but finished first.

Still, Hedden knew he had a problem: "Can he make it or will
we run him off?" He worried that, at any point, Rodman might walk

away and never come back. In fact, it looked like this was in the cards, since Hedden was committed to teaching every player not only what he *had* to do, but also what he *could* do, and would therefore never let up. That's when Coach Reisman stepped in. He understood it was the assistant coach's job to be "a buffer zone—someone the kids can come to for support." So, after each practice, he would visit with Dennis and try to bolster him. "Dennis, you're gonna make it," he would urge. "It won't be like this forever. You know we're gonna scrimmage and put offense in pretty soon. Right now, you're being tested. Remember, I told you: 'You can be a pro someday.' But you gotta pay the price." Dennis always responded to this boosting; he sensed that Reisman cared.

Nevertheless, Dennis's intermittent slacking-off continued for days. Then something unexpected occurred. Near the end of the "14 Days of Hell," Dennis approached Hedden after practice with a confident look he hadn't shown before. He said, "Coach, I'm glad you made me do all that runnin'." Surprised, Hedden asked why, and Dennis replied, "'Cause I ain't never been pushed like that. I never knew I could work this hard." Hedden was delighted and relieved, especially given Dennis's immaturity and self-doubts. He knew that even players further along in both training and self-control didn't often see the light so soon.

So Hedden felt he'd just learned a lot about Dennis: mainly that he *could* be pushed. And he knew now, also, that Dennis *had* that toughness inside; it would just be a matter of drawing it out.

From the Riches' farm, Worm had returned occasionally to his dorm for two or three nights. But having no other friends at school, and feeling lonely and bored, he would call to ask Pat or James: "Are you comin' up to Durant? If you are, could you come by and pick me up?" At Bryne's constant urging—"Please go get Worm; I really miss him"—they'd go pick him up and he'd stay several more nights with them. It was beginning to seem like the farm was his dorm, and the dorm just a place to visit. Dennis didn't care; he liked being out there, and he preferred Bryne's company to anyone else's.

Now that basketball was under way for Dennis, and would begin shortly for Bryne at junior high, they both decided they needed something to do at night when they had the basketball blues. Since the court outside wasn't lighted, that left only one alternative at the house: *Nerfball*. Kmart plastic mini-hoop with hand-sized spongeballs—perfect for housebound competition junkies. So, in the spirit of their best trampoline fantasies, they invented their own version of what Pat would later aptly term: "The NBA Story."

First, you need your standard "NBA Story" Nerfball court. Simple: the living room—attach the hoop to the back of Barry and Mike's door. Next, your classic "NBA Story" parquet playing floor. A no-brainer: the thickly padded living room carpet—left out-of-bounds, the kitchen bar; right out-of-bounds, the couch; center-court, the chandelier. But for an official "NBA Story" game, you must also have your State-of-the-Art Public-Address System. No problem: the heavy cardboard tube off the new Christmas wrapping paper gives that muffled, fake-amplified sound you need to announce yourself to the imaginary crowd at The Forum, Madison Square Garden, Boston Garden. But you *still* can't play a bona fide "NBA Story" game without your regulation electronic clock, replete with end-of-period buzzer. Easy: Pat's microwave—five-minute quarter, buzzer sounds, take it out and serve.

At first they played when no one was home, but once Dennis had been around a few months it was virtually every night. They dressed in T-shirts and jeans because, to equalize things, 6-8 Worm had to play on his knees to shrink to Bryne's standing 5-3; and because, as Bryne quickly learned, Worm would be tripping and shoving him down—playground rules: No Blood, No Foul, No Mercy. It was understood: this wasn't just a game—at least not for Worm. He was in it, he guaranteed, to "mop up yo' skinny ass." In other words, to *win*. In the playground, you always played to win.

A typical game would unfold like this:

The hoop is set on the door. The playing floor is "manicured" expertly—by Dennis—with the nap in one direction, pool-table smooth. The house lights go off and court lights come on, with the crowd eagerly awaiting player introductions. Finally, the PA announcer (Worm tonight) begins: "LADIES AND GENTLEMAN, WELCOME TO THE RICH SKYDOME ARENA. GIVE A BIG WELCOME TO—THE LOS—ANGELES—LAKERRRRRRS! Errrrrr-ahhhhhh! (Worm-made crowd noise) AT CENTER, FORWARD, AND GUARD, FROM DALLAS, TEXAS . . . SIX-EIGHT, ONE-EIGHTY, Errrrrr-Ahhhhhh! (Bryne-made crowd noise) . . . NUMBER TEN . . . DENN-ISSSS—RODDDDDD-MAN! ERRRRRRR-AHHHHHH!" Enter Worm, trotting from the kitchen, arms raised, his long index finger swirling a big "No. 1" in the air as he circles the living room, concluding with a lay-up—backboard-rim-and-in. "Errrrrr-ahhhhhh!"

Then Bryne's turn to announce: "AND NOW FOR THE HOMETOWN—BOS-TONNNN—CELLLL-TICS! Errrrrr-ahhhhhh! LED BY NUMBER TWELVE IN YOUR PRO-GRAM, NUMBER ONE IN YOUR HEARTS . . . SIX-TEN, TWO-NINETY . . . FROM BOKCHITO, OKLAHOMA . . . BRYNE—RIIIICH! ERRRRRR-AHHHHHH!" Enter Bryne circling, too, in his best "I'm a bad dude" posture, high-fiving with the walls, finishing with a lay-up cool as Worm's. Next: pregame drills of lay-ups, free throws, and perimeter shots—private psych-up time. Then: removing the warm-up suits and jiggling arms and legs, just like the pros, to loosen up the kinks. Finally: the microwave "BUZZ!" . . . Gametime.

Opening jump ball: on his knees, Worm tosses up the Nerf but lets Bryne win possession. Bryne drives baseline right away—Worm swats at him, careful not to foul, but Bryne covers the ball and scores: two-zip. Worm's ball. He knee-drags in from the foul line, turning his back to Bryne—who hacks him all over—then head-fakes left and twists back right, reaching around for the finger-roll. Good! Two-all. Bryne's ball.

As the quarter plays out, Worm trails 16–10 playing easy and loose. Bryne sails along having fun, imitating NBA greats, especially his favorite, Julius Erving—"Doctor J"—shooting exactly like him, and narrating aloud, "Doctor goes baseline, he holds the ball out, he pulls it back in, he *scores!* Doctor JAYYYYYY! Errrrrr-ahhhhhh!" Second quarter starts with the same strategy for Worm: let Bryne have the lead, joke him around, false sense of security. But then, with two minutes left, time to get him unnerved. "Make him pay" is Worm's new strategy now, as in: "You come at me, you're gonna get hit." So when Bryne next spins for a shot, Worm leans into him hard, gives him a shove, starts talking trash: "You ain't cool. That little schoolboy crap ain't nothin'." All over his case. Bryne takes the challenge and tries to get fancy. As he drives for what appears to be an easy two, Worm yanks his feet from under him and Bryne crashes down with a thud. "Oh man!" he taunts. "How you gonna get anywhere with that kinda move? Get up off your face, clown." Which really ticks Bryne off. So when he gets his next chance, Bryne charges the lane and leaps recklessly to dunk, piling down deliberately onto Worm's head, slamming them both to the floor. "Get up, boy!" Worm rages back. "Your ass is mine!" Which infuriates Bryne into missing more shots, allowing Worm to rally back and regain the lead. Finally: "BUZZ!"—and it's halftime. Short breather for sandwiches and iced tea by the mugful, and some grousing, teasing, and bragging rights.

Just before resuming, Dennis announces to the crowd the pertinent first-half stats: "DENNIS RODMAN: TWENTY-SIX POINTS, ELEVEN REBOUNDS, THREE FOULS—POSSIBLE PLAYER OF THE GAME. BRYNE RICH: EIGHTEEN POINTS, SIX REBOUNDS, FOUR FOULS, THREE 'I'M GONNA TELL MY MOMMA IF YOU DON'T QUIT BEATIN' ON ME'—DEFINITE CRYBABY OF THE GAME." Bryne won't stand for this: "You're *mine*," he threatens lamely through gooey peanut butter.

Fifteen minutes later—"BUZZ!"—and the second half begins . . . viciously. Worse than one-on-one outside because, in here, there's no room to maneuver. Worm roughs up Bryne mercilessly, like in the rec center at summer camp—to teach him some toughness. Suddenly,

Bryne falls behind, forced to resort in frustration to holds and tugs, trying to counter the hammering by Worm. By the third quarter, they're playing for blood. Thus, with increasing physical contact comes sharper repartee:

Worm: "Boy, you can't hold me! Don't be bringin' that Farmboy crap in here!"

Bryne: "You can't push me, girl!"

Ad-schoolyardium . . .

Fourth quarter: mouths flapping, elbows flashing, bodies bumping, furniture tumbling—serious action. With Worm secretly orchestrating, the game comes up for grabs at the end. Even with Bryne trailing by a seemingly impossible ten points, Worm's defense strangely falters and Bryne gets suspiciously easy shots to tie the score with ten seconds left. Ooops, Worm blows an easy one; Bryne's ball again. He eyeballs the microwave and waltzes around, killing the clock, then lets one go. But Worm blocks it and knocks him on his rear, forcing him to the foul line—two seconds to go, game on the line.

Nerfball free throws are difficult at best, laughable at least. The little spongy ball is too airy and insubstantial to be influenced in flight by old reliables like "rhythm" and "feel." Mostly, you just aim and toss and hope for proximity. But if you can't influence your *own* free throws, who says you can't influence your *opponent's*—like Worm does with obnoxious psych-out babble.

"You can't make it," he mutters as Bryne takes aim. "Choke, choke." Theory being that if Bryne bricks the first shot, he will also eat the second, and Worm can then raise hell and rattle him into more mistakes to cost him the game. Of course, if Bryne somehow makes it, he'll get right back in Worm's face: "Your *momma!*" Gloater's Heaven. Or just: Your Everyday Standard Official Regulation "NBA Story" Nerfball Game.

Day by day, their general game-playing at the house intensified. When football season kicked off in September, they would place couch cushions and pillows across the living room carpet and play their version of "The NFL Story"—tackle football, mano a mano: "You gotta get *by* me to score, and you *ain't* gettin' by me." Naturally, they went all out. Bryne, for instance, would take running starts from the kitchen and hurl himself in the air, trying to clear Worm in his goal-line stand—or goal-line *kneel*—with no time on the microwave. Then there were the more casual, though still competitive, noncontact games, like "Flies and Skinners"—throwing a small ball in the air or "skinning" the floor with it, to see who made the most errors and would therefore suffer the consequent verbal abuse—as well as Wiffle-ball hockey and Wiffle-ball golf.

Although she had witnessed only a little of this, there was so much activity that first fall that Pat began to fret about her dishes, furniture, and cabinets. But she did her best to tolerate it silently—until the day Dennis accidentally smacked her Bonanza ceiling fan with his hand and slightly bent a blade. She noticed it when she turned the fan on and the whole thing wobbled and shook. So she confronted Bryne and Dennis together: "Well, you have really done it," she steamed. "You have warped my beautiful fan!" She knew it had to be Worm's handiwork, but she still restrained from offending him un-necessarily for fear of affecting his friendship with Bryne. She didn't know it then—neither did Dennis—but this deliberate overcautious-ness would trigger a nagging distrust in him that would take them both years to fully understand.

The first time Pat actually observed one of their Nerf basketball games, she like to come unglued. "Why can't you play somewhere else?" was her horrified response. Though her own three boys had certainly romped recklessly as children, Pat had never had to worry about someone as big and powerful as Dennis wrecking the place. Kids will be kids, she realized; but now she had an *adult* being a kid, and he could do a lot more damage. Plus, household accoutrements, par-ticularly delicate items of sentimental or artistic value, were sources of pride to Pat. She literally took them personally. Such that, in a very real sense, if you chipped her china or crystal, you chipped her, too.

Thus, after days of rising anxiety over what these two hooligans might obliterate next, she finally blew her top. "Y'all are ruinin' everything in my house with this ball business, playin' this basketball and football and who knows what else. You are ruinin' my home! You are gonna break my china hutch or knock my chandelier—I can just feel it. You are makin' a *gym* out of my house!"

Which they were, almost like a duty, Pat believed. Yet, odd transformation: the more she witnessed their kooky Nerfball games, and the more inventive and fanciful they became—eventually even tape-recording their own introductions for the grand illusion of being formally announced by "somebody else"—the more the whole enterprise amused her. Since they always stayed up late to play, she often found herself taking a midnight ringside seat at the kitchen bar, and laughing at the sight of "this big ole lumberin'-around Worm," still taller on his knees than Bryne standing up, with his huge hands flapping, elbows jutting, and long feet trailing behind like big wooden blocks. In fact, over time, and despite her premonitions of household disaster, she frequently erupted into hysterical laughter watching them frolic. She was *so* hysterical once, they threatened to have the "ushers" bodily remove her for "making a ruckus in the stands."

Not one to be intimidated by them, she simply counterthreatened to cancel their stadium lease.

8

Guess Who
Isn't Coming to
Dinner

Since arriving in Durant, Dennis had been acutely aware of white people occasionally looking at him "funny."

Even if he might've imagined some of those looks, there was no mistaking the loud, brutal taunts of "Better watch yourself, boy!" and "Get outta town, you nigger son of a bitch!" hurled from cowards in moving cars. Having grown up and attended high school with whites, Dennis felt no racial enmity himself and, until now, had no trouble absorbing an occasional mindless slur. He'd always chosen to just ignore it as "a waste of my time." And though each slander opened little wounds now, he told himself essentially what he would later tell Bryne: "Oh, they're just ignorant anyway. They're not accustomed to seein' black people here. You're gonna get some rednecks in town, some real fools that think since they're white and from a little country town that, 'Well, this black person shouldn't be here.' So, they just lash out at everyone they see. The whole town ain't like that, it's just a few people that wanna downgrade you and run you out."

But lately, although he tried to keep ignoring it, the feeling that he didn't belong in this town simmered in the back of his mind. Which was another incentive to spend as much time with Bryne as possible, especially at the farm. Aside from the friendship and meals and free-wheeling recreation, he found acceptance there as a human being, an absence of not only pressure but also animosity. He rationalized that he was visiting the farm so often now because he didn't want to disappoint Bryne; but he also went for other reasons. Not the least of which was that he savored the Riches' lenient, open attitudes—especially when contrasted, in his mind, with the way his former Dallas pals had pulled him one way while his mother tugged him another.

In casual conversation with Coach Reisman, whom he had grown to trust, he described his developing emotions about the Riches this way: "I never met people like them before. They act so natural, like they don't have nothin' to hide. Everything is: 'Here's what you're supposed to do and now it's up to you to do it.' They don't *make* you do nothin'. They love bein' around each other and they seem to like everything they do together. Man, the country is a lot better than city life. There's hardly any pressure out here at all. Whereas in the city you always have the monkey on your back: somebody always wantin' you to do somethin'. The country is more free and easy and loose."

Certainly, that's what he felt like at the farm. But was this really representative of "the country"? Or was it mainly Dennis's handy haven of safety, to which he could retreat when reality pressed too close? Likely a little of both. For, at the moment, he was impelled to spend even more time with Bryne than before, basketball practice notwithstanding. Thus, just before classes began in September, he urged Bryne to ask Pat—pegging her, as usual, as more vulnerable to their schemes than James—if Bryne could spend a weekend with him at the dorm.

"Worm said I could come up and spend the weekend with him if I wanted to, Mom," Bryne proposed. "Would it be okay?" Pat thought it would, but she had to ask James. After conferring, they both agreed that with Bryne being so young, they ought to check out Dennis's dorm room first.

The campus was familiar to Pat; she'd been enrolled at Southeastern since 1979, taking classes part-time in increasing increments while working in her home-based beauty shop. For years she had yearned to return to school; "I work hard in my shop," she'd told James, "but I have to take on a lot of heads to come up with a good salary. I don't want to just be a country girl and stay cooped up in a little patio beauty shop. There has to be something more to life than this. I want to get out there and explore and see what life is all about, and better myself."

Fine with him. So she went part-time until she got adjusted. First, six hours a term; then nine; then twelve; finally eighteen. In her late thirties at the time, she thoroughly enjoyed the lively "college atmosphere" and—eager to prove something to herself—relished the challenge of making good grades. Not surprisingly, she became a dedicated student who not only outstudied younger classmates but, in many cases, outperformed them, too. No fool in practical matters, she proved no lightweight intellectually; she was zeroing in on two degrees: a bachelor's in education and a master's in behavioral science. "It's weird," she told a friend who worked in the Registrar's Office. "In the town where I live, you'd never know I was even educated."

One factor motivating Pat to seek more education, particularly in behavioral psych, was the new situation with Dennis and her family. She had always been interested in the way people behaved—why they acted and thought as they did. And "I want to understand *me*, too," she used to say. But, at this moment more concerned with understanding Dennis, she applied some behavioral psych to the current scenario, believing that his dorm room would reveal something about the type of person he really was.

The room was small and bare, but tidy and clean. There were two thin beds and a little dressing table, on which he'd set photos of his mother and sisters. His bed was made; the floor spotless; the photos neatly in place. Pat was impressed: "Good habits," she thought. "Probably means good upbringing." And then she considered: "Well, the college atmosphere wouldn't be bad for Bryne. It might even be good for him." James—whose only reflection about the room was how small it was—was already impressed that Worm was at college on scholarship and playing basketball, trying to do something with his life. So he and Pat gave their okay, and Bryne spent his first weekend in Worm's dorm.

Come September, Dennis had his schedule all figured out. Week-days: classes, then basketball practice, then out to the farm for the night. Weekends: either at the farm or the dorm with Bryne. Great carefree life: chores; pinball and video games; "NBA Story"; "NFL Story"; "Flies and Skinners"; pool hall and go-carting with Barry and Mike; home-cooked meals and his favorite french fry snacks courtesy of Pat; and clean clothes (she not only took him shopping for clothes now with Bryne, she also cleaned everything for him, too—even wash-ing his size-14 "clodhopper basketball shoes" separately because he was such a stickler on having them "new-like clean.")

Life of Riley.

Until the first hint of conflict in September, culminating in the unfortunate Thanksgiving mess.

It started, almost imperceptibly, with Pat. Every September through June, she looked forward to going to college in Durant. It was her only extended private time, a rare commodity for a mom raising three teen-aged sons, managing a household, and running a beauty shop on the side. Part of the benefit was having the freedom after class to go brows-ing or shopping in Durant or nearby Sherman. But since Dennis had grown more at ease around Pat, he emerged from his shell and started taking liberties. For instance, instead of calling for lifts from school, he took to staking out her Mercury Marquis and leaving her notes, like "Hi, Miss Rich. Can I ride home with you today?" Or hollering to her from across the parking lot: "Miss Rich! Miss Rich! Wait for me! I wanna ride with you!" It embarrassed her; she knew a lot of people from Bokchito and Durant who were attending Southeastern. What would they think about this black guy begging rides home with her all the time? What bothered her more—though she never would have hurt Dennis's feelings by telling him so—was that once he pegged her for rides, she had to forfeit her shopping time to take him home.

Thus, even though they'd grown closer over the months he'd spent at the farm, she resented his intrusion now on her precious free time.

The first time it happened was on a Friday, Dennis all eager to spend the weekend with Bryne. The following Monday, Pat naturally offered to shuttle him back to school with her, so they got in her car and headed toward town. As she pulled to Bokchito's only stop sign at Highway 22 and Main, she noticed what the locals called a "Farmer Jones"—an old farmer in overalls—standing on the corner by the First State Bank, chewing tobacco and spitting and idly looking around. And when he stared hard at her familiar car and unfamiliar passenger, she realized this could mean trouble.

Sure enough, days later her sister Rachel, a city hall clerk, stopped by to visit and to announce: "I heard a guy at city hall say, 'I saw Pat and a nigger drivin' through town the other day.' " Rachel chuckled, amused. But Pat shot back, "That's not so funny!" And she wasn't referring to the thoughtless use of the word "nigger"—a reflex expression that most people here took for granted, like "Farmer Jones." Although Pat genuinely liked and enjoyed Dennis out at the farm, and always found him funny, polite, and, most of all, respectful, she worried now about being seen with him "out in society." Because where she formerly had only her suppositions about people staring at them wherever they went together, she now had an actual substantiated rumor on her hands—and that changed the mix for her.

All that night, she agonized over the fearful implications—real and imagined—of that rumor. "By tomorrow," she speculated, "everyone in town's gonna be sayin' something like, 'Pat rode around town with a colored guy in her car.' And they'll start making things up and it'll embarrass me to be seen with him. They'll say, 'There they go again,' and they'll stare at me and I'll just want to hide." She was doubly stung, first by the outrageous gossip about her private life—she couldn't tolerate "people who made your business theirs because their business wasn't interesting enough to keep 'em busy"—and second by her inability to ignore the prattle as petty and irrelevant. Although she realized "there are a lot of jealous troublemakers with warped minds that thrive on starting soap operas in other people's lives, just so they can watch 'em go through it," she hated the fact that she still felt susceptible to this nonsense. She'd thought she'd finally been able to embrace James's advice to quit listening to it, and yet here it was plaguing her again.

Now, however, the issue surpassed petty rumor. Because now it wasn't just about falling prey to outlandish allegations she knew to be false; it was about something almost elemental in her soul. If not, why had she found Farmer Jones's childish proclamation so profoundly repugnant? Why was her gut roiling like never before? The answer—though she did not reflect on it very much then—was almost as repugnant: she didn't want people to think she would have anything to do with . . . a Black Man. She knew this deep down because even before she'd felt outrage over the fact that the rumor had spread, her first, response had been shame. ("That is what really hurt most," she would later regret. "Because he always treated me with respect. A lot of times he would come in late and I wouldn't know it, and I'd be dressing or taking a bath, and he never accidentally opened the door or made an excuse to see me in any way—that is one thing I respected Worm for.")

Pat's shame was a complex matter, and beyond her ability, at the time, to decipher. For one thing, she had no bigotry in her heart; she'd never considered herself "above anyone else." For another, she especially prided herself, secretly those past few months, on not seeing color where Dennis was concerned. She had even felt "motherly" toward him at times, and she was grateful beyond words for all he'd done for her son. Bryne was a totally different person now; he seemed whole again—and Pat openly credited Dennis's companionship as the chief reason for that. So it struck her as odd; out at her house, Dennis's color had never come up after the first night's jolt. And now she cooked his meals, washed his clothes, changed his linens, made his bed—which was her *son's* bed; she'd had no problem even with *that!* And yet, in the wake of only a rumor, she could be transformed into someone else, someone suddenly ashamed of being seen with him.

The reasons for this ran as deep as her roots to home. To her, it had nothing to do with prejudice; that wasn't how she felt. In fact, she and Dennis had spent long hours getting better acquainted at home—sometimes alone, sometimes with everyone in other rooms— talking openly, "like mother and son," about sensitive black-white issues, without anyone's feathers getting ruffled. Dennis would come back from class, or else be home early on a day off from practice, and if he had something on his mind he would sit on a stool at the kitchen bar to let her know he wanted to chat. In their first talk, which was typical of so many others that followed those first few months, they shared a lot about how they had each grown up. Dennis talked about coming up in all-white neighborhoods and all-white schools, and about how he didn't have to deal with much prejudice from whites. Pat recounted her early years with "Hot Tod" Lucy and Chester and Reesa, and how her dad hired black workers, and how comfortable she and her sisters had always been around the black people they lived by and knew.

"The only thing," she finally qualified, "was whites and blacks just didn't mix socially. That's what we were taught, so we didn't know any better. Our parents were afraid if we hung around with blacks, we might end up dating or marrying one, and that was not acceptable. But not because they was prejudiced; they weren't—they treated black folks just like they treated whites. It was because they was concerned about the prejudice *we* might get from other people who wouldn't accept blacks and whites bein' together. They didn't want their children ostracized by their own kind, and bein' made outcasts in their community. That was what *they* were taught: blacks do with blacks and whites do with whites. Because they knew if anyone in the family got mixed up with a black person, the rest of the family would flat disown 'em on the spot. And they were fearful of that ever happening."

"But, Miss Rich," Dennis softly objected, "it don't make no difference. If you like someone, you like 'em and that's it. Don't matter what other people think."

"It *does* matter, Worm. If it didn't matter . . . Okay, let me put it this way: if God meant for whites and blacks to mix, He would've made us all the same color. That's what I believe. Why did He make us look so different, if He didn't mean for us to stick with our own?"

Dennis had no answer for that. But he wanted to get under her skin anyway. He knew that Pat liked listening to black singers and especially loved watching Michael Jackson on TV, so he teased, "Miss Rich, you would marry *Michael Jackson*."

She laughed, "No, Worm, I would *not* marry Michael Jackson. I like to watch him dance, but that does not lead to marriage, Worm. Just keep on dreamin'."

"Oh, Miss Rich, I know if Michael Jackson came to Bokchito right today, you would marry him, Miss Rich. He has money and everything—you would marry him. You know you would, too."

"No way, Worm. I told you I would never marry a black guy. If he came up here in a Cadillac and offered me the world, I would not marry him. I know what you're doing, Worm. You're testing me. You really think, 'Well, she says she wouldn't marry a black, but if it was a famous, rich guy like Michael Jackson, because she really likes his singin' and everything, if he were to come up here and ask her to marry him, she would.' Well, you are wrong. Wouldn't make no difference if it was Michael Jackson or Stonewall Jackson or Abraham Lincoln . . . " And they cracked up when she lost the thread right there.

To Pat, though, in mind and heart and outward attitude, "skin" really wasn't the issue. It was chiefly about her accepted place in the community; her identity here, and reputation. She knew that a single rumor like this could cost respect, friendship, even business. The last thing she needed now, while she was trying to earn extra money with the beauty shop to send her boys to college, was clients talking about her and a black boy, and then staying away because they didn't approve. But because this dilemma had grown so complicated and troublesome, she couldn't share it with anyone, not even James—and certainly not with Dennis.

And then her behavior toward him—at least in public—suddenly changed. The morning after she heard the rumor, for instance, she had already decided to shield herself from further gossip whenever she rode in a car with Dennis. So, preparing to take him and Bryne shopping for clothes in Sherman, she asked Dennis to drive—which he loved to do—and she climbed in back. When they approached the stop sign by the bank and she noticed a few local stragglers at the corner, she slumped down and, on impulse, grabbed the *Durant Daily Democrat* off the seat and opened it across her face. She figured if anybody stared in the car they'd only see Dennis and Bryne, and that would be fine. Then, when they had turned onto Main and were pulling away, she peeked back over the top of the paper to see if anyone was still watching her car. She stayed behind the paper until the outskirts, when Dennis finally needled, "You can put the paper down now, Miss Rich. We're through town."

She felt ridiculous. "I know how that looked," she tried to explain to Dennis, genuinely humiliated. "I'm sorry; I feel terrible I did that. I just don't want people talkin' about me, that's all. They've already started a rumor on me and you, Worm. But I don't want you to think I'm ashamed of you, because I'm not. It's nothing personal."

He just shook his head and remarked, "I understand." And he did—and kept driving coolly to school.

Things got worse. One time, instead of driving the normal route to school with Dennis—west on Main and out to Durant—Pat decided to take the back alleys. That night, returning from school, she tried it again, reversing the route. When Dennis asked pointedly, "Miss Rich, why are you dodgin' town?" she spun a big excuse: "Oh, I have to get back to make an important call, Worm, and it's faster this way." She thought he bought it at first, until the next time she tried it and he said, "I know what you're doin', Miss Rich. You just don't want people seein' me with you." She denied it, of course, but he knew.

And she continued her masquerade whenever she felt prying eyes boring in on her car. Once, as Dennis drove them back from school, Pat closed her eyes for a quick catnap. "I'll let you know when we get close to town, Miss Rich," he teased pointedly. "Then you can duck down with your paper over your face."

She felt small, yet helpless to change. Here she was clumsily hiding in Dennis's presence, and yet he was not only not openly offended, he actually had a nice little sense of humor about it. Out of both shyness and respect, Dennis always treated these small gestures of rejection as just silly things that she did. Pat didn't realize however, that, deep down, Dennis resented them. In her heart, she wished she were stronger—she prayed for that strength—but right now, this was the only way she knew how to cope.

It didn't help, either, when she told James how troubling it was to dodge town and be shamed by Worm, and James dismissed her feelings offhandedly. "You're worryin' too much about what other people think," he advised. "It don't make any difference what they think, so just ignore 'em."

That was easy for James to say, she thought, because he had no idea what she felt. So she tried a different tack to convey her dilemma: "I rode through town the other day with Worm in the car, and I waved to Rachel and she saw me and she didn't wave back! That really hurts when your own *sister* don't wave at you. And other people are doing it, too. I ride through town with him and nobody waves—that hurts me real bad, James, it makes me cry. You just don't understand how that feels."

One thing James did understand was Pat's vivid imagination; he thought she was exaggerating. "I've waved at people before and they didn't wave back."

"No, these people have always waved back at me. My sister *always* waves back."

"Well, you know what you do?" he reasoned impatiently. "If you see somebody just lookin' at you funny when you drive by, you start thinkin' they're talkin' about you. I think you create a lot of it yourself."

"I didn't create it, I saw it. You can't say I'm imagining things, James."

"I didn't say that."

"Yes, you said I created it. But I *didn't* create it; it really happened. And you know how sensitive I am. I mean, it's only me that's on the line. Worm doesn't care what people say. He has nothing to gain or lose: 'Bye-bye, I'll go back to Dallas, I can just disappear if I want to.' But I have to live here. And I know how, if some of these people get a soap opera going in their heads, they won't accept you and they'll give you the cold shoulder when you go to some kind of society thing in town. And I want to be accepted, because I have friends here and I don't want to lose my friends."

"Well, I think you're carryin' it too far."

"All I know is, we have just come through all the stress and suffering over Bryne's tragedy, and I'm tryin' to cope with that and help Bryne by letting Dennis live here, and I'm not even over that yet and now this other thing is piled on top of it. You don't know the half of it."

James wouldn't dispute it, because it irritated him to hear about. He felt he had too many other burdens—working at the post office and managing the farm—to listen to this stuff, too. Ignorant behavior was ignorant behavior, and you just had to forget about it and do what you do. And true to his philosophy, when a coworker had recently tried to get his goat by wisecracking, "I seen your *stepson* in town yesterday," James had just shrugged it off with: "No, he ain't my step-son. That's my son from my first wife." And that shut the guy up tight. He wished Pat could handle it like that.

But she couldn't; it wasn't her nature. Everything personal, petty or not, affected her, especially where her reputation was concerned. Which was something that, as a man, James didn't have to worry about. And she wanted him to realize that. "Oh, and your buddy, Marty," she added, particularly outraged about this. "He ran his mouth to Charles that, 'James is hiring a *stud service* out to the house!'"

"I never heard that," James replied, surprised.

"That's 'cause Marty was just wantin' to be devious. He wanted to stir somethin' up because he knew if he said anything to my brother-in-law, it would fly all over town. And it did."

There was more she didn't bother to tell James now about the pressures building up on other fronts. For example, certain women were "throwing little slings at me about 'the colored boy' they heard about." And James had never had a customer cancel a beauty parlor appointment "because you have a black boy livin' in your house." He'd never experienced that, but she had, and it galled her something fierce. " 'Pat and the nigger,' 'Pat and the black boy,' " she ranted, frustrated, at James. "That's all I hear. What am I supposed to do about that?"

But the worst pressure on Pat was being applied by her own kinfolk. Problems had been brewing since Dennis came to the farm, especially with Pat's brother-in-law, Rachel's husband Charles. He'd been dropping scornful and even ugly remarks about it to Rachel—like: "I don't know what that black guy is doin' with them" and "I think somethin' is goin' on with Pat and that black guy." Rachel, a rigidly parochial woman with whom Pat had once been close but with whom she now too often feuded, disapproved as strongly as Charles, and pointedly conveyed her sentiments to their parents. Pat resented that, but said nothing at first.

Her issues with Rachel went way back. In Pat's view, just because Rachel was the eldest sister, everyone in the family had held her up high. So, whatever Rachel said or did, even today, the other sisters usually followed suit. All through her youth, this mindless obeisance caused Pat to feel like "the little baby in the family that nobody paid attention to." And, since she usually subordinated her feelings to those of her sisters in order to keep peace in the house, she'd done nothing to change that equation—until Dennis Rodman arrived on her doorstep. Now she was ticked off that not only was what she did or said around her sisters new fodder for their speculations, but apparently so was the way she ran her own home.

Pat's dad, Roy, a retired lumberyard laborer and farmer, and her mom, Jessie, a former nurse's aide, had a tough row to hoe on this issue. They had both met Dennis numerous times, when Bryne proudly brought him out to visit them, and they'd always treated him cordially, if not downright solicitously. Roy always got a boot out of the way Dennis picked potatoes for him in his little potato patch. Dennis would stand around scratching himself, scanning the neighborhood, plucking a lone potato and dumping it into the can, and gazing up at the sky. "What is he doin' out there?" Roy would muse aloud. "Countin' the *birds?*" Then Dennis would idly pick his nose—and another potato—before stopping to scratch and stare some more.

Roy really liked the bashful young man—he even named one of his calves "Worm" in a whimsical tribute. Jessie liked him a lot, too. A high-strung, sensitive woman in the classic country-matriarch mold, she delighted in serving him food and tea and homey advice about school. She'd developed a soft spot for Dennis, not only because he was so quiet and polite, but also because of his relationship with her favorite grandchild, whom she always called "little ole Bryne." She knew, through Pat's glowing reports, that if it hadn't been for Dennis, Bryne might still be a mess. For that, she would always consider Dennis a wonderful godsend. As for Dennis, he liked Jessie and Roy, too; he was more relaxed around them than around any other adults except James and Pat.

But lately, this stream of good feeling between them was being polluted by a barrage of complaints from Charles and Rachel about "the black boy stayin' at Pat's." Jessie grew unsettled; the thing she dreaded most was conflict in the family. In fact, in the past, whenever the sisters bickered in her presence, she would end up gasping for breath, as though literally choking on the discord. That registered with Pat; it was a big reason she held fire more often than not.

In October, nearly a month in advance, Pat had told her parents she intended to bring Dennis over for Thanksgiving dinner, and they, of course, said fine. But now came the capper—a firm ultimatum from Charles: "If they bring that black boy over there for Thanksgiving, I ain't comin'." And if he wasn't coming, obviously neither was Rachel.

So, a week before the event, Jessie had a private talk with Pat. When she related Charles's ultimatum, Pat was livid, but kept her cool for fear of upsetting her mom. Pat had known for some time that Charles had what she called "a thing against blacks."

As for Rachel, Pat believed she'd always been a little jealous of both her and James, because of "the nice setup" Rachel thought they had on their farm. Pat suspected her sister's resistance to Dennis was just another petty way for Rachel to get back at her. After all, her modus operandi, Pat knew from experience, was "to play a kind of cutthroat game to turn all my sisters against me." And that is what Pat thought she was doing now: aligning the whole family against her and her plan to bring Dennis for Thanksgiving dinner.

"I was expecting somethin' like this," Pat replied to her mom. "I just don't see why they have to act this way. Especially Rachel—she grew up around blacks; she's *never* acted like this. I think they should be ashamed of themselves, that's what I think. I can't help it, I just think it's really disgusting." Jessie probably agreed, but felt she had no choice. With tears in her eyes, she had to inform Pat, "I love little ole Bryne, and Worm, too. And so does your dad. He's welcome in our house anytime. I wish there was some other way, but I really do believe that if he comes to our dinner, it will cause a split in the family. So, to keep the peace, I wish that you would try to talk to Worm and tell him not to come, because it will just cause terrible trouble."

Pat had no recourse but to honor her mother's request. So she went home and told Bryne first. Naturally, he took it hard. "Why do *they* get to keep him away?" he pleaded. "They don't even *know* Worm." Pat tried to explain it was for the sake of keeping peace in the family, but Bryne didn't care. "All I know is," he threatened, walking away, "if Worm can't go, I ain't goin' either." Pat admired his loyalty; she wished she could've said the same thing to Rachel and Charles.

Now the hard part: telling poor Worm. She sat him down on his usual stool at the kitchen bar, and drew a deep breath. "Worm, you'll never know how much this pains me to tell you," she said, holding back tears. "Now, you know that my parents like you, Worm, and they are thrilled about the way you and Bryne get along so well, and all that. And you know how James and I feel about you; we feel like you're becoming part of our family, and I think we have shown you that. But, Worm, there's some members of my family that don't know you like we do, and they been runnin' their mouths and tellin' my parents that if we bring you to our Thanksgiving dinner, they won't come."

Worm seemed unmoved, listening quietly, eyes cast down. She went on: "I just want you to know I don't agree with this, Worm. I don't like it one bit. But my family is important to me, and they've asked me to please explain this to you because they care about you. It bothers my mom and dad, too, but they just think if you came, it would cause a big split in the family. So I said I wouldn't bring you."

"That's cool," he muttered, not looking up.

"Well, I feel so ashamed to tell you this, I just hope you can forgive them and forgive me. Because I don't mean for this to hurt you, Worm. You are welcome in their house and my house anytime you want. You know that, don't you?"

"I know that," he said flatly, leaving to go find Bryne.

Thanksgiving night, Pat kept her promise not to bring Dennis, and everyone else showed up: her sisters and their husbands; her brother; all their kids and grandkids; Barry, Mike—and Bryne, too. Pat had coaxed him into coming for the sake of family harmony, and so her mother wouldn't get upset. But Pat felt a knot in her stomach the whole time; bad feelings got passed around with the food.

Since Bryne still felt it was a betrayal, and never intended to stay, he ate hurriedly, scooped a handful of food onto a big plate, and slipped away for home. When he arrived back at the farm, Dennis was watching TV alone, and he lit up when he saw Bryne. "What you doin' home? You ain't *done?*"

"Yeah, I am," Bryne grinned, offering the plate. "Brought you some supper."

Showing no emotion, Dennis examined every item of the unexpected feast. "Hold on," he said, mock-suspiciously. "This ain't no *calf fries*, is it?"

"Yeah," Bryne countered, playing their usual game. "You ain't good enough for no *turkey*, son."

And the little laugh they now had together was on the family that night. Because Dennis and Bryne knew in their hearts that the real Thanksgiving was taking place *here*.

9

"This Thing About Blacks and Whites": Pat's Version

PAT RICH: Dennis thought I was ashamed of him because he was black, but I wasn't. I was just scared about my reputation.

There were times in the car with him and Bryne, when I was in my ducking period, and Dennis would say, "Look at your momma, Bryne. She's back there hidin'. She don't want people thinkin' we're a family." Well, we *were* a family, so that made me think: "Why am I so tied up in knots over this? What have I done wrong?" But then I went right back to ducking again.

The whole issue was that when Dennis came into our lives, people didn't have any earthly idea where he came from or why he was here. And you couldn't go around and preach to the whole community, "He is staying here because he is good for Bryne, and everyone is growing from it, and Worm is doin' good and Bryne is doin' good and our whole family is doin' good." It just sounds like you're ramblin'. All at the same time, people knew I had a black guy out at my house: "Why is he living there? What's goin' on that we oughta know about?" So right away, they started rumors on me, and everywhere I went I had to watch my step for worrying that somebody else would go run their mouth and start another rumor and ruin my reputation some more.

I really cared for Worm; I showed that in every possible way. But I knew that his and Bryne's friendship was the important thing, so I just let him go with Bryne and tried to stay out of the picture as much as I could. And everything was fine, until I got thrown into these other situations. Like, I remember in early 1984 I took Worm and Bryne up to Dallas to shop at a mall. Worm drove and Bryne sat in front with him, and when we hit the city these black guys stopped by our car and they waved at Worm and gave him the "OK" sign, like, "Well, you're doin' okay. You got a new car and you got a white boy and a white wife." Worm noticed it, too, because he laughed about it; and when we got up the road he said, "Miss Rich, those guys think you and me are married and Bryne's our little boy."

Then, when we were buyin' shoes at the mall, the salesman came over and asked me, "How does your son like his shoes?" And I said, "That's not my son." So then he said to Dennis "Is she your wife?" There it was again: you put Dennis and me and Bryne together and it was like, "What have we got here? A little kid and a big older guy with a woman—must be a family." So I got a little paranoid after that, and whenever I took 'em shopping in Durant anymore, I was always thinkin', "Well, if people in Dallas who don't even know us think that, what will people think about me around *here?*"

The next time we were in a department store in Durant, I went up to the clerk to write a check, and I had Dennis and Bryne on either side of me, and I was real uncomfortable about what this girl was thinking about us. So I just come out with, "This is my son and this is my other son." Dennis was shocked; Bryne was shocked; I was shocked. But the clerk just crinkled up her eyes, like: "Oh sure. We know what's goin' on here." So next time we went shopping, I ducked away from Bryne and Worm and hid behind a bunch of clothes. And I was peeping through the cracks of the clothes at the clerk, and I started plottin' in my mind how to go pay the check alone. But darned ole Worm, he was so excited to be gettin' all these neat clothes—the same good stuff as Bryne—he started waving things around and callin' out my name in this big boomin' voice, "Miss Rich! Miss Rich! Can

I get this, .*too?*" And after he found me hidin' behind the clothes, he said, "What you doin', Miss Rich? You tryin' to duck your 'son', Miss Rich?" Made me feel about yay-high.

What eventually happened was, Worm's presence became a blessing *and* a burden. And I inherited the burden because I was the one getting exposed—I was the only one out on the limb. See, it was okay for me to be out someplace with Worm as long as James was along. But if it was just me and Worm, or me and Worm and Bryne, that's when people *really* stared. I am a woman; I'm not like James: he could be seen all over town with Dennis and there wouldn't be a word said. But it was different with me bein' a woman. 'Cause if a *woman* goes downtown with a black man, people sit up and take notice. And I was the *mother*, too; it was always *me* taking Worm everywhere: out to eat, out to buy him clothes, back and forth to school. So somebody was always saying somethin'.

James thought I made a lot of it up, but I heard it myself—in the local stores or my beauty shop, even at the health club I went to in Durant. Like this one time, I was in the sauna there, and no one knew who I was, and this guy said to his friend, "You know that Dennis Rodman that plays for Southeastern? Well, he come out to my trailer one night with a little ole white boy. I don't know why in the hell a family would let a little white boy run around with a sorry black son of a bitch like him." And there I was, the mother of that little boy, and I couldn't say anything back. But I said in my mind: "God forgive you. You're just ignorant. You don't have no idea how much good Dennis Rodman is doin'."

For a long time, I had all this pressure directed at me like an arrow. It got so bad that whenever I did anything, somebody knew about it. One day, I was in Durant and I ran into someone I knew and we decided to go get a cup of coffee. So we sat in a restaurant about fifteen minutes and talked. Come to find out next day: "*Pat Rich is seein' a lawyer!*" Somebody saw us in town and assumed we were having an affair and that he must've been a lawyer because he was a nice-lookin' guy. First off, it was my sister Elaine's husband, and we talked about their kids—that was the extent of our big "affair." Second, he wasn't a lawyer, he was a retired businessman.

Right away, my mother calls me—one of her roundabout friends told her about it—and she says, "I heard you was in town yesterday with a good-lookin' lawyer." I said, "Well, if you call your son-in-law a good-lookin' lawyer, I guess I was." And I was thinking, "My mother likes Worm. If *she's* callin' about these rumors, what are other people thinking that *don't* like Worm?" That's what I worried about.

People are always drawing their own conclusions. One of my teachers taught me this once in college. He gave us an example: "A man opens a car door for a woman and she staggers around a little bit, so he carries her into a building. Draw your own conclusions." Somebody said, "She was drunk and he carried her into *his* house." Somebody else said, "She was sick, she'd been in the hospital, and he was her doctor and he carried her into *her* house." Somebody else said, "She was drugged and he was taking her inside to try something funny on her while she was out." It was hysterical. Kind of like that party game where one person whispers something to another person—"On Monday, the sky will be blue"—and then that person whispers it to another person, and so on through a bunch of people, until it finally comes out: "A man had honey on his nice blue suit," or something ridiculous like that. Well, that's the way it was for me. Everybody said what they *thought* they saw, or what they *wanted* to see. "Idle mind's the Devil's playground"—that's the saying. And boy, I'll tell you, when all this stuff was happening, the Devil must've been havin' a *field* day in *our* little town.

So, everywhere I went with Dennis, I had it fixed in my mind what people were thinking or saying. And that was the reason I started ducking him—not because he was black. It's a real fine distinction, I know; and I wish I could've been a lot smarter about it then. But I was worried about my status in the community; that came first. I figured the less I was seen with Dennis, the better off I would be, emotionally, status-wise, and every other wise.

Under those circumstances, it was a wonder I didn't have a nervous breakdown. I came pretty close. The pressure from rumors, and then from my family, just about wiped me out. I'd come home from school so upset sometimes, I'd break out in a rash. Or I'd have to lie down because I felt so sick and drained. Or else I'd go in the bedroom and cry. My family would hear me in there, but they didn't understand my private struggles. I couldn't explain it to Bryne; he was too young and he was still recovering from Brad. I did try to explain some of it to Worm, in our little heart-to-hearts in the kitchen, but he always thought I was too touchy about it, which I probably was. And I couldn't tell James; he wasn't getting the flak I was, so he didn't take it that seriously. He didn't know how bad it was for me. And I couldn't understand everything that was goin' on myself—why people acted like they did and why it upset me so much. All I knew was, I had it coming at me from every side at once, and I had no idea how to deal with it.

First, I had some things happen at home, in my beauty shop. I had this business, and I knew people wouldn't understand why Dennis was here, and I was afraid they might start assuming things, like: "Something's goin' on between Pat and that guy. Otherwise, why is he here?" Especially because Dennis looked older than even my own kids. If he was a younger boy, people wouldn't've thought so much about it; but it looked strange for a little boy like Bryne to be involved with a twenty-two-year-old guy: what could they possibly have in common? So, when people would come to get their hair done, I didn't want 'em to see Worm around, makin' 'em feel uncomfortable. I had a right to think that way because that was my livelihood, and I was very particular about it. I had a large clientele from different counties, and a lot from Bokchito and Durant, and I didn't want to lose any of my customers because of Worm bein' there. I couldn't afford it; I needed every single one of 'em. So, when I was working in my shop and Worm was in the house, I would just draw up in a knot, hoping nobody would see him.

Boy, he got on my nerves, though. He was fascinated with what I did in that little shop, so he liked to watch me work. I'd be working on someone's hair and he'd come up to the sliding doors that connected to my bedroom, and he'd peep through the crack with one eye and watch. He'd have that big ole eyeball glued to the crack, and he'd be watchin' and wrigglin' around, and you could hear his toes poppin'—and oh, that made me so nervous. I'd quick turn the chair away from the doors and start worrying: "Oh no. I hope this little girl don't see that eye peepin' through the crack or hear those toes poppin', 'cause she's gonna really think it's strange."

Sometimes, it was just plain funny, even though I couldn't take it that way myself. Like one time I had a girl in the chair, facing the window that looks out over the patio, and I was combing her hair to the right. Well, all of a sudden, there was Worm on the patio in his warm-ups, stickin' his hands down the back of his britches and scratchin' his rear. I thought: "Oh, no!" and I spun the chair around so she wouldn't see it and be embarrassed, and I started combing her hair to the *left* for a while. I was furious, and nervous, and I kept watching him out there, thinking: "I just hope he goes back in the house." But he didn't; he kept scratchin' away.

Well, he had no idea we were watching; he didn't know we could see him from there. So he just stood around lookin' across the hay field, starin' up at the sky, stretchin' and scratchin' and picking his nose. . . . I couldn't let her see all this, because I didn't want her thinking: "Who is that black boy out there? And what is he doin' here, anyway?"

So I had to keep twirling this poor girl around in her chair—I just kept twirling her and twirling her and prayin' for Dennis to get off that patio. She must've thought I was crazy. And maybe I was. If it was one of my other customers that I could've had fun with, and let my hair down and said, "Hey, look at Worm out there," that would've been different. But I knew this girl; she was the type that I had to protect her—she was so picky and straitlaced. If she had seen all that stuff goin' on out there, she would've snarled her nose at it and never come back to get her hair done again.

While I was going through all this at the beauty shop, I had other stuff happening to me at school. It got real intense for me after Dennis got popular in basketball and everyone on that little campus knew who he was. On top of that, he had started to date white girls, which was a big issue between us, because I didn't believe in it. And people was talkin' about it because he was the only black guy on campus doin' it, and plus these girls was always seeking him out. It was a real sticking point for me. It probably went back to when one of my best friends from Bokchito ended up goin' to Southeastern and started dating a black guy. Well, I had this thing about blacks and whites. And I had known her all my life—we were very close friends—so when she started dating that guy, it just devastated me.

So the way it all began at school was this: Dennis and I already had this routine going, with me driving him to and from school. We knew each other pretty good by then, so instead of him waiting by my car like he always did, he started looking me up all over campus. He would look hard for me until he found me. I'd park my car at different buildings, so he'd peek around and find my car, and then he'd just come into the building and look for my class. This one time, I was coming out of class when I saw him walking across campus on those big long legs, and I knew he was gonna head me off and ask for a ride. The campus was full of people I knew, so I thought: "Uh-uh, no. I am not gonna have him come up to me here in front of all these people and have them start dreaming up all their juicy scenarios to spread around campus. No way." I decided to duck into the library. It was just too personal having him track me down like that on campus. It was too much for me to handle at that time.

Well, I got in the library and hid from him behind the bookshelves, and started lookin' for books. I felt so foolish. I thought: "This is ridiculous. What am I doing? A grown woman hiding behind bookshelves." Evidently, he saw me go in there, because here he was, walkin' up and down the aisles lookin' for me. I could hear his toes crackin'—it was so funny; I could always hear his footsteps because his feet made weird noises. I was doin' a pretty good job of hiding from him behind those books—you can get lost in the library—so what he did, he just said in a real loud voice, "Miss Rich, you can't hide from me. I know you're in here." When he said that, I came out because I didn't want him to keep hollerin' to everybody in school, "Miss Rich, I know you're in here!" I don't know whether I was more embarrassed at myself or mad at him for finding me out. But he wasn't upset at me because all he said was, "Hi, Miss Rich. Can I ride home with you today?" He didn't care a bit; he wasn't self-conscious about it at all. So while I walked alongside him with my head down like I was "Miss Nobody," he walked right on outside with me, straight and tall, just like he was "Mr. King."

Every day, just about, I tried to hide from Worm on campus; I was always ducking behind buildings when I saw him coming because he was so tall he could see all over. I kept tellin' myself: "I know he can't see *over* a building, anyway"—and I'd duck over here and duck over there. I really didn't feel hypocritical about it, though. I knew he knew that I liked him because of how I treated him at home, and because of everything I had done for him. I just couldn't hold my head up in his presence because I didn't want people to think we were together. And I remember there was another white girl at school at the time who was going with a black guy, and it was pretty heated, and they talked about her all over campus like she was a dog, a no-body, just low-class trash. I didn't want people saying the same things about me.

Another time, I went shopping with a friend from school, and she knew about Dennis dating white girls and she didn't like it much, so when she got in my car she had this distant look on her face, like: "Don't say anything about him around me. I heard all about him and I don't wanna hear any more." She had this sneer on her face and she acted real cool to me, and I was hurt. So I got to thinking about all this. I enjoyed having Dennis in our lives and I knew he was good for Bryne and they both needed each other, but there was another part of me that didn't want him there because of all I had to go through.

I really and truly didn't feel I was better than Dennis—that wasn't it. But when it came down to maybe losing business, and good friends like her, I had to say to myself: "I better watch it because I need these people in my life. To lose my friends over him, and maybe my reputation—it isn't worth it to me." So, in my mind, I chose my friends over bein' seen with Dennis because, at that point, I had nothing to gain from it and everything to lose. I didn't know he would still be close to our family ten years from then; I just thought: "He might fly the coop for Dallas at any time. And I can't lose my respect and my decency over bein' seen with him." That was just the way I came to feel.

Well, not long after that, I was in my home ec class and I happened to look over to the door, which was open slightly, and I saw this big ole long leg and I thought: "That leg looks familiar." I looked at it and looked at it, and then I thought: "Oh no. It's Worm's leg. He's waitin' for me to get out of class to take him home." The teacher went on with her lecture, but all I could think about was: "When I walk out, Worm's gonna be standing there waitin' on me, and I can't escape. And people will think I am with him and we're having an affair, and they're gonna start pointing their fingers at me." The class was full of women, and a lot of 'em had already seen him riding with me in the car, so I just knew if I went out there now, they'd be sayin', "I bet she *is* having somethin' to do with him. Everybody knows he dates white girls, and she's older than him, so he's gotta be seeing her, too"—and all of that. I was so nervous, my heart was pounding and I could hardly sit still for thinking: "How am I gonna get around this? Is there a back door anywhere? Is there a hole to crawl in? Lord, do I really have to go out there?"

What no one understood was I had all this other pressure in Bokchito and now I was in a different town and I thought: "It's gonna start up here, too." And then, I had to worry about what my teacher would think about me. I really believed they would give you bad grades if they thought you messed with a black fella, because it would automatically lower their opinion of you. And I knew nobody would know why I was walking with him, or why he was riding in my car; they didn't know Bryne; they didn't know anything about it at all.

It was so hard for me to do, but I got up and took a deep breath and walked out of the classroom, and kept my head down. Dennis just walked beside me and we didn't say a word. I tried to get ahead of him, but he would take two big steps and catch right up with me. I walked this way and that way, hoping to ditch him someplace, but he stuck with me like a horsefly. So we went on down to the car, and he got in—I didn't say anything to him and he didn't say anything to me—and we headed toward Bokchito in total silence. It was weird; we didn't say a word the whole trip back. And when we reached the outskirts of town, I thought: "Well, maybe he's more sensitive about this than I give him credit for. Maybe he knows how hard this is on me and he's not thinking about his own needs so much, and he's showing me by bein' quiet that he really understands."

And, all of a sudden, he looks over at me and says, deadpan, "Miss Rich, will you fix me some french fries when we get home?"

10

Big Worm and
Little Worm

Dennis knew Pat was fast becoming a head-case over him.

It made him uncertain about her real feelings. On the one hand, he understood her attitudes—without accepting them—and figured at first: "That's Miss Rich. It's just the way she is." And since she obviously had a conscience, and could even laugh at herself sometimes for how silly she acted, he sensed she cared deep down. On the other hand, the blatant rejections hurt him: "Well, she can't like me as much as she says 'cause she keeps actin' ashamed of bein' around me." He couldn't understand how she could treat him so well at home and do things for him that only a mom would do, and talk to him like she cared, and then turn around and duck him at school. And because he couldn't know that the main reason she hadn't stood up to her family when they'd excluded him was because she was reluctant to distress her mom and dad, he concluded that she really liked him more for Bryne's sake than for himself. But rather than run from this adversity—as he had so often growing up—Dennis made it a challenge. He decided not only to stick around but to find a way to make her admit the truth: that she really *did* like him just for him.

Despite his suspicions, he had come to feel comfortable enough around Pat to start teasing her more often. For instance, about her food. She enjoyed cooking his favorite treats—particularly pancakes, french fries, and corn bread—and he knew she wanted him to say how good they were. So he would set her up by sitting at the kitchen bar and starting a conversation—usually about some pretty white girls he liked on campus—and then asking her if she'd fix him something to eat. One time when he requested pancakes he set her up by saying, "Miss Rich, I know how to fix pancakes better than you do." To her amazement, he proceeded to show her how, and she's made them that way ever since.

That little episode opened a crack in the communication door between them, so he kept putting his foot in farther. For example, he would brag about his grandma's corn bread being better than Pat's. She would then rustle some up and challenge, "Okay, Worm, does that taste like your grandma's?"

"Not quite," he would hedge.

And even though she suspected that he was just pulling her leg, she would always try to cook a better batch. But, not without a conscience, Dennis also found little ways to make it up to her. For example, Pat would come home after church, or sometimes after school when Worm had already hitched a ride back, and she'd find the whole place had been spotlessly cleaned: clothes picked up, garbage tossed, lamps dusted, floors mopped, rugs vacuumed, toilets scrubbed—as though the place had been attacked by a team of maids. It was one way of saying he appreciated her, even if he didn't always understand her.

But then other events would put him off again. Like when Pat would occasionally use the word "colored"—without edge or connotation—to refer to black people. But one day, when Pat said to James offhandedly, "I saw this colored guy in town today," Dennis felt comfortable enough to gently reproach her. "Miss Rich," he said softly but firmly. "You always say 'colored' when you talk about us. But we don't like to be called 'colored,' 'cause we *ain't* colored. We ain't red, white, or blue; we're *black*. So just say 'black people.'" And she understood.

Tougher for him to swallow was her use, though infrequent and inadvertent, of the word "nigger." Finally, one day he explained, "Miss Rich, we hate that word. It's the worst thing you can call a black person." When he outlined why, she looked it up in her dictionary and realized for the first time how intimidating and hurtful that word could be. She'd always thought it was just another way of saying "colored person," though she did know, vaguely, that some considered *that* reference offensive, too.

It came up again later. One evening, with Dennis in view on the couch, she was talking on the phone with a friend when she uttered a thoughtless colloquialism: "You think *you* worked like a nigger today!" Instantly remembering Dennis, she became tongue-tied and started stuttering, "Well, you know . . . I . . . I . . . " She was so mortified, she had to hang up. Which is when Dennis yelled, "Bryne, listen to your momma! Did you hear what your momma just said?" Dennis knew it had just slipped out and she didn't mean anything by it, so he lightly deflected the sting. Still, Pat apologized profusely: "Worm, I am really sorry. My friend said it first and I just repeated it. It's something we say around here, but we don't mean anything mean by it. I know you don't like that word and I'm sorry I said it. I'll be careful and not say it anymore."

"Okay, Miss Rich," he replied evenly, holding no grudge.

Curiously, however, the term affected him more deeply coming from her than it did from James, who somehow, though he rarely used the word anyway, made it sound harmless. For instance, while James virtually always said "colored" or "Negro"—which Dennis would simply correct with, "No, Mr. Rich, we're black"—on occasion he would slip. Like the time they were all watching a pro basketball game on TV and James blurted out, "Boy, that nigger can shoot the ball, can't he?" But immediately, he gave Dennis an embarrassed grin and said, "Oh, I mean 'that *black person*.' " And Dennis said "Yeah, yeah," and laughed it off, unoffended. That was partly because, while he still distrusted Pat's affections because of her overriding concern with the opinions of others, he considered James not only guileless but also a fatherly model.

As for Bryne, who was supersensitive about what he and his brothers called "the N-word," and who always jumped on Pat's case whenever she let it slip—he only crossed the line once in the time he'd spent with Worm. It happened during a Nerf basketball game, when they'd bent the plastic hoop and wanted to fix it and refasten it to the door. Without thinking, Bryne suggested, "Well, let's *nigger-rig* it up there," which was redneck slang for "jury-rig." Since Bryne was no redneck, and because of their remarkable bond, Dennis joked it away with a satirical, "Oh, is *that* how it is?" But even though Dennis was okay with it, Bryne still felt deeply ashamed. "I didn't mean it like that," he offered, scared of losing Dennis's respect. "It's just one of them things you say around here, and no one thinks about." Dennis shook his head and said, "So what you thinkin' about it for, son? Ain't gonna help you *beat* me." And the situation dissolved into their usual volley of sarcastic cuts and playful shoves.

This led Dennis to explain to Bryne how blacks use the word. He said a lot of white people didn't understand that blacks can call each other that name—like in a pickup game where they might say, "You can't hold me, nigger," or "Damn, that nigger is fast." *But*, he pointed out emphatically, it wasn't cool for a white person to talk like that—unless he hung out with the brothers and was considered a brother himself. Which was what Dennis wanted to try to make Bryne someday. Literally.

Bryne already considered them brothers. One way he showed it was by spending time with Dennis that he used to spend with Barry and Mike. Another was by bringing his friends home to play with Dennis too. So, all through that first year, the Riches had a houseful of rowdy thirteen-year-olds playing tackle Nerf football and pickup basketball with Worm. Or else they'd all hang out at the go-cart track where they made quite a sight: this tall, gangly, black boy overflowing his tiny cart, racing all these little, cotton-topped, white boys around the dirt track, laughing and screaming like banshees.

The kids were so surprised how much fun Dennis was—he acted silly, just like them—that their awe of the Big College Player quickly wore off. They didn't know that in many ways Dennis was living his childhood for the first time through them, because he'd never played these games as a kid. That was why playing with them came so natural to him, yet felt so new. More surprised were Pat and James. Even though they'd observed Dennis for months, and Pat was beginning to wonder if his attachment to Bryne wasn't "a supernatural thing," they were still amazed at how easily a twenty-two-year-old, black college kid could fit right in with these little white adolescents.

Dennis was surprised, too. At first, he wondered what all those kids were doing there; he felt "like a toy Bryne brought home for his friends to play with." But then he realized it was just like basketball camp, where the kids loved him because he smiled and laughed and patted them on the back with encouragement, and put quarters in his ears. So he relaxed into that mode again and enjoyed himself. His only concession to the age gap, in fact, was lowering the outdoor basketball hoop from ten to eight feet. But then they'd still play roughneck-style: two-on-two or three-on-three, No Pain, No Gain. And Worm would act all the roles: the strutty, arrogant adversary; the patient counselor; the barking coach; the "hype-guy" teammate getting them all pumped up: "Yeah, kick his butt!" and "Take it to the hole!" Bryne's little friends couldn't get enough. Fooling around with Worm was the highlight of their day.

It was also the highlight of Bryne's life. In fact, they had grown so close now, Dennis was aware that Bryne almost wished *he* were black, too. So, during their private playtime, Dennis decided to toughen Bryne up in their Nerf and outdoor basketball contests, so that Bryne would be ready someday to play against his black friends in Dallas. Thus, he would rough Bryne up more than usual and try new taunts, like: "You don't think you can pull that white move on no black kid, do you?" Or: "You wanna kick a black boy's butt? Then watch me do it and then you do it like me." And Bryne would practice and practice, trying to play "black" like Worm.

Off the court, Dennis tried to get him more "hip" in other ways, like teaching him how to walk cool and talk jive. Bryne loved this intriguing instruction; he immediately took to strutting and jive-talking at home and at school. He got so good at both, it spread to his friends, like a fad. So, until an English teacher finally complained about it to Pat, for a few weeks a bunch of little white country kids comported themselves around the junior high like tough-ass city blacks, parroting Bryne's "Worm-isms" left and right. For example, they constantly greeted each other in class with, "Hey, brother. S'up?" or "Say, homeboy"; when a teacher gave an easy assignment, Bryne, and then his pals, started uttering "Cool breeze" under their breaths; instead of "That's all right," they said, "That's awright"; in the halls, they constantly hurled cuts back and forth, most often "Crazy as a mug!" or "Fat as a mug!" or "Dumb as a mug!"—"mug" being Worm-slang for "the mother-f word," something they couldn't bring themselves to pronounce publicly; and when one of them was nailed as a culprit for anything in class, out would fly Dennis's personal favorite: "No, Lord, not meeee!" This he used most often at home whenever Pat or James accused him of something—like if they asked pointedly, "Worm, did you leave the door open?" he'd give them the innocent eyes and a dramatic, "No, Lord, not meeee!" At one point, this phrase was so much in vogue at the Rich home, the whole family used it regularly:

James: "Pat, did you pick up my car keys?"

Pat: "No, Lord, not meeee!"

Pat: "Bryne, would you please go clean up your room?"

Bryne: "No, Lord, not meeee!"

Bryne devotedly imitated other Worm mannerisms, like the hilarious smacking noise he made with his lips; and the way Dennis would drum a rhythm deftly on his thighs or on the hollow spots and studs on walls; and singing loudly in the shower. Pat used to get the biggest boot out of listening to Dennis sing. He had told her once that he had a pretty good voice and that he'd sung a few times in his mother's church choir as a kid, but he wouldn't sing in front of anyone anymore. So Pat would wait until he went into the shower, where he'd get all wired up and really let loose, and she'd sneak to the living room couch nearest the bathroom door and listen from there as he beat a spirited rhythm on the stall and projected a beautiful voice that mesmerized her, especially when he hit the soprano notes "so pretty and smooth."

It was hard to imagine, she used to think in moments like that, how a person so shy and remote and "weird-actin' " could have so many interesting sides to his personality. Too bad there was nothing in her psychology books about "a Worm that could cuss so bad and sing so sweet."

Bryne and Dennis were inseparable now, in their own little world, day and night. Dennis still had no close friends on campus, including on the basketball team, because instead of hanging with the guys on the team he either stayed by himself or met Bryne someplace. He had this "thing" at the time that except for Pat and James, he didn't want to be around adults. And neither he nor Bryne cared how strange their companionship appeared to others. Bryne, who sought Dennis's approval in almost everything, was too young and attached to feel the uniqueness. Besides, he had always played with his older brothers pretty much the same way before Dennis came along. So it wasn't a big stretch for him to treat Dennis as a brother—though he was more like a brother his *own* age. Whenever someone did raise the issue of their strange friendship, they both liked to say, "Well, we're on the same wavelength."

Which they quickly exploited to their own advantage. For example, the closer they got the more alike they wanted to be, even in their mode of dress. Since Dennis hadn't brought much with him from Dallas, he rarely wore anything but T-shirts and jeans or warm-ups, even to class. So Bryne started wearing the same things. Then Dennis became interested in the nice new polo shirts that Pat had bought Bryne, Barry, and Mike for school, and would occasionally help himself to one of them and wear it to college. But since clothes were at the bottom of his priority list, too often the shirts would end up lost. Even if the boys didn't realize it, Pat certainly did—and it ticked her off because it was hard-earned money down the drain.

This initiated another conflict in values for Pat. If she continued to go easy on Dennis simply because of his importance to Bryne, she knew she would never be able to control his behavior in their home, or instill the values by which they lived. So occasionally she treated him to the same items she bought Bryne. Apparently, it wasn't enough; he still borrowed the polo shirts. Finally deciding that Dennis had been around the family long enough to start taking more responsibility, she confronted him directly on the matter. "Worm," she put her foot down, "I don't want you wearing my boys' polo shirts anymore, because you take 'em off when you go to gym class or wherever, and you don't bring 'em back. So, please don't want wear their nice clothes, because they cost money and I can't afford to replace 'em." And she stayed real strict with him about that.

As usual he took it cool outwardly; but in his mind, he considered it another strike against Pat for not treating him the same as she did the other three boys. That was undeserved, however; Pat was right about the principle. And although it didn't occur to Dennis, what she had told him was nothing more or less than what she would've told Bryne, Barry, or Mike in the same situation. Dennis was acting irresponsibly with someone else's property, and this wasn't acceptable in the Rich home, period. Plus, Pat was worried about the message Dennis's behavior might send. If he could borrow these shirts and not think twice about losing them, even though they belonged to people he cared about, what did that say? She would have liked to raise this with him, but she didn't think it appropriate at the time. Besides, it seemed more a quirk than a pattern, and Dennis was still so much fun to be around.

Dennis obeyed Pat's edict a while, but eventually maneuvered around it and started wearing one of Mike's new blue polos every so often—partly because it made him feel like one of the brothers and partly in childish spite of Pat. They got past this, but Dennis was soon driven to further maneuverings. For instance, still desiring new clothes, he secretly wanted Pat to buy them for him. While it might have appeared as though Dennis was hoping to "use" Pat by having her buy him something he could probably afford himself, that wasn't the case. The real issue wasn't clothes, it was *belonging*. Dennis had grown increasingly attached not only to Bryne but also the family. He still had a deep, consuming need for a father, or at least a father figure, so it stood to reason that if he could feel like a more integral part of this family—in any little way, even getting attention at the cost of disapproval—he could legitimately feel he *did* have a father in James. This notion would manifest itself more provocatively later on.

So when Dennis got the urge for new clothes he would tell Bryne, who'd then tell Pat that *he* wanted new clothes, and he would stay on her case until she finally gave in. Once Pat took them shopping, Bryne's agenda included buying Worm the same things he got—so, of course, how could Pat refuse? Thus, at least twice a month, she would end up taking Bryne and Dennis to the sport shops in Durant and Sherman—the boys adopted the motto "Shop Till Ya Drop" for these jaunts—spending hours searching for the really crucial items: T-shirts, warm-up outfits, sweatshirts. At first, Pat shopped almost exclusively for Bryne, once in a while picking up an extra shirt or maybe some socks for Dennis. But gradually the boys teamed up to play her soft heart and guilty conscience like a violin—Bryne cajoling, "Momma, we can get Worm a pair of warm-ups, can't we?" or, "C'mon, Mom, let's get this for Worm, too, while we're here," and Dennis dropping sincere but obvious hints like, "I sure would like to have that." Little wonder she would always buckle under their "soap opera pressure" and say, "Well, I guess we can get one more," thinking she'd buy Worm an item or two like Bryne's, just to get them off her back. But by the time she would get everything up to the counter, there'd be several pairs of warm-ups, and four shirts, and six sets of socks she didn't even know they had.

Again and again, Pat had to stretch her carefully planned budget of about $60 to more like $120. And once they had her on the ropes for that much, they would go for the whole nine yards, deciding—for a slight extra charge—to letter all their new shirts. Only not with your ordinary single-lettering design; but rather with your more expensive, blue-on-gold, *double*-lettering design—to more dramatically emblazon such important proclamations as: GO FOR THE GUSTO; RUNNING WILD ON ME; SOUTHEASTERN SAVAGE POWER; WORMALISTIC; and WOR-MAZOID.

One time, Dennis held up his and Bryne's identical sweatshirts and asked Pat, "Miss Rich, what do you think about what we should put on these shirts?" She happened to be thinking of the movie *Ghost-busters*, so she came up with a creative idea. "Put on there: 'Who ya gonna call?' " she said, thinking as fast as she spoke. But then, instead of finishing with the obvious "Wormbusters," she accidentally blurted "*Wormbastards*." Major Freudian slip. But Dennis responded like always: "Bryne, did you hear what your momma just said? She said, '*Wormbastards*'!" And he got a big bang out of that. But they went ahead and ordered what she *meant* to say. Meantime, Pat sat down to wait for the shirts to get lettered, and started laughing uncontrollably over what she'd just said. The more she thought about it the more she cracked up, and pretty soon everyone in the place was staring at her, including Bryne and Worm. Then they cracked up, too.

Another day, on a whim, they had identical shirts lettered separately: BIG WORM for Dennis and LITTLE WORM for Bryne, and later, BIG WIGGLE and LITTLE WIGGLE—their two sets of favorites, which they started wearing everywhere. Later still, Bryne had some of his own shirts lettered: RICH: B.K.A. [Better Known As] LITTLE WORM and RICH: B.K.A. LITTLE WIGGLE. Pretty soon, they'd amassed an impressive casual array of matching, lettered warm-ups, sweats, and "tees," along with multicolored basketball shoes. So their next adventure was wearing identical outfits and shoes to the stores to shop for . . . more identical outfits and shoes. "There's those two 'Worm' guys," an amused shoe clerk liked to point out when they bopped by. Which was exactly what they were.

So much so that it spilled into Dennis's basketball life. Once the season rolled around, it had become of paramount importance to him that the Riches, especially Bryne, attend his home games. Two weeks before, he had brought it up at dinner: "Are y'all gonna be comin' to see me play?" James answered, "We'll be there, Worm. Don't worry"— which reassured him. But they weren't really into it big-time; they had no idea yet how good he was.

To prepare, Dennis and Bryne developed a ritual: before every game they would shop together for either a new sweatshirt, T-shirt, or warm-up suit, and buy identical items and wear them together the day of the game—all their shirts displaying their separate trademarks: BIG WORM and LITTLE WORM. At home doubleheaders they would show up at the gym early and sit in the stands to watch the women's team— the Southeastern Savagettes—play the first game. Naturally, their cool shirts drew giggles and stares—almost as much attention as the odd couple themselves. After a while, they knew that newspaper photographers would start snapping away, so within the first few games, BIG WORM and LITTLE WORM became an item—a poor man's Jack Nicholson appearance at a Los Angeles Lakers game.

Soon, every Southeastern fan in the area had either seen or heard about the big black player and the little white kid in their identical shirts with insect names.

11

A Tree
Waiting for
Rain

Dennis had never been so nervous before a basketball game.

On the three-hour ride north to tiny Langston University for Southeastern's opening game—his first organized game ever—he felt queasy and jumpy, worried about how he would perform at center for the first time. Would he remember the plays? Would he make the right post moves at the right time? Although he was feeling the high school butterflies he never had a chance to feel in Dallas, it didn't show until just before tip-off, when he approached Coach Reisman and admitted tensely, "I hope I don't let you down tonight." Reisman was impressed; he'd never heard a star talk like that; not a trace of the usual prima donna ego. It meant a lot to Reisman. The first time they met, he'd sensed that Dennis had "emotion and heart"—and this pre-game statement just proved him right. It was also the first time he knew for sure how much this opportunity really meant to Dennis.

Langston, a predominantly black school with a small brick gym, was a tough place to play. Sound reverberated piercingly, especially the blaring soul music and persistent chants and cheers. Reisman and Hedden wondered how Dennis would handle the pressure of such commotion. They quickly found out. In the first half, he played superbly, with only minor lapses in concentration, like not being ready for passes and fumbling easy rebounds. But he more than made up for it by playing with reckless abandon, diving for loose balls in crowds, not just on the floor, but into the bleachers; running the blocks tirelessly and posting up as taught; storming the boards; whipping the outlet pass to ignite fast breaks.

In the second half, he gave more of the same, but Langston stayed close. With just under two minutes remaining, Southeastern clung to a three-point lead by shifting into a "four-corners" delay—positioning players at the half-court corners to spread the defense and slow the pace. Dennis played one of the corners, where he was simply to catch a pass and swing it back quickly to the point guard, who would swing it another way to prolong the stall. This was a telling moment to Hedden and Reisman: it was the first time Dennis would handle the ball in a key, pressure situation.

Reisman was particularly apprehensive. Dennis had no experience with this tactic, other than in practice. The one thing he hoped Dennis wouldn't do was put the ball on the floor and risk a turnover that could cost the game. Thus, when the pass to Dennis finally came, Reisman fretted, "Get *rid* of it. *Move* the ball." But instinct took over; instead of doing the expected, Dennis did the sensational. He took what Reisman would later describe as "that magnificent, first quick step that he has," put the ball on the floor, and dribbled for the basket, twenty feet away. "Oh God," Reisman panicked, "he's gonna dribble off his foot, he's gonna kick it off his knee, he's gonna turn the ball over to Langston and they're gonna go down and beat us." But none of that happened. Dennis took two giant steps to the hoop and thunder-dunked it home to finish Langston off. Awestruck, Reisman turned to Jack Hedden and said, "Boy, is *this* kid special!" And they both knew they'd found the big-pressure player they needed to keep them in games.

Final score: 56–55, Southeastern. Dennis's numbers: 24 points— a stunning 43 percent of the team's total—and a remarkable 19 rebounds. A world of promise. In the locker room afterward, Reisman found Dennis beaming his trademark ear-to-ear smile, and gave his player a hug. The kid had worked hard all summer—surviving school and all the arduous practices, constantly debating: "Is this worth it?"— and then had come here to Sherman and performed like that in his very first game. It had certified something about Dennis's "heart" that Reisman would only articulate years later: "You never motivated Dennis Rodman for a game. There was no pleading with him to play. When that ball was tipped, no matter what the competition was, you got forty minutes of the greatest basketball you could ever imagine." To Jack Hedden, the tantalizing thing was: "If that's what this kid can do with *no* experience, what'll he be capable of once he really knows how to play?"

They got a taste of that the next game—with a big boost from an unexpected source. Since Langston had been so far away, and Bryne had school the following day, he hadn't been able to attend Worm's first game. But now he begged Pat to take him to the next one, against Austin College in Sherman. Of course, she said yes. But since they had to go first to watch Barry play for Bokchito High in a Bryan County tournament game at Southeastern, they didn't make it out to Sherman until the start of the second half.

During the half they'd missed, the Savages dragged and Dennis scored an uninspired 15 points, too often looking for teammates when he had easy shots. It was frustrating to Hedden and Reisman; Austin was well-coached but a nonconference, nonscholarship team—presumably easier to beat than conference foes. In other words, Dennis should've eaten them alive. Maybe he played subpar because he hadn't perceived yet what his teammates already had after the Langston game: that he was to be their leader and star. Or was it the emotional letdown of not seeing the Riches there when the game began? In some ways, having them there was more important to him than the game itself. He had never felt so pumped up before; never been in the spotlight like this for people who cared about him; never felt so acutely the need to perform for people *he* cared about.

Thus, when he finally spotted the family entering the gym as the third quarter began, and Bryne gave him a little wave, Dennis's heart jump-started, and in storybook fashion he went on a tear. The Savages came alive with him, flying to an impressive 81–67 victory on Dennis's powerful wings: game highs of 13 rebounds and a whopping 40 points in only his second collegiate game. His on-court transformation had been so startlingly obvious, the electrified team manager, Billy Conaway—destined to be Worm's roommate the following year—told Pat and James after the game, "Boy, I don't know what it is, but when Bryne walked in here tonight, Dennis just lit up like a candle and really turned it on. I never seen anything like it." Struck by this, Pat suddenly realized that Bryne and Worm's relationship really *was* a "supernatural thing." She thought: "There *is* somethin' special goin' on here." She would ponder that more and more over the course of the year as she constantly strove to understand the reason why Dennis Rodman had been thrust into their lives.

Outside, Pat, James, and Bryne were accompanying Dennis toward the team van, discussing his fantastic performance, when Dennis asked if Bryne could ride back to Durant with him. Pat said, "Well, the coach may not approve of that," so Dennis impulsively hollered to Jack Hedden, "Coach, can Bryne ride back with us?" Aware of their bond, and despite mild reservations that Dennis might be spending too much time with the Riches, Hedden said, "Yes, I guess so"—and Bryne was ecstatic. Everyone piled in the van, and Bryne and Worm sat together like teammates. The whole ride back the other players joked with Bryne; bought him hamburgers at McDonald's when they stopped; mussed his hair and pulled his ears and generally treated him like a valued mascot. He fell in love with the team that night. In fact, aside from having Worm as his pal, that van ride home was the greatest thrill of his young life.

Following the team home in their car, Pat and James discussed Dennis's performance. Pat, who'd developed a pretty sharp eye for technique from watching her sons play for so many years, was puzzled by Dennis's "bad hands"—how, when he was positioned under the basket, he would let so many passes slip through his grasp and fly out-of-bounds. James's studious eye perceived something more subtle: even though Dennis had rebounded exceptionally well the first few games— never nabbing less than nine—James didn't think he'd played hard enough. "Sometimes he looks like he's doggin' it out there," he concluded, sure that Dennis could do more.

When Dennis and Bryne arrived home after that second game, they all sat around a while watching TV and reviewing his performance. By any objective standards he had played spectacularly, especially given his lack of experience. Even so, James felt compelled to offer Dennis his first critique, in typically frank style. "Only one thing, Worm," he launched into it. "I watched you out there and you don't *jump*. You ain't gettin' off your feet. You just stand there waitin' for the ball to hit you in the head before you go after it. Get in the air and grab that thing soon as it hits the basket. You can't be planted underneath the basket like a tree waitin' for rain. You gotta be aggressive, Worm. You gotta want that ball in your hands more than anybody else out there."

Dennis was speechless; it was a lot to digest. "Mr. Rich," he replied timidly, "I want the ball. I *got* thirteen bounds."

"I know you did, Worm. But maybe you could've got *twenty*, you ever think of that? Maybe twenty-five or thirty. But you ain't never gonna know, playin' the way you are now."

"I played okay."

"Yeah, you played okay. But you didn't play nowhere near how you *could* play. You can rebound, Worm. That's the most important thing you can do out there. But you can't just stand flat-footed under that goal and wait for that ball to come to you. It ain't gonna just fall down in your arms if you don't jump after it. You have to get off your feet and rebound that thing. Make it *yours*."

"I will," he promised, determined to please. Interestingly, where only a year earlier this kind of harsh truth-telling might have alienated Dennis, he now seemed to relish hearing it from James.

"And another thing," James offered, concerned. "You can't hold the ball. They throw you a pass underneath the basket there and, boy, it slips right on through. You gotta *get* them balls, Worm. You gotta tell yourself: 'I'm *catchin'* this pass.' It's all in your mind, how you play."

"Well, maybe not all," Pat cut in with another idea. "Worm, let me see your hands."

"You gonna tell my future?"

"Oh, hush," she said, studying his enormous palms. "Well, no wonder you can't hold onto that ball. Your hands are like leather. You probably can't even *feel* the ball."

James took a close look and was amazed: Dennis's hands were coated with callus. "Man, they feel like chips," he said. "You could toss them things in the fireplace and start a good fire with 'em." Ho-ho; joke finally on Dennis. Which, of course, Pat enjoyed. But she'd also made a good point. So James suggested trying some hand lotion.

"Lotion's not gonna do much good," she insisted. "I think he needs some hot-oil treatments." As a beautician, Pat not only styled and cut hair, she was also expert at hand care. And she knew the same thing that worked on women would work on men. Dennis looked intrigued. "Worm, I got some electric manicure gloves. It helps women's hands; I bet it would help *your* hands to get more flexibility and sensitivity, and everything. I bet you can get a better grip on the ball. Let's go in here and put some oil on your hands and those hot gloves on."

Game for anything, he followed her into the little shop, where she proceeded to soak his hands in beauty oil, sheathe them in thin plastic gloves, then heat them in a pair of electrified manicure mittens. Dennis laughed nervously at first, but he obviously liked the pampering—so much so that they started doing these treatments before every game. And they seemed to make a difference; everyone agreed that Dennis was holding on to more rebounds and passes, and his hands actually looked and felt softer. He believed it, too. When Pat would forget before games, he would pipe right up, "Miss Rich, I need to put my hands in that oil. Would you do my hands, Miss Rich?"

■   ■   ■

From there, Dennis's curiosity grew. One day, after Pat had finished with her last client, he ventured into her shop with a new request: "Miss Rich, would you do my nails?" She said yes; she'd thought to herself a while ago that his nails could look nice if they weren't so jagged and brittle. And now the oil treatments for his hands had softened his nails, too, making them easier to work on. So she sat him in the chair—for which he was much too wriggly and way too long—and she clipped, filed, and polished his nails meticulously. Afterward he was astonished, and proud, at how elegant they looked. It wasn't often people did anything so personal for him; it made him feel accepted and special, and raised his self-esteem.

There was one more favor from Pat he hadn't the courage to ask for. So he sent Bryne to do it. "Mom," Bryne inquired one day as she cleaned her shop, "would you give Worm a haircut?" She agreed; but she warned Dennis that she'd never cut a black person's hair. Bryne explained to his mom that Worm wanted his hair cut "in a nice V in the back." So she sat Dennis in the chair—he'd grown to love being groomed like this—and as he traced a V for her with his fingers, she tried to shape it with the clippers. Since he also wanted a part, he had to teach her how to create one. She had to hold the clippers steady and then painstakingly clear a thin strip in the thick, curly foliage. He insisted it had to look even; when he sensed the clipper going off line, he ignited in horror, "Miss Rich, you're gettin' it *crooked!* You're gettin' it *crooked!*" After they disputed that for twenty minutes, he trained Bryne to do it instead.

One day when Bryne wasn't home, Dennis was desperate for a haircut, because he had a game that night and the players were expected to always look groomed. Though he didn't trust Pat to do it right, he let her try again—but he made her too nervous with his taskmaster commands. Then, unexpectedly, Barry volunteered. "Mom, let me have the clippers," he said, lighting up like a kid at Christmas. "I can cut Worm's hair; I can do the top of it. Worm showed me how."

Later that evening, this was how Pat would describe the fiasco to

James: "You know how he and Barry like to act silly and giggle all the time. Well, Worm didn't trust Barry with those clippers. So Barry takes the clippers and starts makin' noises, like 'Yrrrrn-yrrrrn,' and this was scarin' Dennis because he thought: 'I ain't gonna have no hair left.' So then Barry giggled and showed Worm he was just kiddin', and then he started in to really clipping. Worm looks straight ahead in the mirror and turns his head real slow while Barry's clipping away. Everywhere Barry moves the clippers, Worm's followin' him with his eyes, watchin' like a chicken hawk.

"So Barry had a real steady hand and he was doin' a good job and he kept sayin', 'Now be still, Worm. You gotta be real still.' And Barry starts snickering 'cause he thought it was so funny, and he goes, 'Buzzzz-buzzzz'. And Worm, he wants to see what Barry's doin', so he keeps lookin' up. Barry says, 'Worm, I can't cut your hair if you're gonna try to watch the clippers. So please quit watchin'.' And here's poor Worm watchin' those clippers like they was a branding iron, and Barry got all tickled again, just 'cause he was cuttin' Worm's hair, and he starts giggling real hard. Then he goes, 'Buzzzz-buzzzz' again, and about that time Worm looks up to see what Barry's laughing at and Barry accidentally runs his head into the side of the clippers and a big wad of hair falls out on the floor.

"Well, I was watchin' from a chair and I got so hysterical I couldn't even get up. And Barry was laughing so hard he got weak and he couldn't hardly hold the clippers. 'Cause here he just clipped a big chunk out of the side of Worm's hair. So Barry started cracking up, and I saw that chunk and I said, 'Oh no!' and I was laughing so hard I was holdin' my stomach. Worm goes, 'What y'all laughin' about? Y'all done somethin' to me. I just know you done somethin' to me.'

"So he gets up and looks in the mirror and sees that big bald spot, and he turns and looks at Barry with those big ole eyes: 'Barrrrrr-y! You gapped my hair! You ruined my hair! Look what you did!' And we just all laughed so hard, he couldn't really be mad. Well, then I tried to straighten it up, but the more I cut the bigger I made that spot. So Worm said, 'No, stop it! Stop it! Just let it be!' And he went to the game like that. I thought I was gonna bust my gut I was laughing so hard."

That night the family went to the game. Whenever Dennis took a shot and turned his head their way, they saw the big gap in his hair and they started cracking up. All through the game, whenever Dennis made a dunk they'd stand up together and yell, "Way to go, *Spot!* Slam-dunk it, *Spot!*" And pretty quick, the people in the stands around them caught on and laughed along, too.

From that moment on, Dennis permitted only Bryne to cut his hair. But he had to promise never to go, "Yrrrrn-yrrrrn" or "Buzzzz-buzzzz" while he clipped.

Following their two opening victories, the Savages had lost their next two games in the season-starter Midwestern Tournament, even though Dennis scored a total of 55 points and grabbed 20 rebounds. Was it just coincidence that Bryne wasn't at those games and they lost? Worm never said. From then on, however, at supper before every game Dennis asked urgently, "Miss Rich, are y'all comin' to watch me play tonight?" Invariably, James would say something like, "Well, how many points you gonna get tonight, Worm?" Or, "Okay, I'm comin' to watch you tonight. But I guarantee you, if you stand there flat-footed waitin' on that ball to drop on your head, I might just get up and leave the game and go on home." And Worm would love that byplay; so James and Pat got in the habit of deliberately setting quotas for him to live up to.

"Worm, now look, you can't get under twenty tonight," Pat would say over dessert. "Yeah," James would add in a serious tone. "And give us twelve rebounds while you're at it." And Dennis would take it all to heart and actually try to get twenty and twelve. There were other times when every member of the family, unbeknownst to every other member, would lay the same request on poor Dennis for a particular game:

James: "Let me see three slam-dunks tonight, Worm";

Pat: "Give me two of your slammer-jammer specials, Worm";

Mike: "I want you to slam me a slam-dunk—a *big* one, Worm";

Barry: "Make a nice slam-dunk tonight, Worm";

Bryne: "Your momma wants five 'In-Yo'-Facers,' Mr. Jive."

And Dennis would take *that* to heart, too, thinking he could deliver all those dunks—knowing, of course, he'd be lucky to get just a few. Yet, after each big slam he'd lope upcourt like a colt on the loose, pointing a triumphal finger at the family in the stands. And until they finally caught on, each one thought, "He got that one for *me!*" and felt special and proud, like him.

Observing Dennis's newfound enthusiasm, Pat and James shrewdly decided to boost their quotas every couple of games, to give him incentive to always try harder. Bryne showed up regularly now for home games—as did Pat and James and often Barry and Mike—and Bryne even went to some road games in the team van. After the Savages went 10-2 over the next twelve games, the players started kidding Bryne that he brought them good luck. Dennis believed it, too, because he knew that Bryne's presence kindled a deeper motivation in him to excel.

Bryne was his biggest fan, and after every game, win or lose, he would rave, "I'm tellin' you, Worm, you're gonna make All-American for sure. And then you're goin' pro." Though Worm would predictably balk, "Naw, I ain't good enough," he thrived on this support. It wasn't just that Bryne's opinion mattered like a brother's, it was also a matter of justifying his faith by never letting him down. Even if Dennis didn't believe in his own ability, something inside him wanted to, and Bryne inspired that desire like no one else. In fact, over the next three years, the more Bryne would drive home the praise, the more Dennis would allow himself to think: "Well, if *he* thinks I'm so good, maybe I am."

More reinforcement followed. Dennis had started a postgame ritual with the family by suggesting they all meet up after home games at Ken's Pizza in Durant. Dennis's love for pizza inadvertently provided James with another incentive angle to prod him to play better. "I'll tell you what, Worm," he used to say. "You make me twenty points and fifteen rebounds tonight and I'll buy you a big pizza supper after the game." And after the games they'd all devour pizza and evaluate Dennis's performance, which steadily improved: "You done really good tonight, Worm. You made a lot of points and you're gettin' off your feet for those rebounds now. You've done really well." And like a movie script, the more they bragged on him, the better he played.

Less than halfway through the season, at Dennis's urging, Coach Hedden made Bryne the team water boy. So Bryne started showing up proudly for games in his official "Savages" warm-ups with "WATER BOY" printed on the back. The whole team enjoyed his presence all season. Years afterward, they would remember how they were always so touched, on the long trips back from road games, by the tender sight at 2:00 A.M. of little Bryne sound asleep in Dennis's lap.

Bryne had been so thrilled at the honor of being made water boy, it was all he could talk about at home that night. Pat's heart leapt; in little more than a year Bryne had lost a part of his soul through an unimaginable tragedy that sucked away his spirit and youth and spun him into a chasm of despair, and then found an equally unimaginable new friend with whom he seemed to play catch with life itself. James thought it wonderful, but didn't look a gift horse in the mouth. To him, all events were like the weather, the crops, and the land—destined to be what they'd be—and he was equipped to handle any outcome.

But Pat had been searching for the hidden meaning of Bryne's attachment to Dennis ever since she saw them coiled in bed together in that protective embrace. To her, Bryne's rejuvenation was more than she'd hoped for, which was simply, in prayer: "Please let Bryne laugh and smile and enjoy life like he used to." It even seemed more than the miracle she'd told her minister it was. She just couldn't pinpoint what.

Next evening, Bryne raved again about being water boy and a part of the team, right there on the bench with Worm. Later that night Pat couldn't sleep, so she sat in the living room staring out the window at the new moon beaming back at her, shiny as a silver dollar.

She recalled the prayer she had made to God to send Bryne a little brother, and it suddenly struck her as ironic that the furthest thing from her mind—until just this second—was that God may have answered her prayer by sending . . . *Dennis Rodman.* Just as she'd first assumed that Bryne's 'counselor friend' at camp was white, she'd also assumed that any little brother sent from God—which she never ruled out as impossible—would also be white. So she had to chuckle when it came to her now as clear as that shiny new moon: "See, this is the mysterious way You work, isn't it, Lord? You don't just send us things all rosy and glamoured-up. You have a real sense of humor. Instead of sending us a little white baby, maybe You sent us a big black '*Worm*'."

Dennis sat at the kitchen bar as Pat prepared dinner the next evening. Reflecting on the night before, she was suddenly struck by another bolt. Surprising even herself, she wheeled around to face him squarely and declared with deep conviction, "I know now why you are here, Worm. I have wondered all this time and I couldn't understand. But now it's beginning to come to me why you are really here. *God sent you to take care of our family in our time of need. You're here, for a little while, for all of us.* But one of these days, Worm, you're gonna go to greater heights. Something wonderful will happen to *you*, too. I don't know what it is, I just feel that it will."

Dennis looked startled, and embarrassed. Pat had the split-second thought right then that if his face hadn't been so black . . . Lord, it would've probably glowed red.

12

One in a Million

Halfway through that first season, with Southeastern at 11-3 and Dennis averaging a consistent 26 points and 12 rebounds, it was clear the team had an extraordinary talent.

Though Dennis remained remote, his teammates appreciated him not only for his dominating skills but also for his modest, unselfish attitude. For example, even though Dennis had stolen some of his teammates' limelight, they admired his talent too much to hold grudges. They knew attention would be trained on Dennis, but felt he deserved it because he excelled every night, without boasting or seeking out praise. More important, he always worked to set his teammates up for success even more than himself, and if double-teamed or off his shooting game, instead of brooding or grousing he attended to other key parts of his game that the team required to win.

This had been forcefully demonstrated early on, in the finals of the East Central Classic against Oklahoma Baptist University at home. Attempting to nullify Rodman's quickness, Baptist ran a 1-3-1 trapping defense instead of a conventional man-to-man or zone, trapping Savages—particularly Dennis—all over the floor. Hedden countered with a 2-1-2 set, positioning Rodman farther out on the baseline, which negated some of his explosive rebounding. Although Dennis scored what was to be a season-low 15 points, he nevertheless played a complete game to lead Southeastern to a difficult 68–60 win. Aside from pulling down 13 boards, he did all the other little things: dove into crowds for loose balls; made precise passes; boxed out; keyed the breaks. From that game forward the players rallied behind Dennis, riding an almost tangible emotional momentum toward, they now dared to hope, their ultimate dream: a berth in the national championship tournament at Kansas City.

Enthusiasm also swelled in Durant. There had not been so thrilling and dominating a player at Southeastern since high-scoring Jim Spivey thirty years ago. The school's only three-time All-American—whom the locals still remember today for, as sportswriter Harold Harmon once put it, "standing the NAIA basketball world on its ear"—had fallen just short of single-handedly producing a national small-college title in 1956. Hope was high here now that Worm Rodman might finally deliver that prestigious title.

Basketball chatter raged throughout Bryan County. Older Southeastern alumni who recalled the electricity generated by those Spivey- and Jerry Shipp-led teams, under the tutelage of legendary coach Bloomer Sullivan, started coming out of the woodwork to games again, just to see this Rodman kid. The exalted Sullivan, a member of the NAIA Hall of Fame, would have loved him. After all, it was Bloomer's brand of patterned, passing offense that his devoted disciple, Jack Hedden, used to Rodman's advantage. Unfortunately, Sullivan had died the year before Rodman arrived. Hedden's biggest regret, he'd stated midway through this season to Reisman, was that Bloomer never got the enjoyment of seeing the passing game he invented with Dennis Rodman at the center spot. However, in increasing numbers, thousands of others were now experiencing that enjoyment.

As the Savages prepared to start conference play, they were living up to their nickname behind Dennis's infectious intensity. For one thing, his rebounding proficiency—especially offensively—had established them as a great rebounding team, which, according to the coaches, had also improved their shooting. Psychologically, every player knew that if anyone missed a shot, Dennis could grab the rebound and put it back in. They came to rely on that. Also, Dennis could shot-block, run the floor hard, and finish off most passes they threw to him. Lastly, he lived to win; it was more important to him than personal stats. This ethic, practiced as it was by such an obvious star, motivated teammates to think the same way. And when they heard the overflow crowds cheering Dennis wildly every night, home and away, their desire to excel soared, too, often lifting them to a higher level of play than even they thought they could achieve.

It affected the team in another key way. Hedden and Reisman's goal was to win twenty regular-season games and an Oklahoma Intercollegiate Conference championship—they talked about it often for motivation. The previous year their Rodman-less team had finished a disappointing 15–13 overall; so, at first consideration, that much of a leap this quickly seemed farfetched. But, surging now, the coaches and players were talking about not only winning the conference championship but also of actually having a realistic chance to win a *national* championship. All because of Dennis Rodman.

But it wasn't so easy. Of their final thirteen games, the Savages won just seven, finishing a frustrating 4–4 in conference play. However, they closed the regular season with their eighteenth consecutive victory in "The Snake Pit"—their home-court gym—over Southwestern Oklahoma State on Dennis Rodman's brilliant 27-point, 20-rebound performance. And with Dennis finishing ninth in the nation in scoring and fifth in rebounding, and the team closing at 18–9 overall, they felt they were just now starting to bloom. Hedden and Reisman were excited and pleased. The team was jelling under Rodman, who, it was now clear, was made to order for their run-and-pass game. He ran both sides of the lane like a gazelle, posted up big, and rebounded everything around the hoop except the sweat. There remained just one more test of the team and its burgeoning star: The Playoffs.

Southeastern's opener came against conference rival Northeastern Oklahoma State in Tahlequah, where the Redmen had squeaked by the Savages a week before, 65–64, on what Lonn Reisman still recalls disgustedly today as "a fluky bank shot at the buzzer." Both Hedden and Reisman knew the Redmen couldn't beat them twice—especially with Rodman at the top of his game. In fact, the team was now extremely eager to redeem its earlier loss.

It did so handily, swamping Northeastern 86–68. Dennis put up big numbers—36 points, 16 rebounds—and dominated inside, while the team shot blisteringly from the floor. It was an exhilarating win that not only satisfied its need for redemption but also tested its mettle, for the first time, in a must-win situation.

Next, the Savages traveled to Weatherford to face another conference enemy: the tournament's No. 1 seed, Southwestern Oklahoma State again. The Savages destroyed them, too, 81–64. Dennis was sensational: 42 points, 24 rebounds. Whenever he dominated the boards like that, the team was virtually unbeatable. As if to punctuate this, late in the game he delivered a play that Lonn Reisman, even after fifteen years of college coaching, still terms "the most amazing exhibition of athletic quickness and skill I have ever seen, by far."

The game was no longer in doubt by that time; Southeastern was in total control. Dennis had just rebounded the ball and outletted to point guard Phil Stephens on the baseline. Though Dennis usually ran the middle of the floor upcourt, this time for some reason he sprinted up the outside lane. Reisman was screaming, "Slow it down!" because as a conservative coach he never believed he had a game won until the buzzer sounded. Oblivious, Stephens took two dribbles and stopped abruptly at the top of the key, while Rodman flew to half-court. Then Stephens did the unthinkable: he hurled the ball three-quarters the length of the court—some seventy feet—to, apparently, no one.

When it first went up, Jack Hedden couldn't believe his eyes; he thought Stephens had gone crazy and thrown it away. Reisman was also stunned, and ready to explode on Stephens. But then, as if in a dream, Rodman zoomed to the hoop, leapt over the rim with his back to the basket, caught the ball midair, and stuffed it behind his head—all in one motion. When he hit the floor, he was already bolting back downcourt, pumping his fist and waggling that index finger, and the crowd was roaring and clapping and screaming for him. It was not lost on those privileged fans that in District 9 ball you didn't see this calibre athlete every day, never mind that kind of astonishing play. Next day, in his *Durant Daily Democrat* headline, Harold Harmon boldly proclaimed: "*The Juggernaut Strikes.*" And he wasn't referring to just the team.

Actually thinking of themselves now as a juggernaut, the Savages came home on a high. Their once farfetched dream of being the first Southeastern team to make it to the Nationals since Bloomer Sullivan took them there in 1963 was palpable now: a sign over their gym exit—SNAKE PIT 18–0—reminded them of their two-season home-court invincibility, reinforcing their heightened sense of destiny; they'd just crushed the tournament's No. 1 seed; they were actually on the brink now, a single game away from going to K.C. Accordingly, Hedden advised the team before the game, "We want to win this game tonight 'cause you don't know if you're ever gonna get this opportunity again." When the players left the locker room, they were convinced that this was their time; they were going to K.C. because they believed they couldn't be beat in "The Pit."

But disaster struck: Phillips University shocked them, 65–59. And suddenly their national-championship dream had burst; everything they'd worked so hard for was gone. "It was a very strange basketball game," a dismal Reisman informed reporters. "They did a good job on Dennis, even though he got twenty-three and twelve. Every time we got a run, I thought Coach Wilson did a great job controlling his time-outs and the little details they needed to beat us." What Reisman didn't say was that, inexplicably, his kids had lost the intensity they'd showed in the previous two games. Neither he nor Hedden knew why. They figured their players had been pumped so high from beating Southwestern that maybe they never came down, and had just drained themselves too soon. Immaturity, inexperience, maybe even a touch of youthful arrogance. Plus, of course, the key unanticipated factor: Phillips played the perfect game to beat them.

Afterward, Dennis bawled in the locker room, distraught and disbelieving. He had desperately wanted to win a championship in Kansas City, more to prove something to his mother and sisters and Bryne than for himself. There was no consoling him, even though the coaches told him he'd had a sensational year and played above everyone's expectations. Hedden was proud of him, and Reisman reminded Dennis of something he'd told him before he'd ever played a game: "Always keep that gleam in your eye for the pros. Because one day you're gonna get that chance." He knew it was crucial to keep Dennis motivated.

The coaches' only consolation was the positive press their team had received in major newspapers, like the *Daily Oklahoman;* and they now knew exactly what they had in Dennis Rodman. Their end-of-year assessment: they had never coached a player with Dennis's enthusiasm, instincts, and talent. They discovered he could consistently score from six to ten key points a game just by rebounding and beating everybody down the floor. Plus, he could rebound and quickly fire the outlet pass, and by the time his teammate caught the pass he was so instinctive and fast, he would be almost at half-court. Also, he played so hard he always looked like he was playing the last game of his life. It wasn't showboating, it was the fervor he generated for the game. And he loved to play hard for the team. In other words: *One in a Million;* Coaches' Dream; Meal Ticket to a possible national title.

The trick was to make certain that Dennis maintained his enthusiasm through the off-season. Hedden and Reisman's biggest aid in that quest was the announcement that Dennis had been named a First-Team NAIA All-American. Coming at the perfect time, after such a devastating season finale, this honor was a great surprise not only to Dennis, who could barely believe it, but to his coaches as well. After all, the team hadn't made it to Kansas City, where most of the top players enjoyed their first exposure to the national press and NBA scouts. And while Dennis's stats were outstanding, the selection committee rarely chose even the most exceptional sophomores for First-Team All-American, opting in its "Let's-wait-and-see-what-he-does-next-year" approach to name them to the Third Team instead.

Then more great surprises, as Dennis was named Oklahoma Intercollegiate Conference Player of the Year and then District 9 Player of the Year. Now, finally, he had major awards of his own to show his mother and successful sisters, as well as Bryne and the Riches—an immeasurable boost to a constantly flagging self-esteem. These accolades also helped focus him through the summer on what he might achieve next year, and provided him with an inkling of how good he could be. Of course, he would never acknowledge this to anyone.

That spring, the coaches expected Dennis to stay focused in school. (Hedden hadn't left that to chance the past year. Aside from running grade-checks every two weeks, he'd often roused Dennis from his room to see that he made it to class; arranged for instructors to provide extra assignments so he could make up work that he missed; and had Dennis write class papers in the basketball office.) They also expected him to remain in shape and stay clear of "problems" outside the program. Which was a euphemism for "dating young white girls." Just before spring semester ended, in fact, Coach Hedden had a little talk with Dennis about that.

He said he'd received a couple of calls from outraged mothers of underage girls, who'd insisted frankly: "Keep that black boy away from my daughter!" Hedden explained his position: "Dennis, this kind of thing might be acceptable in Dallas or L.A., but, unfortunately, not in Durant, Oklahoma. You need to conduct yourself with that in mind. It's not just a black-white issue, it's also about statutory rape. There's strong feelings about blacks and whites in Durant. And even though I don't agree with it personally, and neither does Coach Reisman, we have to recognize that it's here. And so do you."

Dennis stared at the floor silently, sensing déjà vu. He was recalling his mother's advice when he'd phoned her about all the white girls calling him for dates: "Momma would rather see you stick with black girls, Dennis. I don't want you crossing over. Mind you,

Oklahoma is not the place you want to get tangled up with white girls. Black men have been picked up for lesser things. And you hear stories about blacks getting lost in those jails and nobody ever finds them again."

He was reviewing this when Hedden concluded his appeal: "Most people around here will like you and respect you and treat you well, Dennis. But there's others that won't. Like some of these parents. Now, I told 'em, 'I'll have a talk with Dennis but, hey, it's your *daughter's* responsibility, too.' But you really need to stay away from these young girls, Dennis. People know who you are now. Believe me, it's for your own good."

Hedden was right about one thing—people did know who Dennis Rodman was now: his popularity on campus had soared. Yet, between practice and games and constantly hanging with Bryne, he'd left no time for dating, though he contemplated it often. Just for fun he would occasionally wander campus and fix on a particular girl and start trailing her around—for weeks sometimes—without ever saying hello. He wasn't afraid, just still painfully shy. Also, it was a much more complicated issue for him than for most. Assuming he wanted to, how would he find black girls to date, since there were very few around? And of those, how many would be available, attractive, and interested in him? However, this was not the main deterrent; he strongly favored white girls anyway, despite knowing that dating them could be risky in Durant.

Eventually, his new popularity and the constant attention from attractive coeds finally emboldened him enough to take some risks. That was when word started whirling through Durant and Bokchito and, eventually, back to Pat, compelling her to initiate long talks with Dennis about the morality of the issue, as well as the potential dangers. She wasn't the only one: Lonn Reisman had sat him down, too, and said, "Dennis, you know this is a town without very many blacks. And you're gettin' to be kind of a celebrity, so there's gonna be some white girls lookin' to get close to you. But you have to be careful. These people around here mean business." Even James brought it up, emphasizing essentially: Do what you want, but be discreet, because there are too many people who won't understand.

Dennis listened to everyone, but continued dating whites anyway. As Pat knew and would later acknowledge with candor: "He was just a young man with hormones and you can't control that, you just can't." Sometimes, though, he would do his thing a little too close to home. For example, there was the outrageous time when one of Pat's sisters showed up at their parents' house, where the family regularly gathered to visit and play dominoes, and griped to Pat: "I told you about that black boy. I seen him parked down the road in your farm truck and he had this white girl in there and he was kissin' on her." Everybody seemed awkwardly stunned. "I *saw* that!" she added hastily, as though it verified that *everyone* knew, and cared, what Dennis was doing.

Pat was incensed. She didn't know if it was true or not—she thought it probably was. But what really galled her was that just because her sisters didn't approve of Dennis's behavior they felt free to throw it up to her, as if insisting: "You need to do something about it. You need to get him away from here because he'll give the family a bad name." Always a peacemaker, James tried to defend Dennis to the sisters: "Well, it ain't entirely his fault, though. These white girls do the chasin' after him; they don't hardly leave him alone. They call him, more than the other way. Right, Pat?"

"Yes, that's right," she chimed in. "I've answered the phone myself, so I know that they're the ones doin' all the calling."

"There's nothin' he can do about them girls likin' him and callin' him up all the time," James concluded reasonably.

But as far as the sisters were concerned, there certainly was: Dennis should just quit messing with those white girls, if he didn't want more trouble than he could handle.

"Listen," Pat said, barely keeping her cool, "none of y'all really know Worm—he's not living with you. He has a wonderful personality around girls that they just like. I'm not saying I approve of him goin' around with white girls, because I don't. But I can't control him. It's *his* choice; it isn't mine and it sure isn't yours. So I would really appreciate it if you would just keep your slurs to yourself. And that's all I'm gonna say about it because I'm starting to get upset."

So it was dropped for the moment. But it nagged her day and night that she had more to say on the subject. She just didn't know what she needed to say, or who to say it to first.

13

"Once You Go
Black
You Never Go
Back"

One day in the kitchen, as Pat cooked him a hamburger, Dennis rhapsodized about a pretty white girl at school who liked him, and then Pat tried to dissuade him from dating her.

They were emotional double agents at this, weaving feeble webs of deceit. For his part, he was both fishing for advice about his love life and yanking her chain on her intractable attitudes. She had a hidden agenda, too. While she was happy to proffer a "mother's" advice, she also used these opportunities to try to steer him away from white girls.

"Miss Rich, she's crazy about me," he dug in. "She would go with me. I could go with her any day."

"Well, I wish you'd date black girls, Worm. You know that people around here don't approve of blacks messing with whites."

"I ain't messin' with 'em. I only know a couple."

"Well, I'm just afraid somebody's gonna try to hurt you, or somethin'. One of those white girls' dads is gonna get mad at you for dating his daughter and you might get hurt." She was surprised that he seemed so unconcerned. "Why won't you date a black girl, Worm?"

"Miss Rich, if you knew black girls you would understand why."

"Well, I don't. So please tell me."

"They just act dumb sometimes. You ain't never been around it. But you would feel that way too, if you was."

"What do you mean?"

"They just act so different. White girls treat you right. If you make a date, they won't stand you up. They just have more common sense. You can't get comfortable with black girls, they're always changin' their mind on you. I get along better with white girls."

"Well, what does your mother say about it?"

"Oh, she's always sayin': 'I want you to marry a black woman,' and: 'I don't know why you date white women.' Stuff like that."

"See, she thinks like I do. We *both* can't be wrong, can we?"

"I guess so. 'Cause I still like datin' white women better. So you *must* be wrong."

"Is your mother against all white people? Is that why she wants you to stick with blacks?"

"No, she ain't prejudiced at all. She's worked with white people all her life and she has a lot of white friends. She just thought it would be a lot easier for me."

"She's right, it would be easier. And it would be easier on the people you care about, too. Don't you think she had your best interests at heart when she gave you that advice?"

"Oh yeah, I know she did."

"But you didn't take it, did you."

"Nope. I said, 'Mom, if you can't cope with it, there's nothin' I can do about it. I can't sit here and try to please you, and say, "Well, I want you to like this girl that I'm datin'." ' I don't care if it's my mother, father, or whoever is close to me, they can't tell me who I can date and who I can't date. That's *my* decision."

"Yes, it is your decision. But people who love you want to help you make the right decision."

"I don't care. If she says she loves me and she don't care what I do as long as I'm happy, she should accept that I can date the opposite color."

"Well, I hope you marry a black girl. I would like to see your kids have a nice life and not have to go through all the prejudice. Just stop and think: if you married a white girl and had children, who do you think will suffer more—you or your children? So I wish you would think about it a little more."

"Miss Rich, you should come to Dallas. It goes on all the time in Dallas; people don't think nothin' of it. You should pack up this whole town and take 'em all down there. They'd have plenty to talk about then."

She had to laugh at the truth in that. But the issue lingered in her mind. The rest of the school year, though mostly in humorous ways, she kept dropping hints and pointed remarks about it at home. Her emotions were hopelessly mixed: for one thing she wanted Dennis to be "popular and well-thought-of and respected," not only for himself but also because he lived with her family and his behavior reflected on them. Second, she thought: "If he stops dating white girls, there won't be any controversies and everything'll go smooth for everyone."

She decided at first to tease Dennis to keep him focused on the issue. "Worm," she'd prod gently, "there's some cute black girls on campus. You want me to introduce you to one?" Or preach: "If you marry a black girl, Worm, they won't end up teasing your kids in school." Or moralize: "I talked to this one girl at college that's dating a black guy and she said, 'It's caused me so many problems with my family. I can't go home; my parents won't accept me now.' And she swore up and down if she had it to do all over again, she wouldn't do it."

But Pat couldn't dent his attitude. In fact, since she'd become so obsessed with the issue, he knew he could easily turn everything she said around and manipulate her. For example, at the end of spring term one day when Pat was cleaning the kitchen, Dennis sat at the bar with something on his mind:

"You know, Miss Rich, I'd sure like to go on a picnic today."

"That's good, Worm. Go on a picnic."

"Well, I got this problem. I like this girl, and she's a really beautiful girl, Miss Rich. But she's leavin' town and I wanna take her on a picnic before she leaves 'cause this is the last time I get to see her."

"Worm, don't beat around the bush. I know you want something. So just spit it out and save a lot of hot air."

"Well, could you fix me up a little basket? You know, just put a wineglass in it—I'm gonna buy her some wine. Can I get one of those wineglasses you got in your cabinet there?"

"You know I'm particular about my glasses, Worm. You start taking my crystal and not bringing it back, I will really get mad. I have paid for that all my life."

"I know. But I ain't never liked a girl like this. I really wanna take her out to the lake and have a nice picnic with her, Miss Rich. Those crystal wineglasses would get me in good with her, too. Can you put one in there?"

"You want me to fix you up a basket so you can take a pretty white girl out on a picnic? You know how I feel about that, Worm."

"I know. But she's special. And it's real important to me."

So she started feeling sorry for him now, because she knew he'd been lonely. And though she disapproved, she didn't want to alienate him. "Okay, Worm, I'll fix you a basket and I'll put two nice wineglasses in there. But you better not break 'em. And bring 'em back. Will you bring my basket back, too?"

"Oh yeah. But, you know, I need to use your car, Miss Rich."

"Oh, I don't know about that. James might not like that. We need to ask James."

"We don't have time to ask him. He won't be home till later on, and I need to go soon. I need to go now."

He didn't want James' little, dusty Subaru anyway; he was really maneuvering for Pat's big Grand Marquis, to impress his girl. Aware she was being played, Pat relented anyway. And off he went with picnic basket, wineglasses, tablecloth, sandwiches, and drinks. And her Grand Marquis.

Another irresistible opportunity for manipulating Pat on the "white girl" issue arose whenever this group of pretty Bokchito high school girls came over to her beauty shop. Pat had a reputation in the community as the best trainer and groomer of young women entering Bryan County Fair talent shows and the prestigious "Miss Bokchito" beauty competition. She'd become so proficient at coaching them to act out monologues—from her drama training at college she knew where to get the skits and which ones would win, and even how to block and direct the scenes—or in securing professionals in Durant who taught music or dance, that the prettiest girls in the area flocked to her for help.

In preparation, they came to Pat's house for makeup and grooming, her real expertise, unaware that Dennis was often observing through the crack in the door. He was fascinated with girls then, particularly these girls, because they were so attractive and straitlaced— and such close friends of Pat's. The girls were cordial to Dennis, but nothing more. So when they graduated and a few went to Southeastern, Dennis decided he'd try teasing them like he teased Pat.

So he occasionally tracked them to their classes and talked to them in front of their classmates, knowing they were as reluctant as Pat to be seen publicly with him. He had more fun, however, riding Pat about them. He'd say, "Miss Rich, you know who I saw on campus today? I saw Lorinda Lee"—a lovely little blonde who had her hair done often at Pat's. Or: "Miss Rich, I saw Sue Ellen Green today." Pat always played along. "Oh, well good," she would say, pretending disinterest. Then he'd spin stories about talking to them on campus and how much he knew they liked him, just to get her goat. But he didn't succeed. So one day, he came home with a wild story he thought would do the trick.

"Miss Rich, you'll never believe what I saw on campus today."

"What was that?"

"Well, this is really gonna shock you, Miss Rich. Because it's about one of your friends. You won't believe this, you won't ever guess what it is." He got her all built up, with her curiosity "burnin' steam"— exactly what he wanted.

"Well, come on and tell me what it was, Worm."

"Miss Rich, you won't believe this, but I saw Susie Matthews walkin' with a black guy on campus."

She didn't believe it. "Oh really," she said, tossing it off.

"Yep. They walked right across campus together and went up to his car. And he was drivin' this real fancy new Monte Carlo, and you know what he did? He opened the door for her and helped her in. They started laughin' and she was smilin' at him and I thought they was gonna kiss right there! Then he went around to his side and got in and they drove away."

This was Worm, Master Manipulator, laying in specific details to try to convince—like the Monte Carlo, which Pat knew was a favorite of young black men in Dallas. It didn't work. Though, years later, she would admit that he did have her going: "The question was in my mind, even knowin' Susie as well as I did as a totally spotless virgin who never made a mistake in her life, and also how strict her parents were on her." But she caught herself at the last second.

"Worm Rodman," she said, suppressing laughter. You have told me a lot of things in life, and you suckered me and I believed 'em. But this is one thing that you won't sucker me in on. 'Cause I know this girl better than that. And she wouldn't even be *walking* with a black boy on campus, let alone get into a car with him. You're lyin', Worm Rodman. You better back up and tell another one 'cause that one won't get it."

"No, I ain't lyin'," he lied again, barely keeping a straight face.

"You know, Worm," she added, "that's what you *wanted* to see, isn't it? That's what you *wish* you could've seen. But it didn't ever happen."

"Yeah, it happened," he said, keeping the ball in play.

"No, Worm. That will never, ever, *ever* happen. No way. It will never, ever happen—not in *this* world or in any worlds to *come!*" Realizing the game was up, he fell off the bar stool onto the floor and rolled around laughing. She cracked up, too . . . finally concluding another of "our big drama scenes over blacks and whites dating."

But it didn't deter Dennis from trying other ploys. Like his famous

"Con Game"—psychological warfare that capitalized on an opponent's most obvious weaknesses, a technique he'd learned growing up with people older and more streetwise than himself. Pat's obvious weakness in this instance was her children—especially Bryne. For example, she often felt compelled to remind Dennis, "Worm, you know I don't want my sons dating any black girls," because she was never sure what Dennis and Bryne did together when they went out. And Dennis would expertly stir those fears by parrying back, "Miss Rich, I don't care. I'm gonna take Bryne out to date a black girl real soon, you wait and see." Which would have her in knots.

Since Pat was such an easy target, sometimes Dennis couldn't resist going further with the tease about Bryne: "It's like they say, Miss Rich," he would taunt melodramatically. *"Once you go black you never go back."* And that would really curl her hair; because it was *she* who'd told that to *him* after hearing it from "some roughneck cowboy in town."

Something else Pat had told him in their comical Michael Jackson dialogue lingered in Dennis's mind: *"If God meant for whites and blacks to mix, he would've made us all the same color. Why did He make us look so different, if He didn't mean for us to stick with our own?"* This nagged him and he couldn't let go of it. Something inside—like the need to make her admit she liked him for himself—urged him to disabuse Pat of this notion. He discovered one way, almost accidentally. When spring term rolled around and basketball had ended, he had a lot of free time on his hands. So, naturally, he went looking for Pat more often at school again, mainly for rides to the farm. Which gave him more chances to pester her.

It started one day as Pat walked to class and heard in the distance: "Miss Rich! How ya doin' today?" Looking around, she saw Dennis fifty yards away, waving wildly as he walked with a black girl. Pat thought this was a ruse: "Yeah, sure, Worm, that's a good one. You're with a black girl; okay, I see you. But she's *homely* and you like 'em pretty. There's no way you're dating her. You're just yankin' my chain again." When she related these thoughts to Dennis later at home, he could only hold his stomach and laugh.

He knew from the food-teasing games in the kitchen that she knew this was partly a game, too, no matter how polarized their positions or solemn-sounding the issues. Which only made it easier and less risky for him to keep challenging her in other ways. For example, recalling how vulnerable she was to him at school, and particularly her panicky response that time he'd stood outside her classroom door, he knew he could rattle her just by letting her see him. So several times a week he started showing up during Pat's school day to make his presence known. Had she been more rigid on the matter, this ploy might've had an extreme effect, like tormenting her into an unforgiving rage. Instead, it eventually disarmed her into seeing the light.

One afternoon, Dennis stood outside a large, bleachered, third-floor classroom where Pat happened to be reciting a short scene from *Macbeth* in her Introduction to Acting class. The assignment was: perform a speech with which you can personally identify. Unaware of Dennis's prying eyes, she stood there, hands slicing the air, playing the wrathful Lady Macbeth scolding her husband for vacillating in their murderous plot:

> " . . . Art thou afeard to be the same in
> thine own act and valor as thou art in
> desire? Wouldst thou have that which
> thou esteem'st the ornament of life, and
> live a coward in thine own esteem, letting
> 'I dare not' wait upon 'I would,' like the
> poor cat i' the adage?"

After she finished, she sat down to await her grade. That was when her professor glanced at the door and announced to the class, "There's some black guy peepin' in here." When she heard that, Pat thought: "Oh no. That's probably Worm. What's he doing here? The teacher's gonna think this is really strange." Then she spotted Dennis holding his stomach and laughing so hard he nearly fell to a knee. She could imagine what he'd found so hysterical; she must've looked like a fool waving her arms and ranting, in her thick Southern drawl, all that fancy Shakespearean stuff. "God," she thought, relieved, "if I'd seen him *during* my recital, I'd've freaked right out." She learned days later from Bryne that Dennis said that after he saw her performance, he about bent over double going back down the stairs, and nearly tumbled three flights down.

There were other maddening episodes. Although Pat was not a sports-minded person, she had decided to broaden herself spring semester by taking a phys ed class called Individual Coaching where she would learn badminton, archery, and tennis. Her badminton class started in the gym. Coincidentally, as a phys ed major with most of his classes there, Dennis was always hanging around the gym. One day, with him propped in the doorway observing, Pat had to perform some fundamental badminton strokes with her partner for the day, an athletic phys ed major who also played on the women's basketball team.

While her partner played perfectly, Pat played perfectly awful; this was as foreign to her as shooting a Nerfball. She thought: "Worm is such a good athlete and he's so used to always seein' me cooking or cleaning or bein' a mother, he can't visualize me playing sports." Her fear was that, with him watching critically, she would feel too self-conscious to do her best. As a result she tightened up, thinking: "I just wish he would leave." But he wouldn't, of course; he could read her like a book. So she had no choice but to stand up there and hack away at the fluttery little shuttlecock, missing it wildly—"like I was just swattin' at flies." Getting it anywhere near the net seemed too much to hope for. And, as she expected, Dennis launched into his patented laughter, embarrassing her almost to tears.

Then there was archery class. They were out on the grounds close to the gym, so Dennis—alert for more opportunities—saw the class and strolled outside. Meantime, preparing to take her first shot with the bow, Pat was thinking: "Oh, I hope he don't show up." Her teacher had just finished instructing how to properly hold the bow and release the arrow so the bowstring wouldn't snap back and black-and-blue their arms. That's when Pat noticed Worm moving through the little gathering audience, observing along the fence. "Oh God," she panicked, poised to shoot. "There's Worm. Now I'm gonna no-tellin'-what with this thing."

Stepping up to shoot anyway, she tried to block out his presence and remember the right technique. She raised the bow up, drew the arrow back, and . . . THWAP! Followed by "Ouch!" as the bowstring snapped back on her arm. She could hardly bear to watch as the arrow arched high over the target and landed way beyond. Foiled again, and publicly exposed. When she heard Dennis' annoyingly familiar giggles, she felt like aiming an arrow at *him*. Funnier yet, she actually thought: "Well, I *would*. Except I'd probably end up shootin' the thing into my foot."

It developed into a regular haunting. Pat would improve in the next class and then Dennis would show up again to watch, just as she aimed to shoot, and she'd crumble and "make the biggest blunders you have ever seen." Then the air would ring again with his guffaws. But she was too mad, too proud, too determined to give up; no, she'd show him, one way or the other. Sure enough, after a few flustering sessions she gradually improved. Eventually, Worm or no Worm, if her arrows didn't always hit the bull's-eye mat, they always came close. That seemed triumph enough.

It also told her that if she really concentrated, maybe she could learn to block Dennis out altogether. This was immediately put to the test when he managed to show up a week later at her first tennis class, taught, coincidentally, by Lonn Reisman. Later that evening, she shared the ordeal with James: "We were all in our warm-ups and we were doing this little jitterbug thing to make you more agile, where you stomp your feet up and down pretending you were running and holding the racket like you were fixin' to hit a tennis ball. Then in walks Worm, right on cue. He couldn't stay away 'cause he knew he could come down there and get a laugh out of watching me screw up in a sport. Well, I did not want to get out there and do it with him watching me. But they called my name so I had to get out there and start doin' it. I gave it my all because he was watching and I wanted to show him I could do *somethin'* right with him there hauntin' me, but he just laughed so hard he finally had to sit down on the bleachers. He doubled over, holdin' his stomach like: 'I can't take this anymore. Miss Rich is so ridiculous she's crackin' me up.' So he fell right on the floor, laughin' his fool head off at me. And after it was over, that coach came over to me and said, 'I don't know why Worm was so tickled.' She knew who he was, but she didn't know he knew me. And I am not gonna tell her, either.''

Yet another time, Pat was playing her first tennis game in her class at the outdoor courts. When her partner served up a shot, Pat smacked it "like I was usin' a big ole baseball bat," launching it over the fence and onto the road where cars were driving by. Oddly, Dennis happened to be strolling that road when the ball came bounding up to him. Returning it to the teacher, he spotted Pat and, with big, wide eyes, loudly proclaimed to everyone: "Oh, I know who *this* ball belongs to." Pat drew tight, embarrassed, knowing that if he stuck around he would only have more stories to report to James that night himself, and embarrass her even more. But, as usual, there was nothing she could do. At night, Dennis would always make sure that Pat heard him begin his report to James: "Oh, Mr. Rich, you won't ever believe what I saw Miss Rich do today." She hated it when Dennis made it sound as though she couldn't hit a shuttlecock, or do calisthenics, or shoot an arrow, or hit a tennis ball. It was personal; she didn't want *anyone* knowing that. Worse: James would always play along with the razz. "What did she do, Worm? What did she do now?" And Dennis would describe it and James would reply, "Yeah, sounds like somethin' she would do all right. Sounds just like Pat." Driving it home.

She could take some of the teasing good-naturedly, but when it came to her grades Pat would tolerate no further nonsense. Thus, at term's end, paranoid about Dennis's harassing visits, she decided to issue a warning before disaster struck. "Worm," she threatened without a trace of play, "don't you show up tomorrow because I am gonna take my final exam in tennis. And if you are there, you will cause me to flunk that test and I will never forgive you."

"Oh, I'll be down there," he said to exasperate her more.

"Don't you dare, Worm! This is a hard class for me. I have to do the backhand stroke and forehand stroke and knock the ball over the net in the right positions to get a good grade. And you know I can't do anything right when you're hangin' around there watching me. I am real serious about this, Worm. You come down there and blow that test for me tomorrow and I swear, I will never forgive you."

"Okay," he replied, sounding willing to comply. But then: "I'll see you down there."

Which caused her to storm from the room. And to fret all night that he'd come to her test and cause her to flunk and totally ruin her semester. Next day, she went to her class angry, nervous, and completely convinced that Dennis would show up to embarrass her again.

But he never came. He knew he didn't have to anymore.

As it turned out, Pat aced that course. Coach Reisman was amazed at how much she'd improved in such a short time. His parting words after her last tennis class were, "When you play tennis in Bokchito, tell 'em who taught you."

And she thought: "Yeah. You and *Worm Rodman.*"

14

"This Thing About Blacks and Whites": Dennis's Version

DENNIS RODMAN: I had a lot of opportunities to leave Oklahoma but I stayed—I can't exactly say why.

Miss Rich would always tell me, "You were sent by God. I think God meant for Bryne to meet you." I liked Bryne but I don't think it was because God brought us together. It was just two people who needed to be with each other and we got real comfortable hangin' together. After Bryne's accident, here I come to save him from all that turmoil he was goin' through and relieve a lot of tension and pressure from him. And then, when I had to go through all *my* tension and turmoil, here he comes to save me, too. I don't think it had anything to do with God; it just happened between me and him.

For a while, I wanted to do things more because Bryne looked up to me than for myself. He was probably the only person that really looked up to me that way. Even my mother and sisters, they loved me but they didn't hold me up so high like he did. They wanted me to be happy and everything, but they didn't feel a part of what I was doin' when I was there. I knew right off that Bryne cared about me as a person because he was like, "I want him to be my friend. I like bein' around him. He's fun and he makes me laugh." He just took to me like an older brother and then we wanted to be together all the time. He kept wantin' me to come back and come back, so I kept on livin' there. After a while I just figured: "Well, I guess I belong here."

But with his parents, it took them a while to get used to me. In the beginning, to be honest, I felt like they didn't really want me there. I think Mr. Rich was more like, "It's okay with me, it's no big deal." But Miss Rich was totally different because she made it a point to let me know right off—mainly in her actions—that she wasn't really fond of me. She didn't want me and Bryne to be too close because she was afraid of her friends and the community. I understood it; I knew she was protecting herself and her family. But it troubled me because some of her actions didn't speak as loud as her words. Like drivin' to school when she kept duckin' down in the car. I wanted to say, "Miss Rich, why don't you just come up here and drive and let *me* ride in the backseat."

It bothered me because I was always wondering: "Why would they let me into their home if they're ashamed of me outside?" I didn't think Mr. Rich was ashamed; he's a man, so it was like, "I can deal with it. What's the big deal, you know? People aren't gonna think anything." But Miss Rich was always afraid that people might say, "Oh, that black guy's her boyfriend." But for some reason she didn't make it a point to tell them, "This is Dennis Rodman. He's my son's friend." She just blew it off. It's funny, though, how kids are. Kids can look at a person and not think they're black or white. That's what me and Bryne did, and Barry and Mike, too. This thing about blacks and whites, it didn't make any difference to us. Only the *us* part mattered.

Today, I see Miss Rich a lot different than when I was living in her house. Back then, she could hide a lot in the corner from a subject. Like she didn't condone blacks and whites bein' together but yet she condoned me and Bryne bein' together. *She* was the one that had the problem. It was because of *what* I was, not *who* I was. For a long time, she couldn't get past me bein' black. Sometimes, I thought it was funny as hell. And I had a lot of fun keeping the pressure on her all the time because I knew she really liked me, and I just wanted her to come out and tell me. I knew she had a good heart but she wasn't always listening to it. Like when she told me, "Why don't you get yourself a nice black girl?" I said, "What does it matter if I'm seein' a black or white girl?" She said, "Well, think about it." I tried to tell her, "It don't matter what you *think*. It's what you *feel* and what you *want*."

Funny thing was, you could tell she knew all this. But she wouldn't let *me* know. I never did understand that. Me and Bryne and her had discussions all the time. I used to get real mad: "Well, if you can't care for what I do and who I see, I can't please everybody. You'll just have to deal with it or not deal with it. Where I come from we don't have problems like that. We just live day by day and moment to moment." She knew how I felt but I think she just wanted to please too many people.

Sometimes, she thought that I didn't see what was goin' on. But the way I looked at it when I first got there was: "I'm bein' used." Maybe they didn't use me, maybe they thought I was usin' *them*. Probably seemed that way; I don't know, though, because I never did have a clear picture on it. But it's very difficult to have a stranger in your house all of a sudden. It was very difficult for me to believe, "Well, let's have this twenty-two-year-old black guy in the house. That'll be great." Why would you do that? Not Mr. Rich—I mean *Miss* Rich; she couldn't hardly deal with it at first. But Mr. Rich, he said, "Fine, it's just one night." 'Course, one night turned into three years.

I didn't want it to happen. I knew Bryne was so much younger and that people in town didn't pay me any respect. I had no reason to be messin' around with a white family, except I didn't want to disappoint Bryne because he kept asking me to stay. But I still had the feeling the family didn't trust me. I felt I was continually bein' watched in the house—you know, like they was thinkin': "Is he gonna try to steal somethin' or take our car?" Probably the only reason they let me stay was because, "Hey, he's here trying to help our kid." Otherwise, why was I in their house? I didn't think they cared about me at that particular time. They didn't even know me yet.

It's true that I was affected by them. But that took a while to happen. I think about it a lot now but, back then, I guess I was too caught up in what was happening to *me*. They were there for me whenever I needed somethin', no question. And I wasn't real close to my mother then so I didn't go home a whole lot the first couple of years. It just felt easier to stick around in the country. It was a real tough situation with my mother saying, "I know you're enjoyin' your-self there with that family but I'm your mother and I'd like you to come home a little more"—and kind of feeling left out. I don't think she accepted the fact that I wanted to be where I was at the time. I tried to make her understand, "It's nothin' come between you and me. It's somethin' that is happening for me right now, and these folks are my friends and I ain't gonna stray away and forget you." But she re-sented it a little bit because so many things was goin' on and she wasn't a part of it. I was playing basketball and living with this white family on a farm in the country and she was worried that somethin' might happen to me because I didn't belong out there. She was worried about her baby, I guess. But I wasn't a baby any more.

Whenever I would get a little homesick I would call her and tell her about whatever was happening at the time: "Momma, it's a whole new world out here"—stuff like that. She'd say, "Well, that's nice," but you could tell she wasn't too happy. And I could see why. But I wasn't trying to make her feel bad; it was just that things went downhill for me in Dallas and then I got to Oklahoma and Bryne and his family came along and they helped me a lot, and she just didn't know why *she* couldn't be helping me, too. Because she was my mother.

She had to live with the fact that I wanted what I wanted, and I thought what I did was in *my* best interest and not necessarily her best interests. It wasn't that she raised me wrong, 'cause she didn't; she did everything in the world for me and my sisters. And I give her a lot of credit for bringing us up all by herself. It was just that sometimes in a person's life they may need somethin' to steer 'em in the right direction, and that was my time. When I was in Dallas I needed some-thin' to steer me and I didn't have that, so I came to Durant and everything just went up from there.

I tried to explain that to her: "It's not what you think it is, that I'm really putting them first. I'm just doin' what I think is best right now for me, and, hopefully, things'll work out. But I'm not losing contact with you and I still love you." I never talked to her about Oklahoma that much, so maybe it was my fault she felt left out. I just didn't want her to get mad and start putting more pressure on me than I already had. I was still mad about when she kicked me out—even though she probably did the right thing. I don't know why I was mad; maybe because I always thought she treated my sisters with more respect than she treated me and gave them more opportunities than she gave me. It was just one of the stages I went through. It wasn't worth a hill of beans, really, because she was still my mother and I respected that and I loved her for it, too.

But the Riches really helped me, too, as far as going out and bein' somethin' in life. They always talked to me and gave me advice and tried to straighten me out on some sort of path. I probably didn't show 'em too much appreciation but they helped me just by talking to me about the way they lived and acted toward each other. I just grew with that atmosphere they had around each other: they were pretty patient with me when it came down to it. It took Mr. Rich a while to get comfortable with how to talk to me. First, he treated me like I was the friend that was there to help their son, so he couldn't say no to me. But once he got to know me better, he could put that authority behind his voice like, "I'm gonna bust your ass if you do this again! I'm gonna teach you this!" The first time he yelled at me, I was like, "Why is he yellin' at *me?* I ain't one of his kids." But the more times it happened, the more I felt like one of his kids—and it felt real good. I was practically living there and I guess he decided, "Hey, you're just like anyone else. If you screw up, you're gonna hear about it." After that, I always knew where I stood.

He was a big influence on my life—all the values of right and wrong he taught me, and how you gotta work hard to get what you want. He was always pushing me to get over the hump and do better. Like he used to take me for rides in the truck and give me a lot of man-talks and fatherly guidance that I never had. I remember I told him I didn't have a father for about twenty years and he said the same thing happened to him, and he had to go to work. He could relate to me; he used to say, "I know, 'cause I've been in the same shoes you been in." He started taking an interest in me and bringing me along in my life. Like he would say, "I had to go the hard way. I don't want to see you go the same route. I want you to be more than I was and have it a lot easier. You *can*, too, if you really try."

He would make me feel better about myself because I finally had a father figure in my life that really took a personal interest in what I did and how I did it, and not just put me in the background. In all my years till then I never focused back on myself and said: "I miss my dad. I wish I had one." I never thought about not having a dad at all. Until I met Mr. Rich. Then it came to me: maybe if I had a dad, my life would've been a lot different. I don't think my real dad would've cared about me as much as Mr. Rich. I don't think he would've said, "You have to work hard to get this" or "You can do this if you try your best and don't give up." Because what did *he* do? He gave up on us. I think it was good for me to go through hard times and bad times without a father and develop myself as a person, because that helped me get over the hump. And if I had my dad, I probably never would've met Bryne, or Miss Rich, or Mr. Rich, and gone to Southeastern and got my first big chance to really *do* somethin' with my life.

When I was in Durant, I didn't really know *what* to do with my life. I needed advice; and I know I could've got it from Miss Rich or Mr. Rich. But I never really went to them for any particular advice. I did a little with Miss Rich, mostly about girls. I guess I just felt that whatever problems I might have besides girls, like school or basketball, Mr. Rich would be there to help me take care of it. He would take me for a drive in the pickup and give me advice. Like he told me one time, "I don't think it's a good idea for you to date white girls. They're not too fond of mixing white and black relationships around here." But he didn't feel that way himself, he was just looking out for *me*— just trying to protect me. So I felt real secure with him. He made me feel that I was really part of the family. Best way he did that was by chewing me good when I screwed up around the house. He'd scold me, "Man, I told you not to do this!" *He* did that—but *she* never did, hardly. She wasn't comfortable enough to say things like that to me. She used to take it out more on her sons. She would rag on them but she would never rag on me the same way, even if I was one of the culprits, too. She was like, "Barry! Mike! Bryne! Y'all go to bed!" But she would never say *my* name; she never did pinpoint me out. I guess she felt like, "He's not my son so he can do anything he wants to." It took her some learning to figure out how to deal with me.

For some reason, every time Mr. Rich talked to me I got all emotional. It got to me because I felt like, "He's right." He would always explain what you did, and why you were wrong, and what you *oughta* be doing. I liked that; it was like having your father tell you what was what. So I listened to him more than anyone else, as far as advice and which direction I should go. And here's a guy that didn't go to college but yet, when he talked it made a lot of sense.

And then when I felt low I would tell him, "I want to go home. This place is boring. I hate the way people treat me in town. I hate the school." And he'd find a soft spot in me and tell me I had to work on my future and that I could make it in basketball. He used to tell me, "If you work hard for somethin' and do what you have to, you'll earn it." I didn't believe it for some reason; I just didn't think I was that good. But he'd say, "You got the talent to make it. You gotta keep workin' for your future and stick with it." And that made me want to do it, too. But, in a sense, I really wanted to do it more for Bryne. I wanted to show him I had the toughness and that I could go out there every night and do it. I just wanted to prove to him that I was a winner. I wanted to make him happy and I knew he wanted me to do good and eventually make the NBA. So I started to want it, too.

I remember the best advice Mr. Rich ever gave me: "Don't ever lie to me or cheat. Because as long as you know me, you will never know me to lie or cheat. And remember, once you tell one lie you gotta tell three more to back it up." He had lots of little sayings like that. It was a hard lesson for me to learn, though. Because in my neighborhood cheating was the best way to get over sometimes. So for a while there, I did it anyway—I don't really know why. Like me and Bryne would pick up all the loose change we could find lying around the house and go play video games. Man, we would hunt for nickels and dimes just to play in those tournaments—we won some trophies doin' that. And we wrote out one of his parents' checks when we wanted to go buy food or somethin'. Or I'd go down to the feed store and start charging gas and candy and Coke and stuff on their account, just like they let Bryne do. Only I didn't tell 'em I was doin' it. They'd say, "Whenever you want somethin', just please ask us first."

One time they went to the horse races in Hot Springs, Arkansas, and I was home by myself so I wrote a twenty-dollar check for groceries. I was debating so bad: "Should I do it or not do it?" I told myself, "God, I can't do it." But I sat there wondering about it and I finally said: "Well, me and Bryne always do it." All of a sudden I did it; I didn't have any money and I wanted somethin' to eat. But I knew they were gonna find out about it. And as soon as I did it, I said, "Damn!" because I knew I was wrong. I felt real bad about it. But after that they started givin' me twenty dollars every weekend, and an old Subaru to drive around, so there was no more reason for me to do it anymore.

But I still had that mentality: "I have to have somethin' more than the other guy. I have to be ahead of the other guy." And every time I got in trouble, Bryne would go to bat for me, even when he knew I was wrong, because he didn't want me booted out of the house, he didn't want to lose me. Then Miss Rich would get to me through gettin' on Bryne, because she would say to him, "Go to your room. You can't drive the car," or, "You have to come right home from school," and stuff like that, even though she knew *I* did it.

As far as the prejudice out there, I went through a real tough time with that. It was hard for me to get used to the way people looked at me, and then bein' slandered all the time when I was walking down the street or just hangin' with Bryne. I thought: "Damn. This is crazy.

What the hell am I doin' here?" But I stuck it out. I kept my feelings to myself because I was too proud to let anyone know. I still keep a lot of stuff in—I don't tell people what I really think. I feel a lot of anger toward a lot of things, but I don't backlash on anything. I don't look for revenge. I'm too softhearted for that, for some reason. Sometimes, I might let people run over me because I just want 'em to be happy. And, in certain ways, maybe I learned some of that living with the Riches, because when they would get mad, the next minute they would come back and say, "Okay, that's over," and resolve the problem and everything was all right again. They didn't carry grudges.

There were times I didn't just want to quit and leave, I wanted to go kill people—you know, go to Bryne's house and get a gun. But I used to tell myself: "Don't carry a grudge. Don't lose your temper. You can't do anything about it. What the hell, it's only three years." But I had to have somethin' to fall back on, like the Riches, to help me get over. They would say, "There's nothing you can do about some of these ignorant people. You can't start anything because you'll be playing right into their hands and get yourself in deeper. You just gotta ignore 'em." They told me some white people hung a black guy in Oklahoma about twenty years ago for raping a white woman—and that worked on my mind, too. So I tried to ignore it. But a couple of times I couldn't do it and I almost got shot. I didn't care; there's some things you just can't take.

When it really got bad, Bryne knew what was goin' on inside me. I was his best friend—he could always tell when I was pissed off. He'd say, "Don't pay any attention to them rednecks in town. My family likes you and I like you and I don't want you to leave." Mr. Rich would say he didn't want me to leave either. Miss Rich never said one way or the other. In the beginning, I think she was too busy protecting herself to think too much about me. But gradually she started caring about me for me, not just because I was helping her son, and then she didn't want to see me get hurt. But she really didn't come out and say stuff like that to me. So even when she started warming up and sayin', "We like you a lot" and "We love you" and kissing me and all, I still thought: "Well, it's just because 'God sent you'. . . . " I just thought of her as more of a friend, not so much a mother figure. Sometimes, I would call her "Mom" because she *was* like a mom to me in a lot of ways. But I already had a real mom.

So when you really get down to it, I think it was Bryne that kept me there. *He's* the one I stayed for.

15

Ring the

Message Out

Over the next two years, Dennis started to find himself.

The process carried over to his relationships with the Riches, especially Pat. As they grew more comfortable with each other, things started opening up. It had already begun when Pat realized she wasn't fooling anyone by ducking down in her car and hiding on campus. Disgusted with the petty rumors and ashamed of her constant need for guile, she ceased much of that behavior. She even came to feel that Dennis's mocking scorn helped her to resolve: "I'll show you, Worm. I don't care what they think anymore." But she did; she was still reluctant to being seen with him in her car. Which is why, when they passed the Chevrolet lot on their way to shop in Sherman, and Dennis spotted an old maroon car in the weeds, and gushed, "Miss Rich! You see that '77 Monte Carlo right there? Boy, I'd like to have that car, Miss Rich. I could fix that up *good*," she didn't think it was such a bad idea. She knew that if he had his own car, much of the gossip would stop, lifting *that* horse off her back. "Miss Rich," he played her another time, "I really need a car. I bet if you talk to Mr. Rich about it, he would get me that Monte Carlo"—and she gave it serious thought. Just the idea of it helped her to feel better about him.

In little ways, it appeared to Pat that Dennis also felt better about her. Like the subtle but momentous nuance in a note he left on her windshield one day at college: "*Mom,*" it began instead of "Miss Rich" for a change, "can I ride home with you?" Then there was the strange occurrence one evening in Bryne's room. After she'd tucked Bryne in and kissed him good night and started to leave, she heard a voice whisper, "Momma." At first uncertain, she turned around to ask, "Was that you, Bryne?" When Bryne giggled back she turned to exit again—and again the voice muttered, "Momma." This time she knew: "That was *you*, wasn't it, Worm!" When Dennis broke into giggles, she blew him a kiss. In that split second, she knew intuitively he wanted a *real* kiss, but something stopped her. Was it her nature? (She'd told Worm one time when discussing girls, "I was raised to be affectionate but not showy. I don't go 'round patting people on the back or huggin' 'em or sayin' 'I love you' all the time. But when it comes to the nitty-gritty, I'm there to show my love.") Or was it just the programmed restraint of her youth that "white people don't kiss black people"? Unfortunately, she hadn't had time to reflect; she'd just reacted. Afterward, though, she felt funny about it. A little regretful.

There were other signs. All during Dennis's second year at the Riches', he kept telegraphing that he wanted to feel more a part of the family. An indelible demonstration of that occurred one night when the family went to watch a high school basketball game and Dennis showed up at the farm. Finding no one home, he scribbled a touching note that read: "Mom, dad, little brother: I came to see you but no one was here. I love you. Worm." To Pat, this was special for two reasons: first, because previously whenever Dennis had used the word "Mom" it was always "when he wanted somethin' really bad from me"—money, a car to borrow, permission to do something with Bryne; and second, because "Worm always stayed away from emotional things." Even more heartwarming, it was the first time Dennis had openly referred to them as "mom," "dad," and "little brother." Of course, the "I love you" part wasn't peanuts either. It moistened her eyes.

Shortly after these episodes, Pat noticed other changes in Dennis. As he gradually discarded emotional armor, he grew more sensitive to how they regarded him. Since he and Bryne considered themselves brothers, and he spent more time at the farm than in his dorm, he wanted to be treated like family and not just a guest. So occasionally now he would get mad at a slight, and unload. For instance, one thing that really annoyed him, though he'd never made a fuss over it, was the apparent double standard James applied to how late the boys could stay out during the week. If Dennis wasn't back by 11:00 P.M. James would chew him out good. But Barry and Mike could come in later with impunity.

The difference usually was, however, that unlike Dennis, Barry and Mike weren't driving James's little red Subaru—the car he relied on for delivering the mail. So James—who was always worried about Dennis wrecking his car anyway, or maybe even taking it to Dallas and staying overnight—would stipulate, "I'll let you drive my car, Worm. But just you be careful. And you need to be in by eleven sharp 'cause I need that car for work tomorrow morning." Another difference was that, often, Dennis took Bryne along. So when he'd come back late, Pat and James might *both* get on his case—which really ticked him off.

One night, Dennis kept the Subaru out three hours past deadline with Bryne along, and Pat and James were fit to be tied. When they finally straggled in, James let loose. "Worm, I told you I had to have you back here by eleven. I'm gonna stop you from drivin' the car if you don't get in when I tell you to." Then something unusual happened. Dennis started pacing from the den to the kitchen and back, puffing and sniffling with rage, madder than they'd ever seen him. "Mr. Rich, it ain't fair," he reproached. "You don't chew Barry or Mike out for bein' late, but you chew *me* out. They come in all different times and you don't say nothin' to 'em, and here you are gettin' on me."

"Yes I do," James argued back. "When you go out with Barry and Mike, I don't tell you anything because you're goin' to college and you can get up when you want to. But Bryne is goin' to high school. He's fourteen years old; he needs to be in bed by ten or maybe eleven. And that's the reason I'm on you all the time, because I tell you to come in by eleven and then you don't do it."

Dennis couldn't accept that, even though it was true. As Pat described it later to Barry and Mike: "Oh, he was hysterical. It was so funny, because he wanted so bad to be equal with you. He started acting like a preacher, rattlin' on and then snorting and sniffling through his nose. And he walked past the kitchen and then back to the den and started preachin' again about, 'You handle your kids one way but you don't let *me* get away with anything. You should treat me like Barry and Mike.' And he went on like that—he was talkin' pretty mean and stern, and his nose was all runny. I have never seen Worm act this way before. And I have never seen him stand up and express himself like that to James. He was just lettin' it all hang out, boy. And I couldn't keep from laughin', although I knew it was serious to Worm."

There were other little events. Once, when Bryne asked Pat for extra spending money and she forked over ten dollars, Dennis suddenly protested, "What about *me?*" To which James replied, "Well, we give you money, Worm. But you know, here in the country you don't just get somethin' for nothin', you got to earn it. If you want more, you can work for it and start *earnin'* some more." James was right; in the past, whenever Bryne got five or ten, so did Dennis. Besides, with Bryne's homework and chores he had no extra time for outside work, while Dennis made extra cash at jobs his coaches arranged: handyman at a radio station and car detailer at a dealership. Still, he was always scrounging more cash to spend on food and pinball and video games. So he took up James's suggestion and started working more at the farm for a wage: disking, planting, mending, repairing, cleaning up. He enjoyed these tasks; the cash was great, but the comfort of feeling more like "one of them" meant infinitely more.

This new rush of family-feeling had been stirred, in no small part, by the closer bonding between Dennis, Barry, and Mike. It had developed gradually; whenever Bryne had school the next day and had to be in bed early, Dennis would go out somewhere with Barry and Mike—to a pool hall or maybe just cruising Durant—and they'd return home at 2:00 A.M., laughing and raising cain. Pat sensed he idolized them and wanted to fit right in and be just like them, with their sharp Western clothes and boots and their cool new pickup trucks with the booming pipes. All of which, she believed, added weight to Dennis's mistaken belief that the Riches were as well off, money-wise, as their name implied.

They weren't, of course. The boys saved every dime; their clothes, though certainly quality, were not "high-dollar"; and no one named Rich had bought any pickup trucks: (Years ago, James's aunt Odessa had promised the three brothers that if they graduated from high school she would buy each of them a new pickup. Dennis didn't know that when he first saw the trucks, he just started wanting one, too.) Pat had detected his envy right then, which she'd assessed this way for James: "I think Worm's starting to like bein' part of our family life-style because he's gotten to do a lot of fun things with us that otherwise he'd've never done. So this is one way he thinks he can be more a part of our family, by having whatever the other kids have. You can see he wants to be like Barry and Mike."

"Well, yeah," James had concurred. "Probably 'cause they're a lot popular with the girls."

"That's right. And they look so good in their Western outfits, and they go cruisin' down the road in their new pickups with the pipes sounding so cool. And who knows, from the way he's eyeballin' those pickups, he probably thinks if he's in real tight with Barry and Mike, maybe Des'll get *him* one, too."

They got a kick out of that unlikely idea. But she wasn't far off. Though Dennis hadn't spent much time with Des—plowing the fields last summer, he'd often stopped in to say hi and raid her refrigerator for a Coke and whatever food was on the shelf—he knew Des liked him. Also, Pat had told him, bemused, how when Southeastern played its basketball games Des always invited some of the local "widow-women" to the house, where they all listened over her little radio and cheered for her famous friend, "The Worm."

One thing they all knew Dennis was dying to do was dress exactly like Barry and Mike in Western shirts and jeans and cowboy hats and boots, and go country-and-western dancing with them. He kept asking but they kept putting him off; they knew they'd have trouble getting their dates to go with them if a black guy came along. But Dennis wouldn't let up. Eventually, he drove to Texas and splurged his spending money on stylish, lizard-skin boots and Western shirts and Levi jeans and a Stetson hat, and returned to the farm to try everything on for the Riches and to persuade Barry and Mike. In hysterics at the sight of "long, tall, lanky ole Dennis" in jeans too short for his huge new boots and a big-brimmed cowboy hat instead of his little black cap, they finally caved in. "Well, I guess we better go to the Electric Company now," Barry conceded. "Yeah, Worm," Mike agreed. "That's where all the action is for big ole cowboy dudes like you."

So finally one night, Dennis the Dude moseyed into the Electric Company—one of the most popular country-and-western clubs in Sherman—a little anxious, at first, about how to act. But with Barry and Mike along for support, he worked up the courage to not only stroll around inside but also to dance. Naturally, heads turned to take in the big skinny black guy whirling around the floor. But once he demonstrated, surprisingly, that he could dance the fashionable two-step like them, people watched that, and women literally lined up to ask for a turn. Nobody knew he'd learned the two-step in a phys ed dance course at college, and then practiced constantly at parties.

As soon as the boys returned home that night, the phone rang, and they ended up talking to girls on the extensions for so long that Pat and James went to sleep. Eventually, so did Barry—snoring while still on the phone. Next night, Pat couldn't contain her curiosity. She asked Barry and Mike, "Did Worm have a good time last night?" Mike giggled his way through The Electric Company Tale: "Mom, he was a sight to see. When he got out there and danced, he was really tearin' it up and rippin' and roarin' around. All you could see was elbows and ass". And Barry added, "Man, his arms and legs were so long and everything, people just kinda cleared him out a spot so they wouldn't get elbowed to death. That really made his night, boy."

After that, Mike, Barry, and Dennis became a Mutual Admiration Society: Barry and Mike prizing Dennis's awkward, endearing ways and idolizing him for his basketball prowess and all the attention he got; Dennis appreciating their easy companionship and admiring their popularity with pretty young girls. Nevertheless, when next they drove together to dance at the Electric Company, or Calhoun's in Denison, Texas, or the college dances, Barry and Mike still worried a little that their dates and friends wouldn't accept them in a black guy's company. So they invented what started out as a little game but turned into a farcical, long-running routine for their mutual fun.

It was initiated by chance one night when they asked Worm to drive them around in Pat's Grand Marquis. When they met some girls they liked, one girl asked who the black guy was and Mike blurted, "Oh, that's our *chauffeur*" and Barry said, "Yeah, he's our *butler*, too." From then on, whenever they did the town in the Marquis, Mike and Barry piled in back and Dennis "toured" them around—in Mike's words, "like we was high-class Big Dogs or somethin'"—and Dennis was their hired chauffeur. He played along willingly, too, savoring and often embellishing the ruse by wearing his little black cap and grandly opening their doors. But it wasn't strictly for fun; Dennis also did it to feel more like their equal, more accepted by them as a "brother."

In fact, it was around that time that he mentioned to Bryne that he'd like to be adopted as a brother, as though he believed that was the only real way to be equal with them. Bryne told Pat about it, and while she was flattered, she deflected it. "I don't think we're ready to do somethin' like that," she told them both. Pretty soon, Dennis started teasing about it. "How does Dennis *Rich* sound?" he'd say in a freewheeling mood. Pat believed he meant it, too, but she wasn't sure why he was pushing it. She had her theories, though. One was as a sort of childish "payback" to Shirley for perceived past slights, like favoring his sisters over him as he had always griped. As if he wanted to get back at her by saying, "Look, this is my home now. I have a mom and a dad and a new last name. I'm not Dennis Rodman anymore, I'm Dennis Rich!" Pat found it amusing but didn't treat it that way, because, as a mother, she identified with Shirley. Which is why she always discouraged Dennis's "Adopt me" pleas by pointing out forcefully: "Your mother might be offended by it, or hurt. I know I would be if I was your mom."

Failing to get adopted, Dennis started pressing a new request: "Miss Rich, I want Bryne to go home with me. Do you care if he comes home with me? He wants to go." She asked what they would do in Dallas and he said they'd meet his friends and mostly play basketball during the day and go bowling at night. She said she'd talk it over with James, but she wasn't encouraging. For, while they'd permitted Dennis to drive around Bokchito and Durant, James, especially, was reluctant about Dallas because he thought Dennis drove too fast. That was true; on the open highway Dennis routinely did 80 or 90, passing everything that moved. It was habit; he and his Dallas friends used to drive fast and pass each other like that in their souped-up Monte Carlos. Yet, he was actually an excellent driver technically—Bryne vouched for that, and so did Pat. But she had other objections.

For one thing, Bryne had never been that far away from home without them before. More compellingly, since she knew nothing of that part of Dallas, she was concerned for Bryne's safety. "Well, you know, I don't . . . I just . . . " she hemmed and hawed. "I just don't know what kind of neighborhood we're talkin' about, Worm. I mean, Bryne's pretty young and I know that it's probably an all-black neighborhood and he's gonna be the only little white boy. I don't know how, you know, the *blacks* might react to that." In other words, how did she know someone wouldn't try to hurt Bryne just because he was white? Ironically, this fear was just as myth-driven and over-magnified as Shirley Rodman's black-men-lost-in-redneck-jails scenario had been when she'd worried about *her* son's safety in Durant.

Dennis assured Pat that he would watch over Bryne and take care of him and never leave him alone, so there was nothing to worry about.

But she was still afraid of the unknown, and she finally decided, "Well, I'd rather for Bryne not to go."

This stung Dennis like a personal rejection. "Miss Rich, you're just afraid of black people," he charged, offended now. "You think you're better than we are."

Pat was surprised at his frontal approach. But it worked—she got defensive. "No, Worm, I don't think I'm better. You know that's not it. I'm just worried about letting Bryne go down there because I don't know anything about the community you live in, and I don't know what kind of people are hangin' around there. And if you were a parent of a young boy, you have to admit, Worm, you would probably feel like I do."

But he wasn't, and he didn't; so he just kept hammering them for the next two weeks: "Please let Bryne go. I don't see no reason why you won't let him. I won't let anything happen to him." And Bryne joined in with a relentless barrage of, "I wanna go. Why can't I go?" Finally, under the constant pressure, Pat and James gave in. But only on one condition: *they* would accompany the boys down.

Cruising through South Oak Cliff, uncomfortable with the unknown, Pat grew increasingly tense. So, when she pulled up in front of Shirley's apartment building, instinct took over and she hit the button that automatically locked the car doors. Dennis needled her instantly for that. "Miss Rich, what you doin'? Nobody's gonna hurt you here. Open the doors, Miss Rich."

"Oh, okay," she finally said, feeling ridiculous and popping the locks. "I guess maybe I shouldn't've locked the doors, should I?" She looked at James for support . . . but he was already halfway out of the car. So she got out, thinking: "Okay, he said nobody's gonna hurt me." But she still looked all around her, just in case, before heading inside.

Shirley wasn't home, so Dennis showed them around the neat, immaculately clean two-bedroom. James was impressed with the basketball plaques belonging to Debra and Kim that hung above the living room couch; while Pat enjoyed perusing pictures of Dennis's family, especially those of him as a kid. "Look how *tiny* you were, Worm!" she remarked, amazed, as though he never could've been small.

Eventually, Shirley walked in and Dennis introduced everyone. For a while the main topic was basketball, as James asked more about the plaques and where the girls went to school and how they were doing. Shirley noticed how protective Dennis was of Bryne and the way Bryne's eyes followed him around the room, and she thought: "This kid needs a lot of love." But both Dennis and Bryne were as silent as goldfish, anxious to leave. When Dennis finally said he wanted to go to the mall with Bryne, James decided to accompany them.

Pat stayed because she thought it would be awkward—and rude— if she just jumped up and said, "I'll go with y'all." But she was still nervous about Shirley, and what she really thought about everything that had happened to Dennis after he left home. Shirley felt uneasy, too, because she didn't know what Dennis had told them about her, and she hated pretense and didn't want to have to "entertain." So she made a pot of coffee and took out a cigarette and, determined to be herself, made perfectly clear, "Pat, I smoke. And I am going to smoke a cigarette. So if it's going to bother you, you will have to go to another room." And she lit up and started a conversation.

She said that Dennis had talked about Bryne and his parents and how nice they had been to him, and she was glad they were finally meeting. When Pat inquired about Dennis's childhood, Shirley mentioned his growing spurts and his problems with that, like not seeking dates and staying in the house too much, and how shy he was, and how he always kept his emotions to himself. Sensing that this upset Shirley—and noticing the piano in the room—Pat quickly changed the subject.

"You know, Dennis has talked up a storm about you, and how much you love music."

"Yes," Shirley brightened, "music has been very important to me my whole life. Shall I tell you why?"

"Oh yes, please," said Pat, getting more comfortable.

"Well, I did not think I was very attractive in my youth, because I wore glasses. And at that time, glasses were a no-no, and kids could be very cruel, so my self-esteem was not very high. I used to channel all my energies into my intelligence. I was very smart in school and I read a lot of books—I love to read. But music was my life, and I could play anything. I got in trouble behind that once, when I went to North Texas to train and major in music. Because I was always inventing new music on Bach and Beethoven—which I should have played as written. But I was always trying to add something to it. And my music teacher said, 'No, this cannot be,' so I was stifled."

Pat said she understood; she was in college now herself and she often had the impulse to add something *she* thought about whatever subject they were teaching, but she always held back. "I guess I stifled *myself*, though, didn't I?" And she was surprised at her growing sense of easy intimacy with this stranger. Then, switching subjects, she asked how Shirley had learned to play in the first place.

"From the beginning," Shirley explained, "my mom noticed that I was not a child that liked to play with dolls and things, and that all I liked was music. We didn't have a lot of money, but my first toy was a small piano, and I would beat that piano to death. When I got older I could hear the music in my mind, even though I had never had a lick of training. And now I indulge my music by playing gospel at church every Sunday."

This was a world of insight for Pat; she thought she could see the roots of Dennis's introversion and musical talents in Shirley, and a lot of his stubborn pride. She liked Shirley already and was feeling more and more relaxed. Maybe that's why she could say, "You know, Worm has bragged on you many times that you play and sing so pretty. I love religious music. Would you play me a song?"

Shirley thought: "Oh, good. Here is some common ground we can touch on"; so she had Pat sit beside her on the piano stool. They thumbed through a hymnbook and Pat picked out "Bringing In the Sheaves" and hummed the tune. Shirley played it by ear and sang. Pat was moved by how "the music just flowed out of her so smooth, like she was composing it herself." Shirley played so effortlessly, it brought to mind an amusing memory she impulsively shared with Pat: that the best she had ever played in church was after she came there from a wedding one time, "tipsy on champagne," and she got all these compliments afterward. They chuckled together about that.

"Would you like to sing a song with me?" ventured a more amiable Shirley. "Do you have a favorite?"

"Yes, I do," Pat said, caught by surprise. "Do you know 'Ring the Message Out'?"

"No, I don't believe."

"Well, I can sing it for you, because we sing it in my church all the time. Our little congregation has a difficult time with it because of the intricate harmonies." And she started to sing and Shirley picked it up and joined right in: "Ring, ring, ring. Ring the message out. There's a message strong and true . . . " But then Shirley suddenly stopped abruptly to demand, "Would you get on *key!*" She wasn't scolding or being rude; she was just used to people who always sang on key.

"I thought I *was*," Pat replied, and they laughed together at that. But Pat was a little offended, thinking: "Boy, she will tell you what she thinks whether you like it or not." Yet, she realized Shirley was right; so she had to admit, "Well, I guess I sing about like I play tennis or archery"—an inside joke on herself that Shirley only half-understood, but accepted as true.

"Let's back up here," Shirley said, humming the pitch. Quickly, Pat got on key and they sang it all the way through. When they finished they congratulated each other warmly and then Shirley shifted the mood by swinging into some black gospel—her natural forte. Pat swayed and hummed along, feeling so gratified and touched that her eyes welled with tears. She felt she was fitting right in with Shirley and that this had turned into "a really neat experience." Shirley, who would develop conflicts years later with Pat, would nevertheless always recall this episode as "our best moment together."

About this time, James, Dennis, and Bryne returned, and Shirley quit playing. Pat proclaimed exuberantly to Dennis, "You were right, Worm, your mother really can play and sing beautifully." They sat around until Pat reminded James that they'd better get a motel for the night. Shirley said, "Well, you don't have to do that. You can share Kim and Deb's room. There's beds in there and no one will be here. There's no point in getting a motel room." So they decided to spend the night.

After dinner, Shirley talked about Dennis and how he'd cleaned her house for extra money when he'd lived there, and how pleased she was with his attitude since he'd been spending time with the Riches. Around 9:00 P.M., Shirley showed them the girls' room with the twin beds and said she was going to lie down on her bed now and read. Just before turning in, though, Pat wandered into Shirley's and chatted some more, and it surprised her that in just one day she felt comfortable enough to go into this woman's bedroom and just talk away like an old friend.

When James finally shut off the light and they climbed into their beds, Pat heard noises under hers—and her fears rushed right back. For an instant, she conjured her worst nightmare: a *black man* under her bed! "James!" she erupted. "There's somethin' under my bed!" So he turned on the light; and when a dog suddenly came scampering out, Pat's hair stood up on her neck. It turned out that the dog had been feeding six puppies in a box under the bed, which Shirley had neglected to mention. And now the puppies where squealing and whining, and Pat was jumpy, too. She thought: "Well, this is gonna be some night sleepin' over all this commotion with the mother goin' in and out of the box." But she was relieved it had only been *puppies* under the bed.

Meantime, Worm and Bryne were out on the town, getting ready to bowl. Bryne had been aware all day that he was "the only white person around," but wasn't concerned, because he was with Worm. Earlier, Dennis had explained that they'd be around only black people that day, and some of them might look at Bryne like, "What is this white kid doing here?" But if he avoided staring at them, everything would be cool. Thus, there were no incidents when they played basketball and then video games through the afternoon. Finally, they had met up with Dennis's close friends, Terry, Robert, and Claude, and they all gave Bryne the "brother's" handshake and played pinball with him and joked him around. Starting around 1:00 A.M.—while Pat was still battling her irrational fears—they were bowling at Don Carter's Bowling Alley and having a great time, black and white together. Nobody noticed or cared about that.

Sunday morning, Shirley made breakfast: eggs and bacon and her famous grits. They didn't go to church. Pat wanted to but didn't press it because, unlike Bryne, she couldn't see herself being "the only white person there." After breakfast they all said good-bye, with James offering, "Y'all should come up sometime and we'll fix you a barbecue." Shirley said she might just do that, and they departed, leaving her there alone.

On the return trip in the car, Dennis and Bryne napped in back. Pat stared at them a while, shaking her head, thinking what an odd couple they made, and how far all of them had come. And how far they still had to go.

Inseparable friends: Dennis "Big Worm" Rodman and Bryne "Little Worm" Rich.
(Tim Crews)

A family photograph of Shirley Rodman (front) and her children (left to right): Dennis (age 16), Debra (age 15), and Kim (age 14). Even though Dennis would eventually sprout to 6 feet 8 inches, at this point his younger sisters were taller than he was.
(Courtesy of Shirley Rodman)

Dennis's sisters Debra (left) and Kim (right) were both star basketball players in high school and college. Debra played for Louisiana Tech, one of the perennial power-houses of women's college basketball, while Kim played her college ball for Stephen F. Austin College. (Courtesy of Shirley Rodman)

(Left) Dennis displays the form that has made him a star rebounder, a specialty he perfected at James Rich's suggestion. (Right) He holds up the plaque for winning the NAIA District 9 title. The Southeastern Oklahoma State Savages had many such occasions to celebrate, bringing the school some of its most successful seasons ever. (Courtesy of Harold Harmon)

Bryne became the water boy for the Savages, frequently traveling with Dennis and the team to road games.
(Courtesy of Pat Rich)

Dennis returned as an alumnus to Southeastern Oklahoma State for ceremonies retiring his jersey #10—an honor he never could have predicted when he first visited the campus. (Courtesy of Harold Harmon)

Coach Jack Hedden stood for a photo opportunity with his star pupil. (Courtesy of Shirley Rodman)

Bryne (second from left) and friends take in a ball game. (Courtesy of Pat Rich)

Bryne (left, in dark uniform) developed into a first-rate high school and college basketball player thanks to all those years of competing against a 6-foot-8-inch future NBA star. (Left photo courtesy of Pat Rich; right photo by William Snyder)

Dennis visits with the Rich family around the breakfast bar in their home in Bokchito, Oklahoma. Standing in the back row (left to right) are Barry, Mike, Pat, and James. (William Snyder)

James Rich (left) helped Dennis learn to rebound on the basketball court and in life. Dennis, who was raised in the big city of Dallas, finds comfort and refuge at the Riches' rural home. (William Snyder)

Starring in the NBA, Dennis plays before thousands of fans in packed arenas and millions more watching on television—a far cry from one-on-one games in the Rich-family living room with a cardboard-tube PA system, imagined crowd noises, and dreams of the NBA. Still, Bryne is one of the few people Dennis trusts to cut his hair. (Courtesy of Pat Rich)

Enjoying a second national title after having come so close with the Savages, Bryne and Dennis celebrated in the Detroit locker room after the Pistons' second straight NBA championship. (Courtesy of Pat Rich)

Dennis, never ashamed to cry, was moved to tears when he was honored with the NBA's Defensive Player of the Year Award in May 1990. The award represented an important personal achievement to Dennis, who had already had a terrific season, including selection for the NBA All-Star Game. (William Archie/Detroit Free Press)

16

His Way or

Not at All

That everyone still had plenty of psychological and emotional distance
to travel was to become evident again though 1984 and into '85, Dennis's junior year at school.

However, much of that summer—spent mostly in Bokchito—was
another romp of childish fun. Dennis got to Jet Ski on Lake Texhoma
with Barry and Mike; did his first house-painting job (when Pat
checked on him, he was painting the ceiling in his shorts and had
"white specks of paint all over his face"—one of the funniest sights of
the summer); drove the tractor practically every day; swam and fished
in the pond; and even tried his first horse ride—if you could call it
"riding." (Pat described it this way to Bryne, who'd missed it: "I was
cutting this guy's hair and he had a saddled horse out in his trailer and
Worm asked if he could ride it. So he gets the horse out of the trailer
and climbs on, and here's this big ole long gangly Worm on top of this
short little horse. And he gets goin' and the saddle turns sideways and
there's Worm riding down through the pasture just almost under the
horse's belly! So he gets off and straightens it up and he rides it back.
But instead of getting off and tyin' the horse up, he rides it up into
the trailer and ducks his head and starts lookin' around, 'cause he don't

know what to do. He figured, 'Well, this is where I got the horse from, this must be where I gotta ride it back to.' ") But the highlight was when Pat, James, Bryne, and Dennis went on a weekend vacation to see the horse races, shop, and relax in a spa at their favorite getaway spot: Hot Springs, Arkansas.

Since James's job required him to drive hundreds of miles a week, and Pat wanted to relax in back with a book, Dennis got to drive the Grand Marquis to Arkansas. On Highway 70, as he passed a shiny white Monte Carlo, he turned to look at it again through the rear window and cried, "Mr. Rich! There goes a Monte Carlo! That's the kinda car I want!" Petrified, James hollered, "Get your eyes on the road, Worm! You're scarin' me to death!" From that point on, every so often James would admonish, "Slow this damn thing down. You're gonna wreck us, you're gonna kill us all," to get Dennis's wandering attention as he scanned for Monte Carlos.

Except for this little madness, Pat loved it when Dennis drove; it allowed her to indulge her "secret fantasy dream" from youth: that she had her own personal chauffeur. "Hmmm," she chuckled aloud that Friday. "Here I am in my big private limousine with my chauffeur drivin' me around like royalty anywhere I want to go. Where should we go first?" And everyone snickered, including Dennis. So, deciding to play the role to the hilt, when he pulled up to their hotel, he exited the car in his little black cap, opened her door first, and, with a flourish, assisted her out. Then he did the same for Bryne and James, concluding properly with, "I will go park the car." Pat never forgot the looks on the faces observing from the lounge as the 6–8, black chauffeur serviced his eminent white patrons in their impressive Grand Marquis.

That night, by accident, Pat's old concern with getting Dennis together with a black girl took a new turn. She'd thought it would be neat to go to a dinner theater, especially since Dennis had never been before, so they went over to buy tickets to a show starring comedienne Phyllis Diller. At the desk, Pat initiated a casual conversation with the young black girl selling the tickets, propelled, she believed then, by the fact that the girl was pretty and therefore a potential date for

Dennis. But the real reason, she would admit later, was that she was still driven by her standard of blacks marrying blacks and whites marrying whites.

Pat chatted with the girl and then rejoined the group to press Dennis. "Worm, she's a good-lookin' black girl," she urged him on with a little chuckle. "You ought to go for her, you should try to get a date." But he was too shy, so Pat returned to the desk and resumed conversation, and then called out, "Worm, c'mere. There's a lady here you should meet." Finally, Pat introduced them and left them alone so they could get acquainted. Amazingly, they enjoyed each other so much that they arranged for a date the following evening.

Next night, Dennis drove the Marquis to pick up his date, and Pat was delighted with her handiwork. But he returned within an hour, frustrated and mad. "Miss Rich," he steamed, "I told you about black girls, didn't I? I picked her up and she just changed her mind and didn't wanna go. You always want me to date black girls—well, I told you how they are. That's how they act right there!"

Her lesson finally learned, this concluded Pat Rich's brief, unfortunate career as self-appointed matchmaker for Worm.

Maybe it was fate; maybe coincidence; maybe just human nature. But as if a germ had been emitted into the air of his life when the ticket girl reneged on their date, the ugly issue of race poisoned Dennis's summer of fun. Until then, he thought he'd gotten used to the casual slurs in Bokchito and Durant. But what he hadn't anticipated was that once his basketball stature increased, so did jealousy and ignorance— as though his success had pulled the trigger on hate.

One night in late summer, he and Bryne visited Nickels and Dimes, their favorite video hangout, and afterward drove in James's pickup to the Sonic, a fast-burger joint where you order from your vehicle. While they were eating, two white guys in a rusty truck pulled into the parking area and circled them until one called out, "You don't belong here, nigger!" Then they peeled away. Pent-up anger sparked;

instead of ignoring it, Dennis suddenly wanted revenge. "Did he say what I thought he said?" he growled at Bryne. "I think so," Bryne confirmed.

Seething, Dennis told himself: "I can deal with it, I can cope with it." But he couldn't. So he piled out, climbed onto the pickup bed, opened the toolbox, and removed an ax. Then he jumped back in and burned rubber in pursuit. They tailed the rusty truck out of town and over the dark, back roads before finally losing it. Then they returned to the Sonic, where they sat on the pickup bed for hours, hoping to spot the culprits doubling back on the drag. Dennis was still hot; he wanted to nail these guys and brandish the ax and scare the hell out of them. But the longer he waited, the more he cooled off. "I think we scared 'em pretty good," Bryne finally ventured. "Maybe they saw the ax."

Dennis grumbled, "Oh yeah, they saw it. They about shit their pants." Only days later did he reassure Bryne that he never would have used the ax: "You crazy, son? I wouldn't kill no one. I was just gonna get a little cocky with 'em. Like, 'Now who's the nigger?' "

Oddly, other problems caromed off that one. Like the way prejudice underminded his relationships with two white girls he was really "hung up on." The first—Sheree, who'd grown serious about him—suddenly stopped talking to him without explanation. For two weeks, whenever he called her apartment a roommate answered and said Sheree was out; and when he went there in person Sheree wouldn't come to the door. (They'd only dated a year—only recently in public, which had made her more nervous than him—before the arguments had started as a result of pressure from family, friends, and her white ex-boyfriend not to date a black.) Finally, he ran into her on campus and she told him she couldn't be seen with him anymore, and it ended like that.

So one night about a week later, after learning that Sheree's ex-boyfriend was in town, Dennis drove with Bryne on angry impulse over to her apartment, camped in the parking lot, and laid on the horn and called Sheree's name. She just sent her roommate out to curse and to tell Dennis to leave. He cursed the roommate back, dumping his frustrations on her before going. Later, he felt depressed. To him, it made no sense; it was the first time he had felt in any concrete way the full brunt of prejudice on his personal life.

That fall, Dennis picked up again with CarolAnn, his other school flame, who was living at home in Durant. He was still hurt over Sheree's snub, so despite repeated warnings from Pat to "quit dating that CarolAnn girl, 'cause her daddy's mean enough to come after you with a sawed-off shotgun," and sessions with Coach Hedden, who advised him to quit this girl and get his mind back on basketball, Dennis continued not only seeing her but taking reckless chances in the process. Since CarolAnn didn't want anyone close to her to know about her affair with Dennis, they pretended in public that they were just friends. But they would rendezvous behind closed doors—in Mike Rich's pickup, or her house when her parents were out, or Dennis's dorm room. Sometimes, word got back to the coaches through the dorm grapevine, and they'd have yet another session with Dennis, hoping to get his thinking straight. But nothing worked; just like when he was a kid, he'd do everything *his* way or not at all, no matter what anyone said.

Thus, everyone but Dennis was aware he was courting disaster.

It finally came. One night, CarolAnn's mother was home when Dennis drove up, and she confronted him. "You leave my daughter alone!" she screamed. "She has no business messin' with the likes of you!" An hour later, when her parents had left for the evening, he returned anyway and went inside. While CarolAnn and Dennis were watching TV, he heard the front door slam and her father's voice. "Oh, crap," Dennis gasped, jumping to his feet, "your daddy's home!" And he scurried for the back door. On the way, he heard her mother shriek, "Where's he at? I told you not to have that guy come around here no more!" And then, when her dad caught a glimpse of Dennis slipping out the door, he yelled, "Don't you never come back here, nigger!" Dennis never looked, but he knew from CarolAnn that her dad had a gun. . . . Later, CarolAnn confirmed to Dennis that her dad *had* been wielding a gun—a pistol—when Dennis escaped. And he had threatened that if she ever saw him again, he would kill Dennis and disown her.

Nevertheless, they kept sneaking around for weeks, seeing each other like before. Until one day CarolAnn finally delivered the "I can't see you anymore" farewell—and they were history, too. But not long afterward, something else involving her occurred. She'd told him that her ex-husband sometimes beat her up—Dennis had seen some of the bruises—and that he was getting on her case about dating Dennis and she was afraid he might hurt her again. So on occasion, Dennis would inconspicuously follow her home from school to make sure her ex didn't try anything.

But one afternoon, he spotted the guy shoving her around at a park, while his friend watched. As Dennis approached, he heard the ex-husband menacing her, "Why are you messin' around with him? Why are you leavin' me for a black boy?" Dennis immediately hurried over and challenged him, "She's a girl. You oughta leave her alone." Upon which, the guy's friend grabbed a shotgun from his truck and handed it to CarolAnn's ex who threatened, "I'll tell you what. You better get on outta here or I'll kill you."

"Put the gun down and we'll see how bad you are then," Dennis said, hanging tough.

"I said I'll kill you, boy. And I *will*."

"Oh yeah," Dennis tried shaming him again. "You can kill me that way, but you can't fight with your bare hands."

It worked; he dropped the gun and lunged at Dennis and they started slugging it out. Dennis knocked him to the ground and battered him badly—no contest. Finally, the guy's startled friend urged, "Hey, get off him! You win, okay? Just get off him." And he did, and then walked away defiantly, escorting CarolAnn. "Go on!" yelled her ex-husband. "You go on with your black boyfriend!"

But after that, she told Dennis he'd better forget her.

These incidents scarred him and set him on edge. Gradually, he grew moody, angry, remote, less carefree than before, more irresponsible. He started missing classes regularly; he came late to basketball practices and dragged around as though he didn't care as much; and he often showed up late now for his part-time detailing job at the auto dealership. He continued this behavior even after Coaches Reisman and Hedden both chastized him about getting his act together. In fact, things worsened: he started getting into scuffles and arguments in the dorm, which wasn't like him.

The cap finally blew one afternoon when he and Bryne were minding their business in Dennis's room. Suddenly, a black fellow student started riding Dennis mercilessly about his basketball notoriety, accusing him of not deserving the attention he got. It was mostly nonsense that Dennis would normally ignore. But the kid kept at it, spewing insults across the hall. Finally, when he tried the schoolyard psych of calling Dennis "nigger"—as a brother-to-brother affront—something snapped. Dennis spit the same cut back, with embellishments; and then, suddenly, the kid charged into him, knocking him on his back. When Dennis got up the kid pulled a knife and brandished it at him. "Don't mess with me; I'll cut your ass," the kid warned, fierce enough to try.

"Oh, you're real bad with that knife," Dennis snarled back. "You're so bad, why don't you wait here for me. I'm comin' back for you with a gun."

"That's cool, boy. I'll be here."

That lit the fuse. With a helpless Bryne trailing him, Dennis jumped into James's pickup and raced the fourteen miles to the farm in ten minutes flat. He ran inside and grabbed a loaded 16-gauge shotgun, hurried to the truck, and sped back to Durant. Bryne was scared; he thought Dennis might actually use the gun. "Don't do it," he kept saying, "You don't need that. He ain't worth it." But Dennis ignored him and kept driving toward trouble.

Fortunately, when they pulled into the dorm lot and Dennis yelled for his adversary to come out, no one emerged. Dennis decided to wait. But after Bryne stayed on his case, he eventually agreed it was stupid, and gave the vigil up. Instead, he drove Bryne back to the farm, where they played some vicious games of "In Yo' Face" on the basketball court.

Even throwing himself back into his basketball didn't relieve Dennis's gnawing vexation. No one knew exactly what was bothering him—maybe even he didn't know—because he didn't talk about such things. But his behavior showed wide swings in moods from his usually light and upbeat to mysteriously dark and depressed. Part of the problem was that along with his recent confrontations in Durant, he still felt he was battling for equal respect in the Riches' home. So his resentment and anger sat right on the surface. Maybe his problems were exacerbated by the fact that he still couldn't afford a car and had to rely on the Riches for rides; or that since Bryne was playing high school basketball now, they had less time to spend together; or because he and Shirley still weren't getting along; or because some of his belongings had been stolen in the dorm; or that the racial taunts in town just wouldn't quit. . . .

Compounding all this was new friction between him and Pat. It started one Saturday when a white girl drove him back to the farm and parked in the driveway where they talked and laughed. Pat was in the yard, a little miffed because she was still uncomfortable with this issue. So, when the girl drove off, Pat pulled Dennis aside. "Worm," she said calmly, "I care a lot about you. And I know you been havin' a hard time with some things lately. But I think you should respect my home. What you're doin' is still a problem for me. If you want to date white girls, that's your personal life. But please just don't do it in front of me. I just wanted to be honest with you right up front." He said okay, impassive as always, but it rankled him. Actually, however, had it been anyone but Dennis, Pat might have been sterner. But she suspected he might've been testing her somehow, pushing to see if *she* would try to humiliate him as others had done.

Unfortunately, even she had her limit with him; just weeks later they confronted one another in what she would later term "The Big

One." It was over disciplining Bryne. He and Dennis came home late one night when they had express orders to return earlier. So Pat came down harder than usual on Bryne because they'd done this before and she expected him to know better. She intended to just ask where they were, why they were late, scold Bryne, and let it go at that. But when Bryne told an obvious fib, she went through the roof.

"Bryne, I know you weren't there. Why are you telling me that if it isn't the truth?"

"It's the truth. That's where we were."

"Oh, look, I know you were over to see one of Worm's little girlfriends 'cause somebody saw you there and I know all about it, so you're makin' it up." And then Bryne really caught hell. Until, suddenly, Dennis intervened—angrily.

"Damn!" he protested. "Miss Rich, you gotta let your kids get away with somethin' once in a while. We weren't doin' anything wrong, we were just hangin' out like we always do. And Bryne knows everyone I know. You're just bein' too much of a mother; you're too tight with 'im. God, my mother never did that with us."

That got right through. "Now, you hold on, Worm. You have no say in this. I'm talking to my son right now, so you can just butt out."

Open floodgates. "You're always afraid of lookin' embarrassed," he pressed. "Like I'm gonna embarrass you with your son or somethin', just because he's with me. Like when you hide down in your car."

"I have family and friends in this community, Worm. You just don't know how it is. And anyway, that is not the point. I am trying to teach my son the right thing."

"You can't sit up here and run your kid's life: 'You can do this but you can't do that.' He's gonna do what he wants to do, even behind your back. You can't keep a constant eye on 'im twenty-four hours a day. And plus, when he's with me—"

"No, Worm" she interrupted, inflamed, "my kids aren't gonna do that. My kids . . . I hope they grow up to be better than that."

"No. Not me and Bryne," he needled her again.

But she was so mad she missed it, and turned her attention again to Bryne, thinking she could teach Dennis now, too, through disciplining her son. "Bryne, I want you to tell me where you really were tonight."

But Dennis spoke before he could answer. "You shouldn't be pickin' on him like that. He didn't do anything wrong."

"Yes he did. Now, Worm, you don't need to take up for Bryne when he's tellin' a little white lie. That's not teachin' him to do the right thing."

"Well, Miss Rich, that ain't really lyin'."

"Yes it is. There's just one way of telling the truth: either you're honest or you're not. Listen, Worm, there are three things we taught our kids: not to lie, cheat, or steal. We tell the truth around here; I can't stand it when one of my kids isn't honest with me. And I think you have somethin' to do with it tonight. So don't be teachin' Bryne to lie, don't you do that. I am not gonna put up with it. You might as well understand that and just butt out." Then, turning back to Bryne: "Bryne, I know that little white girl Worm is seeing, and I don't want you hangin' around that girl because she's—"

This sent Worm ballistic. "Miss Rich, you have a big mouth, boy. You're always sayin' somethin' about someone."

Cut to the core, Pat couldn't contain her outrage. "Watch it, *nigger!*" slipped out, catching even her by surprise. Instantly, she felt sorry and tears welled in her eyes.

Too late: Dennis had a wounded look in his eyes. "Oh, that's real good," he shot back. "I guess that shows the type of person you really are." And he stormed outside.

Bryne cringed in despair. "I can't believe you said that, Mom. You're not supposed to say that to him. Look what you caused. You made him mad and he'll be gone and he won't come back to see me anymore." Then he added something she would always remember because of its prophetic irony: "You're gonna be sorry someday when Worm plays pro in the NBA and he won't get you tickets to the games. You're gonna be real sorry then, boy." And he started to cry.

Crying now, too, Pat tried desperately to explain. "I didn't mean

it, Bryne. I'm nervous and upset; bein' around three boys all the time—
four boys—will *get* you nervous and upset. I was trying to fix supper, I
was over a hot-cooked stove, and here I'm getting all this malarkey-
lyin' stuff. And I know the truth, I know where you went and you
were telling me otherwise, and goin' against all the principles that I
taught you growing up."

It didn't help; Bryne was devastated. He made Pat feel so awful,
she hit the road after Dennis, who, she thought while she was trying
to catch up, was "spittin' fire and walkin' fast." So she yelled, "Worm,
stop walkin' so fast! Come back! I'm sorry, I didn't mean it. Come
back and talk to me, we'll work it out somehow. Don't leave mad."
And they kept trekking down the road as cars passed by. When he got
about a quarter of a mile, she pulled her ace. "*Bryne* wants you back,
Worm. He's gonna get all sad without you. Come on back, we can
work it out." That slowed him down, though he went a little farther
to think it over. Then he stopped.

When Pat got inside, she sat down in the den and waited. She
knew that whenever Dennis got mad, he always turned on the TV and
watched from the floor. Sure enough, minutes later he strolled into
the den, turned on the TV, and flopped on the floor to watch.

"I am truly sorry, Worm." she began. "I didn't mean to say that
word." That was only partly true; in fact, she knew it was the one word
that could reach him, and that was really why she'd used it. But she'd
immediately regretted it, especially because she didn't mean it the way
he thought. And, plus, it always killed *Bryne* to hear it, too.

"Miss Rich," Dennis answered in his normal, easy tone again,
"you shouldn't've said that. I've heard that word all I want to. Didn't
I tell you that's the worse thing you can call a black person?"

"Well, I know. But you hurt me, too, when you called me a 'big
mouth.' I have feelings just like you do, you know. And I meant it to
hurt you so you'd know how I felt. You need to think about how *you*
hurt people, too, sometimes."

"I know. But you shouldn't've said that word."

"Well, I'm sorry. I really and truly am. And I promise I won't ever say it again. Because, in my heart, I didn't mean it, and I'm just so sorry, you'll never know."

"Okay, I'm sorry, too." He knew, in his heart, she really was sorry.

They watched TV in silence a few moments. But Pat had more on her mind: "Worm, I need to tell you something and then I'll shut up. I know how you feel about Bryne and all, but when you're here and I'm disciplining my kids, just please don't interfere. Don't ever come between me and my kids on discipline because I am gonna make 'em mind. Otherwise, you and I are gonna go to bats."

"Okay, Miss Rich," he said reluctantly. "But it ain't fair."

She broke a grin and so did he . . . and she let him have the last word.

17

Kiss of Death

Dennis Rodman's basketball showing had been so impressive as a sophomore, and he'd garnered so much publicity, that Lonn Reisman felt compelled to warn him junior year, "You're conference MVP, District Nine MVP, first-team All-America—you're not gonna be a surprise anymore, so everyone'll be gunnin' for you."

That didn't faze Dennis; he was confident in his abilities now. "Don't matter," he said. "I'll be gunnin' for *them*." One reason for his assurance was that he'd evolved in less than a year from a lanky 180-pound frame to 200 pounds of sinewy muscle. Plus, he felt more at home, understood his strengths, knew what his coaches and teammates expected. Reisman wondered only one thing: "Can he duplicate? Can he actually do what he did last year again?"

Auspicious season opener against a helpless Austin College team: in an 83-55 rout Dennis nailed 30 points and 19 rebounds. Next game, against a tougher Oklahoma Baptist—which the previous year had held him to his season low of 15 points—Dennis's size, strength, and 26 points carried the Savages to a convincing 67–55 win. After starting off 4–0, and with subsequent winning streaks of four and three games, they blistered to a 12–3 nonconference record, with Dennis averaging

26 points and controlling the boards at 16-a-game. In other words, the focus was once again on him. Then, when the Savages swept their first three conference games to go to 15–3, Hedden and Reisman could almost taste a year of destiny. Anytime you won twenty on a twenty-seven game schedule in their league, you were cranking on all cylinders. Since twenty was their primary goal, with nine games left—six in The Snake Pit—that seemed a lock. They were already projecting ahead to the District 9 playoffs and then, maybe this time, the Nationals in Kansas City.

However, while Dennis's talent and stature grew on the court, his emotional problems continued to nag off it. They started manifesting themselves, as they had during his youth, in self-defeating behavior. The first notable incident happened one night after Dennis and Bryne finished playing a ferocious game of Nerf basketball. When Bryne emerged from his shower for their usual session of late-night TV, Dennis had vanished—along with James's red pickup. Obviously, Dennis knew Bryne would not have let him "borrow" the pickup this late, so he'd boosted it behind his back. He'd never used Bryne like that before, and it ticked Bryne off. It was not only a small betrayal, but it also put Bryne on the spot with his parents, because he was responsible for Dennis's use of the vehicles. If that pickup wasn't back before James was ready to leave next morning . . . well, he didn't want to think about the consequences. So he stayed up to await Dennis's return.

There was a fatal catch to Dennis's scheme: he didn't know the pickup brakes were faulty. Thus his panicky phone call at 4:00 A.M., which Bryne grabbed on one ring: "The truck won't move! The brakes are locked!" Bryne told him to call a tow truck but to be sure to have the pickup home before eight. Somehow, Dennis got the brakes unlocked himself and sped back, running every red light, making his only stop his last one, in the Riches' driveway. When he finally got inside, Bryne rebuked him up and down.

Then something bolder. Dennis had a weakness for jewelry that only Bryne knew about—in the complex where he grew up, guys al-

ways wore shiny jewelry to look cool. Several times, Pat had caught
Dennis peeking into her jewelry box and admiring her gold-plated
necklaces, but she hadn't made anything of it. She just said, "You're
not supposed to be in there" and he'd slunk away, embarrassed. But
then he started his "borrowing" again, lifting necklaces to wear at
school. He never mentioned it, he just returned them when he was
through. Whenever Pat complained about a missing item to James, he
pointed out, "Well, you know how you're always missin' somethin'
and then you find it somewhere else. Look around and you'll probably
find it." But often lately she couldn't.

Still, she didn't put two and two together until one day on campus
when she saw Dennis wearing every necklace she owned. It threw her
for a loop. More surprised than mad, she considered before approaching him: "I guess I can forgive him for this, because he's never had
nice jewelry and he thinks the only way to get it is to take it." So she
confronted him calmly: "Worm, what are you doin' with my necklaces?"

"I'm just wearin' 'em, Miss Rich. I'll bring 'em back."

"Well, I would appreciate it if you wouldn't wear my jewelry
without asking me. I'll tell you right now, they're not fourteen-karat
gold, they're costume jewelry. But I wear 'em a lot and I would like to
have 'em back." He meekly said okay and returned the necklaces that
evening after practice. Nothing more was said.

But it should have been, because the problem escalated. Every so
often, Dennis would wear Pat's necklaces and bracelets to school, and
she'd have to remind him to return them. He would, but it started to
grate on her. It wasn't the jewelry so much; it was the idea that he felt
he could take things without asking. She'd been sympathetic enough
not to embarrass him with reprimands, yet she couldn't help feeling
he needed a good talking to. And she churned with another concern:
given Dennis's watch-stealing episode in Dallas, and his attitude that
"I'm not really accepted that much, they're just toleratin' me," plus
his constant carping about having no money . . . what if he was *hocking*
her jewelry for cash?

Predictably, Pat's suspicions triggered an overreaction. She was in class one afternoon when Dennis entered and marched right over to her. Despite her best efforts to change, she still cringed with embarrassment. But this time, that vanished instantly. Because when Dennis leaned toward her to ask for a ride home, he put his hand on her desk, and there on his pinky was one of the gold-nugget rings she'd bought Barry and Mike for graduation. She couldn't believe her eyes. "Oh no," she gasped, blanking out everything else. "Give me that ring! That's my son's graduation ring! You're not supposed to wear that!" And she started tugging it off his finger. Dennis looked shocked; he couldn't understand her fury. Many times, recently, he'd told Pat how badly he wanted a nugget ring, because it was the going fad in Oklahoma at the time. So, what was the big deal if he wore one of the boys' rings for a day?

They didn't talk until they were in the car, when Pat asked him, "Worm, how could you steal my son's ring?"

"Miss Rich, I didn't *steal* it. I was just *wearin'* it"—his familiar defense, which, in her present mood, she mistook as an insult.

"Yeah, I know." She shook her head. "You don't steal it, you just wear it and then it disappears."

"It don't disappear. You have it, don't you?"

It bothered her that he couldn't look her in the eye. "Why did you steal it, can you please tell me that? After the way we've treated you in our home, Dennis?"

He seemed confounded again. In Dennis's special perspective it really wasn't stealing; far from it. It was merely one member of a family freely using something belonging to another member. In that context, he actually wore these items like fraternal badges of love. "I didn't steal it, I just took it," he repeated. "I didn't know it was a graduation ring. I thought it was just a ring."

While Dennis never apologized directly to Pat, he did later to Barry, admitting he shouldn't have taken his ring. But just to seal the issue, James took Dennis outside to talk. He was upset, too; his aim was to let Dennis know he was trying their trust. "Why did you take Pat's necklaces and Barry's ring?"

"No, no, no," Dennis protested, offended now, too. "I did not take 'em to steal 'em. I can tell you exactly what happened." He always found it easier to express his real feelings to James. "I just borrowed 'em to wear around. And Miss Rich knew I had her necklaces. But she never came to me and said, 'Give me my necklaces,' because she knew I had 'em and I was just borrowing 'em."

"She thought you might be goin' to sell it. Were you gonna do that?"

"If I was gonna sell anything I would've sold it as soon as I took it. If I sold anything personal of hers like that I might as well just leave. I never sold *nothin'*. That wouldn't make sense."

"Well, why did you take the stuff in the first place?"

"I don't know. I think it was more because I wanted to stand out. Just to prove that I have this or that, like other people have nice things."

"Well, I've told you before: if you want somethin', all you gotta do is just ask."

"I didn't want you to think I was a freeloader, askin' for things all the time. I said, 'Damn, I wanna wear this, I'll just take it and then I'll put it back.' It wasn't like I was gonna keep it and you wouldn't know about it. I didn't think anyone would miss it, or get mad or anything."

James laid it on the line once and for all. "Listen, Dennis. Don't ever take anything from this house without askin' first, because it ain't yours to take. Otherwise, it's gonna be over. We'll never have anything else to do with you. Okay?"

"Okay."

"Okay. Then we're gonna forget about it, startin' right now."

And they did; and for about two weeks things returned to normal again. Or so they thought.

■　■　■

About that time, Coaches Hedden and Reisman had to drive out to the Rich farm to have another talk with Dennis on other tricky matters. As Pat and James listened in, the coaches expressed concern that Dennis was spending too much time in Bokchito and not enough on campus. They discussed his frequently being late for classes and appointments, or not showing up at all, and emphasized his scholarship obligations, not only to the program but also the school. They told him they thought he should come back to campus and stay in the dorm, where he belonged.

Feeling put-upon, Dennis figured they really meant: "Stay in the dorm where we can keep an eye on you all the time." So he said no, he didn't want to be on campus, he wanted to stay right where he was. A heated discussion ensued, Dennis complaining about being told what to do when he knew what was best for himself, and the coaches arguing he needed to think about what was best for everyone. But he wouldn't budge. Which led to another of Hedden's severe ultimatums: "If you don't come back with us now, we'll get you a bus ticket to Dallas." Dennis recoiled defiantly, "Well, *do* it then," and withdrew to Bryne's room.

He cooled off later and returned to the dorm for a while, but with a lingering discontent. Which was partly why he kept showing up late to practice. Which was why Reisman and Hedden chewed him mercilessly day after day: "You don't work hard enough!" . . . "Get over here and do these drills!" . . . "Move it, Rodman! You ain't hustlin'! You ain't doin' crap out here!" And most days he wasn't; the harder they pushed the more resistant he grew and the less he put out. The fourth day, when Dennis straggled into practice later than usual, Hedden blew up. "You come late one more time, you're finished"—and he meant it. In fact, he made it clear all afternoon that if Dennis wasn't there, they could do without him. They couldn't, of course, but they would have to if Dennis forced Hedden's hand. After all, Hedden had already given Dennis plenty of slack in the rope he was tying around his own neck.

At week's end, after only five days back in the dorm, Dennis said the hell with it, this is not for me, and he moved out to the farm again. He was so frustrated and discouraged he announced, "I'm quittin' basketball," but he told only Bryne why. This distressed Bryne terribly; he tried hard to dissuade him. Odd irony: here was a fifteen-year-old high school farm kid, only recently out of his own spiraling tailspin, counseling a twenty-three-year-old college boy from the city, "tryin' to build him back up" by reasoning maturely, "Quittin' isn't the thing. It won't do any good. You got so much talent, you're gonna play pro in a couple of years, and you don't want to screw that up. Plus, you're workin' on a degree and you're doin' real well. You gotta get back with it and don't get discouraged if they get on you a little bit. You just gotta bite your tongue and go on and work twice as hard. That's what you been teachin' *me*."

Dennis didn't care—he'd had enough; he wasn't going back. And for the next two days he didn't go back, he just hung out at the farm. James saw the handwriting on the wall, so he finally said, "C'mon, Dennis, let's go check the calves." That was shorthand for: *a serious talk.* The boys all knew James's method; when he was really ticked off he'd take you in the pickup—alone, so you wouldn't be embarrassed in front of the others—on a casual premise, like checking the calves or feeding the cows or maybe going to town for a Coke. If he turned right, toward town, that's exactly what you'd do; but if he turned left, toward miles of nowhere, you had better be ready for both barrels. It was one of those marker events you would always remember; in fact, the boys sloganeered "take you in the pickup" into their version of capital punishment, as in: "You don't watch out, daddy's gonna *take you in the pickup*"—meaning, roughly: *Kiss of Death.*

James turned left and Dennis knew he was in for it. But James didn't intend to scold this time; he just wanted to offer some hard advice. He wasn't given to analytical lectures or probing emotional depths anyway; he just looked at everything squarely for what it was, and applied common sense. In his pickup talks, James always eased into it with something familiar like, "Hell, I wish we'd get some rain" or "You know that tractor you were on the other day? How do you think it's runnin'?" Then he'd plunge into it and talk straight through till he brought you back. And, as Dennis told Bryne after one of those memorable rides, "All of a sudden you're a born-again person, you're off the hook, like, 'Oh man, I ain't gonna do *that* again!'"

This time, though, James went right into it, with no softening up. "What's goin' on, Dennis?" he fired point-blank.

"Nothin' goin' on," Dennis murmured, reluctant to speak. "I quit, that's all."

"Well, but why are you quittin'? What's botherin' you?"

"I just got fed up with the crap."

"You mean on the team?"

"Not only the team. The people, the attitudes, the way they look at you. Mr. Rich, you know I'm not stupid. If you're black and successful, people aren't gonna come out and say, 'Well, you did a great job but you're still black and we don't want you around.' They're not gonna say that, they're gonna try to kiss your ass until they're done with you. I been seein' a lot of that."

"Well, who's doin' it, exactly?"

"It's just people. They didn't accept me doin' a lot of things until I made it in sports and then it was like, 'Well, he's the star of the team. He can do that and we won't do anything, but we still don't like it.' I'm fed up with that and I'm fed up with bein' pushed around by the coaches. I don't need that crap. So I quit."

"Dennis, you ain't gonna quit. I'm not gonna let you quit. I mean, what're you gonna do if you leave school? Go back to Dallas and work nine-to-five, for two dollars an hour? Are you gonna start bein' a bum and livin' the way you used to, and get into trouble and maybe end up in jail? Is that what you want?"

"No, I don't want that."

"I don't want that either. You know, you got a lot of opportunities to do things, and there are a lot of people that don't have those opportunities. And you came from the streets. Now, I want you to really think and try to take in what I'm sayin' here, 'cause I'm not mad at you, I'm just tryin' to help you do the right thing for yourself."

"I know that. But I can't take it no more, Mr. Rich."

"Dennis, I'm not gonna let you fall back. You got too much to offer. Hey, you got a lot of talent, you can play pro. I *know* you can do it. And this school is your break. So you need to get back in there and make somethin' of your life. If it has to be basketball, it has to be basketball. Go back to practice and show those people what you can do. I mean, you don't want to have to go back home a failure and be just another bum in the streets, do you?"

That hit a nerve, and James knew it. So he gently pressed it for the entire forty-five-minute ride. All the boys knew that James held them to the same simple standard: *If you make the effort to do the best you can do, then I'll be proud and happy for you and I'll stand by you through thick and thin. But if you don't give it your best shot, or you give up a chance to better yourself without fighting, I can't accept that.* So when he and Dennis arrived back at the farm, Dennis felt much better about his life, and also about James. He knew this was James's way of showing he cared, and it came at just the right time. In fact, it was this talk that endeared James permanently to Dennis "like the father I was always missin'."

One thing about Dennis: on the basketball court he seemed to transcend the turbulence swirling through his private life. And never better than in his junior year. Though the Savages lost some of their edge toward season's end and finished a disappointing 4–4 again in the conference, they closed in The Pit with their twentieth win, an exhilarating 87–65 rout of former national champion Bethany Nazarene College, in which Dennis outdid himself by hitting a season-high 39 points and grabbing a school-record 27 rebounds. By then, no one was surprised; they knew he was capable of delivering big games.

In what still felt like a year of destiny, none was bigger than the opener at home of the District 9 playoffs against the same Bethany Nazarene. Surprisingly easy win, 74–58; Rodman: career-high 51 points, plus 19 rebounds. Semifinal versus Oklahoma Christian away—69–50 Savages; Rodman: 35 points, 19 rebounds. Championship game at home against Southeastern's biggest rival, East Central University from Ada, fifty miles away. Biggest game of his career to date; biggest game for the school since the 1960s; springboard to the Nationals in K.C. . . . and twenty-four hours from gametime, Reisman got a devastating phone call from Rodman's roommate, a panicky Billy Conaway. "Dennis is sick, Coach," Billy said anxiously. "Coach, he's *real* sick."

After that, it was a Keystone Cops-type nightmare. Reisman rushed to Dennis's dorm room and took his temperature—104. Immediately, he called Jack Hedden and advised, "I'm headed to the Emergency Room with him. Meet me there." At 1:00 A.M. at the hospital in Durant, they learned Dennis had contracted a mean ear-and-throat infection and was in terrible shape. They had cooled him and pumped him with antibiotics, but that was all they could do. Forget about basketball. At 4:00 A.M., Reisman and Conaway drove Dennis, a virtual zombie, back to the dorm and put him right to bed. "Billy," Reisman ordered, "I want him to take aspirin every three hours. Every three hours, you got it? I'll be right back." He went to the all-night convenience store for ten quarts of Gatorade and carried them back to the room and said, "I want him to drink a full one every hour. *Every hour*, make him drink it. I'll be back to check up." Then Reisman went home to sleep.

He returned to the dorm at eight sharp to take Dennis's temperature—102. "All right, time to get up, Dennis. Take your aspirin." Dennis was laid out, sicker than hell, but Reisman and Conaway hoisted him up and forced him to drink the Gatorade. Afterward, they let him sleep for two more hours. Then Reisman took another temperature—101. "Oh man, got a chance. Sucker's comin' down." More aspirin; another Gatorade; second dose of antibiotic; instructions from the doctor: "Just keep giving him the aspirin, the liquids, and the antibiotics. But, hell, I wouldn't count on him being able to walk, much less play."

At noon, Reisman was back at the dorm with Campbell's

Chicken Noodle Soup, helping Dennis to eat whatever morsels he could bear. Followed by Gatorade, aspirin, antibiotic. They'd pumped so much liquid down Dennis by then, Reisman thought: "Man, it's a wonder his kidneys don't bust." He returned at three and took another temperature—100 on the nose. At six o'clock—with gametime two hours off—they helped Dennis out of bed to find his legs. He couldn't even find the floor. Nevertheless, they hauled him off to The Pit.

Home game, sold out, people throwing $100 bills at the back door to get in. Reisman and Conaway escort Dennis into the locker room and take another temperature: 98.6—*normal*. Of course, they know it's really the megadoses of aspirin at work, and that Dennis is still weaker than hell. Reisman asks him anyway, "You wanna try to warm up?" and Dennis replies, "I'm gonna play, Coach. I'm *playin'*." So they get him dressed, and Jack Hedden comes in and lays down the law: "If he has any temperature at all, he doesn't play."

Six minutes before tip-off, alone with Dennis in the locker room, Reisman takes one last temperature, praying for one more "normal"— Still 98.6. So Dennis plays. They rest him every ten minutes, feeding him oranges and pumping water and Gatorade into him, then sending him back in. Dizzy and weak, he nevertheless plays a phenomenal game: 24 points and 10 rebounds in a 74–68 triumph that sends the crowd home exalted and thrilled. They have no idea what their hero's been through.

After the game, Reisman and Conaway loaded Dennis into the van and rushed him back to the hospital for R&R. Couple of days of sleep and antibiotics, and he was fine again. Later, of course, the game would become legend. In Reisman's excited words the next day: "We get knocked out of going to the Nationals the year before and now, all of a sudden, we're gonna get blown out of going the second straight time? We were wiped out; how could bad luck hit you two years in a row? He's got 104 temperature and he's so damn sick he can't walk, and less than twenty-four hours later he's on the floor playin' the game everybody's worked toward for damn near five months, and he goes out and plays with tremendous guts. It told me

he was everything I ever thought about him: great heart, great courage, great inspiration to his team. He knew what that game meant.
And he took it on his shoulders to get us that win; he wasn't gonna
let us lose because of him bein' sick. So he went out there and played
his heart out, and then he damn near collapsed. That's how bad he
wanted it—for *all* of us."

At the Nationals, riding that inspirational performance—and
Dennis's 40 points and 17 rebounds—Southeastern squeaked past Ne-
braska's Kearney State, 70–67, in its opener to advance to the round
called the Sweet 16. Next up: South Carolina's College of Charleston,
which managed to get Dennis in foul trouble early, cutting his playing
time in half and thwarting his chances to dominate all game. Reisman
and Hedden felt the referees weren't letting him play his game, were
calling too many marginal fouls. And unfortunately, the team didn't
adjust—and bowed out weakly, 60–43. Dennis had a shockingly low
nine points and five rebounds; it was a crushing loss all the way around.

The only plus was that the pro scouts were at the Nationals and
were impressed with Rodman's first-game showing. When word came
down that one top scout's evaluation read, "You hardly ever see a great
athlete like Rodman who will sacrifice his body and dive for loose balls
into the stands," Reisman reassured Dennis, "See, they notice little
things like that." Reisman also pointed out Terry Porter, a pro prospect
with Wisconsin-Stevens Point: "Dennis, there's Terry Porter. He's
gonna get drafted high and he's an NAIA player. See, you can *make*
it from this level. You just gotta be seen like this at the Nationals."

Next day, a favorable write-up in the Kansas City paper helped,
followed by word that the scouts had concluded: "Dennis Rodman is
a legitimate pro prospect." So despite the gloomy season finale, doubly
bitter for last year's collapse, Dennis did reflect on Terry Porter and
the assessment of the scouts. For one brief moment, in fact, he actually
let himself think: "Hey, I *might* get a shot at the NBA."

But by the time he'd returned to Durant, that improbable notion
had passed.

18

How Time Flies

"Daddy, do you think you could help get Worm a car?" Bryne asked James in the summer of '85.

Followed shortly by an eloquent plea from Dennis that here he was a twenty-four-year-old senior in college and everybody else had a pickup or car except him, and he always had to borrow one from them and bring it back on time, so wouldn't it be great if he didn't have to bother them about that anymore? Followed by the setup coup de grace from the architect of this little conspiracy: Pat. "James, why don't you go down there to Reynolds Chevy and sign a note and let Worm borrow the money at the bank and buy that broke-down Monte Carlo he likes so much. Worm said he'd pay it back. We can help get him a car where he can be on his own and not have to bum rides with me all the time. I like my privacy, and I think it's the right time." Her privacy was a key issue, of course—though Pat really did sympathize with Dennis's need to feel independent. In fact, she concluded her presentation on that note: "Let's get Worm that ole car and give him a little bit of pride and self-respect."

Eventually, James prepared to lay out $1,000 for the car, on condition that Dennis pay it back as soon as he could. Few things had ever made Dennis happier: finally he was about to own his first Monte Carlo! However, when his coaches learned of this arrangement, they explained to the Riches that buying Dennis a car broke scholarship rules. So James bought the car in his own name and let Dennis drive it like his own, telling him that after graduation Dennis could buy it from him. Dennis wasted no time detailing James's new used car with fog and runner lights, curb-finders, and spoked wheels—just like Shirley's car in Dallas—plus a blinking light on the antenna. He cleaned it obsessively with Armor All, something James had never heard of, until he got his next bill from the feed store. "What's all this Armor All stuff on my feed bill?" he had to ask Pat. Same old Dennis with the charge card.

Unfortunately, other more significant things stayed the same, too. Like Dennis's bad habit—cured, they had thought—of "borrowing" things without permission. First it was a check from Barry's checkbook, which he cashed for fifteen dollars—after which Barry, who refused to confront Dennis about it, simply hid his checkbook. Then, with the family on vacation in Hot Springs, he wrote a twenty-dollar check on James and Pat for food, acting on impulse after much self-debate, yet doing it anyway—he couldn't say why. When James confronted him about it, Dennis felt terrible, admitted it, and started to cry, promising he'd never do it again. But the dam had broken.

Pat and James considered what to do. Finally, James told Dennis, reluctantly, "Worm, I think you better go stay at the dorm for a while. We just can't tolerate what you been doin' no more. You've pushed us too far." So the next afternoon Dennis packed his clothes and, despite Bryne's vehement protests to his parents, drove with Coach Reisman back to the dorm. For weeks afterward, sorry, ashamed, and miserable, Dennis couldn't bring himself to face Pat or James, although he and Bryne still saw each other every day at school. Then one day in early fall, as Pat came from class, she spotted Dennis standing by himself in front of the bookstore. She hadn't intended to talk to him, because he'd drifted out of their lives and she'd decided to write him off her list and have nothing more to do with him. But as she looked at him standing there so lonely and forlorn, compassion flooded her heart.

Strangely drawn to him, she heard her own voice guiding her: "You ought to be friendly to him. He's a good person. He loves you and your family, and we miss him. He needs another chance." She hesitated, debating what to do. Then, against her better judgment, she approached him and said straight-out, "Worm, why don't you come on back and have dinner with us again sometime. We're not mad at you anymore. Everyone makes mistakes. Bryne misses you and we miss you, too. So come on back and see us." His eyes widened and he cracked a bashful grin and said okay.

A few days later, he came back to stay.

That year, it seemed like conflict was always in the air. One night around the time Dennis returned from his brief exile, while Pat was sitting in the bleachers at Bokchito High School watching Bryne play, a man leaned in to tell her, "Y'all might be sorry you got that colored boy out to your house again."

"Really?" Pat snapped, defensive already. "Why's that?"

"Well, because I heard the KKK's gonna pay you a visit."

These days, that was all it took for Pat to boil. "Well, *good!*" she flared, dripping scorn. "You tell 'em to come on ahead. Let's see what happens when the KKK visits *our* house. We'll see pretty quick who the *sorry* ones are, I can tell you that. You go tell 'em Pat Rich said, 'Come on ahead.' "

They didn't come. But other problems did—once again race-related. For example: the intolerant attitudes of some of Pat's relatives reared up again when they heard about "some colored folks" visiting her house. They didn't know it was Dennis Rodman's mother they were complaining about.

Shirley Rodman had seen a few of her son's basketball games the previous year, but had never stayed overnight. There were many reasons for this, like having to split her free weekends traveling to Texas and Louisiana to see Kim and Debra play, too, and feeling a little resentful of Pat and Bryne—though it wasn't actually them as much as Dennis. He'd called her often, usually for advice about his problems at school, yet it seemed to her that "the more popular he got in basketball the more he talked about the Riches and the less he bothered with me." She had wanted him to be happy and independent at school, and she was grateful for the care and support the Riches had given him, but she still felt jealous. After all, she had been Dennis's "idol" growing up, and now strangers were deflecting his attention away from her. Most hurtful of all: Dennis chose to spend his college summers with them instead of her.

Nevertheless, she'd decided to set her resentment aside and give them a chance. So she drove up to Bokchito late one Saturday afternoon, with her boyfriend, her sister and her aunts, to take the Riches up on their barbecue-and-ballgame offer. It was a big bash, and she was surprised and delighted at how much she enjoyed the company. Before the meal, Pat and James escorted her on a casual tour of the farm, which revealed so many obvious benefits for Dennis. He even rode the tractor around for her and excitedly showed her the cow named "Worm," and she was impressed with her son's carefree manner. "This is not my life to be unhappy with," she reminded herself. "This is Dennis's life." And she resolved that regardless of her own feelings, she would abide by whatever made *him* happy.

They ate supper and talked, and the aunts played dominoes with James until they had to leave for the gym. After the game—an easy win over Arkansas Tech as Southeastern took the Southern Arkansas Classic behind Dennis's 25 points and 15 rebounds—they all celebrated at Ken's Pizza. Shirley and the others were invited to stay overnight but Shirley declined, explaining that she had to play in church the next morning.

The following Monday, gossip reached Pat's relatives. Her sister Rachel and brother-in-law Charles objected about "all them colored people out at Pat's place." When Pat heard that, she knew she'd made a wise decision not to tell anyone that she'd spent a night at Shirley's.

So she just ignored this latest encroachment until it died away. But it started up again when Dennis's sister Kim came up to see him play and spend the weekend at the farm. Kim had done that the previous year, and it had caused a stir then, too. Because on the Monday following a game one day, when Rachel came to Pat's house, she discovered Kim asleep on the couch, and was appalled. Here was *another* colored person sleeping at her sister's house! What would the neighbors say! Rachel left immediately and later reported it to her parents, and as Pat soon learned, made a big issue out of it.

Good thing Rachel didn't pop over *this* time Kim was visiting: because Kim had brought a pal along: her little cousin, Tukey. Following the game, Dennis and Kim went to the homecoming dance and wanted to stay out late, so Pat and James agreed to take Tukey home with them. On the way in the car, with Tukey perched on the armrest between them, Pat chuckled, "We haven't ever baby-sat a black child before. This oughta be an experience."

At the farm Pat made a bed on the couch, turned off the lights, and tucked Tukey in. She was struck by how irresistibly cute the child looked with the pretty red bows in her tightly braided hair. Then Pat turned in, too. But just minutes later she was awakened with a start when something brushed her arm. It was Tukey, grabbing hold and climbing up. "I wanna sleep with y'all," the child squealed, edging in between them. Pat was startled; this wasn't part of the plan; it was so . . . *unusual*. "James," she tittered, intrigued, "what're we gonna say if our relatives come in here and see her in bed with us?" James grinned at the unlikely prospect. "We'll just hide her in the closet," he joked— and they slept on that jest. But funnier still to Pat: little Tukey *snored*.

In the morning, Tukey awakened with a confused expression that asked, "Where am I? Who am I with?" She looked at James and then Pat and rolled her eyes and broke into her cackly little laugh. After breakfast, Tukey played with Bryne. Pat enjoyed watching her so much she said to James, "I'm gonna take this little girl over to my parents' and show 'em how cute and sweet she is." So she drove Tukey over and got out and noticed a neighbor's window shade rising, and she could almost hear the neighbor remarking, "Lord behold!" as she walked to the house leading a black child by the hand.

Inside, Pat unexpectly encountered Rachel and Charles, and just hoped they'd be civil. Her mom made a fuss over Tukey, but Pat grew anxious because she thought Charles was "throwin' everyone hard looks." She was right. Unable to contain himself, Charles pointed at Tukey and scoffed, "Is that what you and *Worm* come up with?"

An uneasy silence gripped the room. Pat was startled, and fit to be tied; she considered the remark cruel and perverse. Still, she just grinned contemptuously to avoid a fight in front of her mom. She knew that Rachel and Charles had been barraging her parents with provocative reports about her, but there was nothing she'd been able to do. So she'd followed James's advice to ignore it as best she could. But it offended her pride and her sense of family propriety; it was one thing to flare at *her* with their ignorant remarks, but how dare they give so much constant flak about her to her *parents!* And after this kind of vicious insult, she could just imagine the garbage her parents had to hear.

But the straw that finally broke her self-control occurred one day when Charles suddenly flared at Pat, "None of this business would've happened between us if you hadn't brought that colored guy into your home!" Pat thought: "That's it. This is gonna stop. I'm fighting back." So she marched to Charles's chair, pointed her finger under his nose, and raged, "Let me tell you somethin' right now. And you can *well* remember this. If I had it to do over, I would do the very same thing. I don't regret that Worm come and lived at my house. Do you understand me? I do *not* regret it. And there is not one thing you can do about it. So you better just chill out. Because *you're* the one that's causing all the problems." That left everyone silent; and Pat huffed away, outraged.

But it didn't end there, because Pat had now decided to start standing up for her rights. Thus, the following week, Pat confronted Rachel face-to-face for the first time. She said, "Will you please tell me one thing? Why do you think Worm is stayin' at my house? Do you really believe those rumors?"

"I didn't hear no rumors," said Rachel, coldly. "I don't know what you do here."

"Well, do you really think he's here because of *me*? Are you gonna tell me you really believe that?"

Rachel admitted, "Why, no. He's here to help Bryne."

"Then why can't you all accept that and keep your mouths shut?"

"I guess because we wasn't raised that way."

"That doesn't explain why you're not supporting me. I need your help and understanding and love, not all this other stuff. Bryne's been through a terrible tragedy, and Worm is good for him. And he's good for our family. There is nothing ugly or indecent about him stayin' out here. I believe Worm was sent here to minister to us and maybe teach us somethin'. But you all want to make it look ugly by causing trouble for me with all your gossipin'."

"We're not tryin' to cause trouble. You're the one boardin' a colored guy."

"Now look, Worm is black. But he's a person and he's got a heart and a soul just like anyone else. And he's gonna be here as long as Bryne and all of us want him here—that's *our* business. You don't pay our bills and you can't tell me how to run my home. So why don't you just stop punchin' and pokin' all the time, and keep your mouth shut and accept things for what they are."

It didn't end there, either. Pat's relatives gathered regularly for family suppers at her parents' house, and over the past year Pat had been bringing leftovers home for Dennis and Bryne. Lately, two of her sisters had begun to have a problem with that. But unwilling to raise it directly, they resorted to murmuring disparaging remarks in Pat's presence. While cooking the meal one night, one of them grumbled sarcastically about Pat carrying leftover food back to "Pat's nigger." She exploded; she slammed her fist on the bar and said, "I want to tell you somethin'. You are coldhearted, and very insensitive toward my needs. You have never been through what I've been through in life, so where do you get off standing over there and judging me?"

They were shocked as she hemmed them in, menacingly, between the refrigerator and the bar, nerves frayed, face pinched, fists clenched. "You know," she threatened, "if I wanted to pull some hidden skeletons out from somebody's closet, I could start on *both* of y'all. I could start pullin' 'em out, now couldn't I? So if we're gonna pull out skeletons, just let me pull a few out of *your* closets."

They didn't want to talk about that. Pat added, "Don't you say anything to me anymore unless you can say somethin' positive or nice. Because I've about taken all I'm gonna take from you. All I've heard is 'colored-this' and 'nigger-that' out of y'all, and I'm getting tired of hearin' about it. Worm is out there to help Bryne, and they're doin' somethin' for their lives. Are you too selfish to see that? Bryne's healthy again; Worm's doin' great; and he has never shown my family, or me, any disrespect. The only disrespect around here is coming from *you*. It's *you* that's causing the shame and disgrace in this family. I think it's about time you *shut your gossipin' mouths!*"

She closed in on them, adrenalized on stress, fury, and offended pride, ready to literally fight them if she had to. But their mother intervened by pounding a fist on the bar and insisting, "I will not have this in my house!" Pat apologized, vowing never to fuss like that again in her home—and not another word was said. And from that day forward, none of the sisters ever mentioned Dennis again to Pat.

Like before, basketball helped Dennis to rebound from personal woes. Working with weights over the summer, he added ten more pounds of muscle that helped turn his senior season into his—and the team's—best yet. After an early-season loss to Wayland Baptist, the Savages actually became the juggernaut Harold Harmon had envisioned them becoming before, winning sixteen consecutive games—including all eight in their conference—closing at 23–3, and being ranked sixth in the nation. Dennis averaged a commanding 24 points and 17 rebounds, the highlight a 32-rebound game against Cameron University to set the NAIA District 9 single-game record.

Next came the district playoffs, every game at Bloomer Sullivan Gym—The Snake Pit. Hedden and Reisman worried about the winning streak. What if the Savages got high too early, like last year, and the pressure to continue the streak withered them too soon? But the players knew the stakes: it was Dennis Rodman's last hurrah and their final chance to reach for that national championship brass ring.

Opening round at The Pit versus Panhandle State. Leading by 19 with less than seven minutes left, the Savages coast to a 76–69 win against a team they've never seen. They win on the poised team play of their zone-buster, "Super Swish" Gerald West, penetrator "CD" Carl Davis, intimidator "Mighty" Myles Homer, supersub Kenny Chaffin, junior defensive specialist Tyrone Thomas, JC transfer Brian Allison, and an extra-animated Worm Rodman, who leads the way with game highs of 27 points and 20 rebounds. "Dennis showed great emotion," Hedden tells the press. "He really wanted this one." True; Dennis had made it his personal goal this season to lead this team to a national championship.

Second round versus the 20–8 Central State Broncos, another team the Savages haven't seen. A tired Southeastern pulls out a squeaker, 56–51. Eighteen straight wins, but wobbly.

District 9 championship game versus thirteenth-ranked Oklahoma City University, coached by former NCAA Division I legend Abe Lemmons (512 career wins). Pro scouts turn out, principally to see Dennis Rodman in his last home game. Beforehand, down on the floor, Pat and James assure Dennis that their suitcases are packed for Kansas City. "You better play good so we don't have to unpack," urges Pat.

"Give me twenty tonight," James throws in as usual.

"No," Pat corrects him. "*Twenty-five.* And I want two big slams."

Dennis smiles. "Okay, I'll dunk it tonight for my white momma." This almost brings her to tears.

The game is a rout. The Savages systematically destroy the usually high-scoring Chiefs, 84–61, behind Gerald West's spectacular 24-point binge, Tyrone Thomas's quiet 20, and Dennis's 19 and 19—including two finger-pointing-at-Pat big slams. Nineteen straight overall; second consecutive District 9 championship; another shot at the Nationals. At the buzzer, two thousand fans pour onto the floor in frenzied celebration. When Pat and James finally shoulder through the mob surrounding Dennis, he hugs them and says, "I love you!" They can hardly believe their ears. Meantime, as an unusually exuberant Jack Hedden proclaims to reporters, "This was a tremendous win! We just kicked 'em around; I don't mind that bein' in the paper! Last season we were happy just to be in the Nationals. This year we wanna *win* it," the crowd is busy chanting the old rock 'n' roll standard, "We're goin' to KANSAS CITY . . . KANSAS CITY here we come. We're goin' to KANSAS CITY . . . "

Opening round of the NAIA National Tournament in Kansas City's Kemper Arena versus Franklin Pierce, New Hampshire. Auspicious start as the Savages steamroll to a 17-point win, with Dennis being pulled early to preserve him for the Sweet 16 game against Huron, South Dakota. He'd performed poorly, so afterward James Rich is concerned. He gives Dennis a little extra motivation. Aware that the tournament record for rebounds is 96, James urges, "You're capable of gettin' that rebound deal if you'll get after it." Dennis says okay, he'll try.

Against Huron the next day, Southeastern breezes by 13 with four Savages in double figures, including a rejuvenated Rodman, who leads everyone with 31 points and 20 rebounds. But now *Hedden's* not satisfied. He tells Dennis, "You're not playin' up to capability. You're tryin' too hard to meet everybody's expectations. Relax and play your game and show these people what our fans at home already know." Dennis wonders what more he can do . . .

Quarterfinals; down to the crunch: only eight of the original thirty-two teams left. The Savages are a crowd favorite for their run-and-gun style, their nonstop pressure defense, and Dennis Rodman's eye-popping athleticism. Pregame—just three wins from the finals—

Hedden preps his team. "We've won two, but we still haven't played well," he surprises some. "We struggled to beat Huron; we didn't play to our potential. We gotta keep our mission in mind and concentrate fully on the task at hand. And that's not just winning *this* one, it's winning the national championship."

The Savages are playing Southwestern Texas, who'd whipped them 51–48 in the second game of the year in The Pit. Another redemption game. Lonn Reisman is uneasy; he knows it'll be a difficult game because the kids from Southwestern are tough and smart, led by intimidating, 6–8 Bobby Deaton, a kid Dennis will have to battle for everything off the boards. Southeastern leads throughout by one, two, or three points, but gritty Southwestern keeps answering, bucket-for-bucket. At the half, Hedden is so intense he rips the team, especially Dennis. On the way out, Reisman shows Hedden the stat sheet. "Goddamn!" Reisman says, chuckling at the irony. "Dennis is leadin' everybody in everything! And we're in there rippin' his ass: 'Play *harder!*' Do this! Do that!'" Hedden just winks and heads back out to the arena.

Southeastern leads throughout the second half. In the closing minutes, the Savages are protecting a one-point lead but Deaton is crashing the boards, crawling all over them, bumping them around— and the refs are permitting it. At the finish, with Southwestern one possession from taking the lead, a defining moment for Dennis. When Southwestern swings upcourt and launches the potential winning shot, it sends everyone crashing the boards for the rebound, especially Deaton, who's already planted under the cylinder. As the shot caroms off, and bodies leap and collide, and a sea of hands grope skyward, suddenly Rodman's hand stabs up between them—higher than Deaton's—and snares the ball midair. He hauls it down in the same motion, shoves it in his gut, and flails his elbows to clear opponents out. The crowd erupts; they can't believe their eyes. Through the screams and applause, the Savages rush downcourt, score again for a cushion, and hold on to win 58–55. Dennis's numbers: 27 and 15.

Reisman is beside himself with joy. He confides to a friend afterward, "That was the most key rebound he ever made. It was one of those rebounds where it takes a great player to win you a big game like that—not the points, not the offensive boards, just that one defensive board when you knew the game was on the line: *Don't give 'em the offensive board.* You know they're gonna climb over your back, and shove and push and elbow, and here comes that big arm to clear the ball one-handed, and wins you the game."

Making the Final Four is daunting; but Hedden and Reisman agree that Southeastern is the most talented team left. They also know that in a tournament anything can happen. So Hedden delivers what is likely to be his last pep talk to his greatest team ever. "Remember this," he drills them one more time. "You have your whole life to run around and do other things. We have this one little chance to win the national tournament, and it's up to us to take advantage of that chance. This is somethin' you can be proud of the rest of your life. So focus on our goal. You may never get this chance again."

But as in the previous year, it isn't to be. Against what appears to be a weaker University of Arkansas-Monticello team, the Savages come up flat, shooting poorly the entire night. Dennis gets 20 and 17—despite the defense doubling-down on him all night—but once again, at least in their own minds, the better team loses, 67–61. It's a bitter pill for Dennis; he cries in the locker room, assuming the weight of the loss on his own shoulders. Hedden can't console him; he considers this the worst loss of his coaching career, and the most disappointing. Reisman, too, knows they'll never have another golden opportunity like this. All year, it has seemed to him like a Cinderella story destined for a storybook finish in which the Savages become national champs. But it eludes them again, despite three years of relentlessly striving for that dream.

Next night, in the third-place game against St. Thomas Aquinas of New York, Dennis decides to end his career with a statement. So he inspires the Savages to one last victory, 75–74, scoring 46 points—second most of his career—and setting an NAIA National Tournament single-game record with 32 rebounds—for a total of 95, only one short of the all-time tournament record James Rich had primed him for. Hedden and Reisman are elated, too: they've notched their thirtieth win—*their* statement of excellence.

Afterward, Reisman drapes an arm around Dennis and says like a friend, "If anybody wanted to know if Dennis Rodman was a winner, they could see it in this game tonight. After such a heartbreakin' loss, you still came out and showed your character and guts and leadership—and that got noticed. Remember what I told you three years ago: you're gonna go pro. Well, you proved me right tonight. So don't hang your head. We wanted to win the last game of the season. And we wanted thirty wins—that was big for Jack and me and the team. And you'll always remember you won the last game you ever suited up for. So walk away proud because that's how everyone at Southeastern, and everyone in Durant, Oklahoma's gonna feel. Proud as hell of *us* and proud as hell of *you*."

On the way back to Durant, Reisman ponders "The Era of the Worm," and how impossible it will be to replace Dennis Rodman. "Somethin' special has passed through this town the last three years," he tells Hedden, "and no one can ever take those memories away. They'll be talkin' about this team in the coffee shops. It won't just be the Bloomer Sullivan days of the fifties and sixties anymore, it's gonna be the Dennis Rodman teams of the mid-eighties now, too." And he consoles himself with that.

Fitting end to a remarkable career: Dennis's 17.8-rebound average leads the NAIA; he's named Oklahoma Intercollegiate Conference Player of the Year, NAIA District 9 Player of the Year, and first team All-America—each for the third straight time. Stats show also that in his three years, the Savages have won 74 games and lost just 22, an extraordinary 77.1 winning percentage. Unprecedented credentials for a kid who never played a single minute of high school ball.

That summer, Dennis plays the major postseason tournaments designed as showcases for NBA scouts to check out players not expected to go first round in the upcoming draft—like the Aloha Classic in Hawaii for the nation's top thirty-two seniors, where he's the leading rebounder; and the prestigious Portsmouth, Virginia, Invitational where, out of nowhere, he's voted Most Valuable Player. Suddenly, he vaults in the minds of the scouts from virtual unknown to potential first-round pick.

Draft day at the Riches: Dennis, the Rich family, friends, TV cameras, and radio stations were planted all over the house, including in Pat's beauty shop. Pat cooked the traditional family meal: barbecue chicken, corn on the cob, potato salad, ranch-style beans—same as they'd prepared for Shirley Rodman's visit. There was no privacy; the TV cameras filmed everything, even the potato salad on the kitchen bar.

In the den, Dennis lay prone on the floor—his usual position—watching the draft with everyone crowded around. When his name was announced—second round, twenty-seventh pick overall—he rolled onto his back, stunned, and covered his face. Bryne bounded up, screaming, "You made it! I told you you'd go pro! I kept tellin' you you'd make it!" Dennis got to his feet and James shook his hand vigorously, smiling like a proud father. Pat was so excited, she grabbed Dennis around the neck and hugged him and kissed him on the cheek—the first time she'd ever done that. Dennis was thinking: "God, I wish I went *first* round"; while she thought: "This is really somethin'. I actually *kissed* him."

Late that night when it was just the family, Dennis sat around with the Riches contemplating the future and reminiscing about the past. During a lull James lamented, "Boy, I can't hardly believe that's the last time we're gonna see you play for Southeastern." After all the triumph and rejoicing of the winning season, they were enveloped now by sadness over a loss that had little to do with basketball. Pat looked at Bryne and sighed. "I was just thinkin' about how you were only a seventh-grader when you first met Worm, and now you're in high school."

Deafening silence, downturned eyes.

Then she added wistfully, more to herself, "How time flies."

19

"How's Rodman?
Is He Down-to-
Earth?"

DENNIS RODMAN: After college I sought to better myself and my life by going to all these basketball camps and tournaments across the country: Montana, Hawaii, Portsmouth, Chicago—and some of 'em even paid money.

I didn't care about the money, I was just hopin' for a shot at the pros. I wanted to prove to people that I could make it. Because a lot of guys I played against in the rec centers back home were down on me, sayin', "You don't have the skills"; "You're too slow"; "You can't shoot the ball"; "You don't have the big-school name behind you." Lot of great players from Dallas went to big schools and didn't make it. So people were sayin', "Dennis is gonna be the same way."

Bryne kept tellin' me, "You're gonna make pro," but I never did believe it. I didn't feel like I could shoot the ball or stay with those guys because on TV they looked faster and stronger than me. I didn't really know, because I never went to an NBA game when I was in college. I just didn't have any interest in it. But when I discovered Julius Erving, I started watching Philadelphia on TV. All you'd hear is "Doctor J! Julius Err-ving!" I said, "God, he's got leaps, he's got glides, he can grip the ball out front, he's got all these weird moves."

He just stood out—like Michael Jordan does today. And everybody always watched in amazement. But once I played in college, the first pro player I really wanted to be like was James Worthy. I felt I was a clone to him, as far as being the first guy down the court on the break, and rebounding, and hittin' the inside lay-ups. Me and Bryne would be watching him on TV and Bryne would say, "You can *guard* him. He ain't that tough; *you* could be that tough." I used to say, "No way. I'm not that good. I'll *never* be that good." But inside I was thinking, "Well, he *don't* look that tough. Maybe I *could* be that good someday."

When the NBA draft finally happened, I watched it on TV at Bryne's with the whole family and about three TV camera crews from stations in Oklahoma. I thought: "Man, if I get picked I'll jump up and down for joy." I was a three-time All-America but nobody really knew about me—not until I won the MVP in Portsmouth and the scouts said, "Oh, this guy can play." But I didn't know if anyone believed it. So just hearing my name at all surprised the hell outta me. When they announced all the names in the first round and then they came back on TV for the second round and they said, "So-and-so, and So-and-so, and the Detroit Pistons pick Dennis Rodman," I said, "Oh my God, I'm goin' to Detroit! I can't believe that! Detroit? Why to Detroit?" But I didn't really care at that point; I was just so happy I got drafted.

Bryne said, "I told you you'd make it! Didn't I tell you?" And we all went crazy. But it didn't sink in until the Pistons called and said, "We need you here today for the press conference." I told the Riches, "God, they want me there *now!*" So I took a plane to Detroit and I was like: "God, I can't believe I'm goin' to Detroit. I'm goin' to the NBA." I was stunned, because I had an offer to play in Spain for about $300,000 a year for two years and my agent said, "You can play in Europe a couple of years and come back and try again." Even he didn't think I could make the cut in the NBA. But I kept tellin' him, "No, I wanna prove to everybody I'm good enough. I don't care how much Europe pays, I wanna go NBA."

When I was on the plane to Detroit, I was so hyper I just wanted to bust out and tell somebody. I never imagined that I would ever be on the same court with all these guys I watched on TV. And yet I didn't know too much about the Pistons, except that they had Isiah Thomas. And to be honest, I never even saw *him* play. I just heard he was a great player—the best point guard who ever played. Boy, I was so anxious to meet him and Coach Daly and Jack McCloskey, the general manager, and everybody at the press conference, I had a 103 temperature. I was so sick from my nerves, I flunked my EKG in the physical and they thought my heart was gonna explode right there. I knew I still had to make the team but I told myself: "I don't care what it takes, I'm gonna make it." All I kept thinkin' about was how everybody shot me down back home that "You can't do this" and "You can't do that," and how James Rich, and then my coaches always told me in college, "You work hard enough and good things will happen." I really wanted to do it for Bryne, too. I wanted to prove to him that I was a winner. I knew he wanted me to make the NBA real bad, so I wanted it, too, because I wanted to make him happy.

I remember my first pro game: I shot three airballs, missed six shots, got four rebounds—that was it. But in those first exhibition games I ended up averaging about 16 points and 10 rebounds. And I was down on the floor doin' all the little things that coaches like to see: diving for loose balls, working hard at both ends of the floor, getting position. Every time I made a basket I'd raise my hand and point my finger, just like I did in college, and everybody thought I was a joke. They said, "He's a hotdog. He's trying to show people up." I wasn't. How could I be a hotdog and only be scoring about six points a game? I wasn't even a star or anything. You never saw me go into a person's face and deliberately point my finger and start talkin' trash. Or point to the other team's bench to rub it in their faces.

But yet, my second year Jack McCloskey called me in and said, "I want you to stop that pointing stuff. It's bad for the league." I said, "That's bull. That's the way I play." He said, "If you do it, we'll fine you," and I said, "Then, you're gonna have to fine me. Because I'm not changin' the way I play." I didn't, either—and they never fined me. Then the fans started catching on that "He's not a hotdog. He's just pumped up. And he's boostin' the team up, too." So then Mc-Closkey came out and said, "You just gotta let Dennis Rodman go. He's something to watch when he waves his finger." All of a sudden, he decided it worked and he accepted it.

I think I'm the farthest thing from a hotdog. Sometimes, when I'm out there, I look around at the fans and the players, and I am awed. I think: "God, I can't believe I'm on this court with all these famous guys in front of all these people." There's times I don't realize what I'm doin' out there—like pointing my finger and pumping my arms as I run upcourt. It's like I'm in a daze. I once said that sometimes it feels like my body is out on the court but my mind is up in the stands controlling my body with a joystick. Like it's not really me out there; because some things I do I can't associate with me. I'll make these weird lay-ups I never made before, or I'll get impossible rebounds, or save the ball when it's already outta bounds, and I'll say, "I can't believe I did that. How did I do it?" Next day, people say, "That was a great play," and I go, "Really?" Because I don't know I *made* that play.

My goal when I got into the NBA was to stay there and prove to everybody that even though all those guys I grew up with failed, and all those guys who went to bigger colleges failed, I wouldn't fail. But nothing I do comes easy—it's all hard work for me. I think I work as hard as anybody in the league just to get a little bit. It's not natural for me; I have to work harder because I play so much defense, and rebound, and I have to stay motivated at both ends of the court with-out scoring a lot of points—even though I can score if I want to. Most of the time, I just don't want to; it's too boring; it might seem like I wasn't workin' hard enough or cuttin' corners. *Everyone* in the NBA can score. But not everyone can do what I do.

Back in 1990, the year I won my first Defensive Player of the Year award, I actually got to the point where I thought I could do anything, stop anybody, anytime, anywhere on the court. I started to really be-lieve that nobody could score on me at all. When somebody did, I got so pissed off I went, "Hey! How did he *do* that?" When I played that way, it motivated me to keep on doin' it. Because then people said, "Did you see that? That was Dennis Rodman. No one *else* does that."

Once you're in the NBA, you have proved that you as an individual can play with the best in the world. So now you wanna win a championship to prove that your *team* is the best in the world. And I can tell you, winning an NBA championship is like a dream come true. Whenever I'd get alone with Bryne I'd even say, "God, I still can't believe I'm even *in* the NBA. And here I got two *championships!*" I was so shocked when we won the first one, I was in a dream state for weeks. During the playoffs in '90, I was still so worried about doin' good and making an impression on everybody, my back started acting up and they had to hook me to a machine that ran heat and electricity through it. That's how scared and nervous I was. Then, right during the finals in L.A., my wife Annie put some trash in *People* magazine and the newspapers about us, and I was under so much stress I couldn't hardly play. (About the only thing that takes my mind off basketball today is my daughter. If things aren't right with her, like if I can't get to see her or be with her, for whatever reason, I can't concentrate on my game.)

So I did what my coaches taught me in college: I worked harder. Night before every playoff game, I stayed inside and watched a videotape of the guy I was guarding the next day. I studied all his moves and figured out what I had to do to stop him. The Pistons made separate tapes on everyone; I had one on Michael Jordan where the camera stayed on him the whole game. Bryne and I watched the tapes together and when Jordan made a real good move, I got all excited and said somethin' like, "Man, look at that move!" Like a *fan*. Because I'm like everyone else; I love to watch all these superstars play. But then I started thinking like a player again and I went "Man, I got to *guard* this guy! I better play way off him because he's so *quick!*"

People think I just go out there and run around like I'm in the playground, like I don't know what's goin' on. They're wrong. I think about everything I'm doin' out there. I even write little reminder notes in my playbooks, like: "REBOUND! WORK HARD!" Stuff Mr. Rich used to tell me, and Coach Reisman. I wanna do things the hard way and earn it. That comes from Coach Hedden and Coach Reisman. They did it the hard way. When I went to practice, Coach Reisman was always screaming at me, "You don't work hard enough!" Even though I was the star of the team he always got on my case more than anyone else's. He'd say, "If you want somethin', you have to work. You have to run and jump and rebound—hustle, hustle, hustle." I thought: "Yeah, right. What's this crazy guy talkin' about? I'm not gonna listen to this stuff."

But in my second year in the NBA it hit me one day: "Now I know what he was talkin' about. God, I'm doin' exactly what he said. It's really working." So I really put the effort forth in saying, "I'm gonna keep doin' it as long as I play basketball. I'm gonna work my butt off and no one is ever gonna say Dennis Rodman didn't work two hundred percent every night." So now, I work on everything in practice and then I do some more work at home. Like I'll visualize a great play I've made before and tell myself: "I'm gonna do it again tonight."

For example, I might visualize taking a charge in my mind and then I know I can get it in the game. Like that charge I took against Michael Jordan in Game Six of the '90 playoffs in Chicago. He had five fouls and I wanted to get him the sixth one, so I kept playin' him and playin' him, hoping to get the one extra step for the charge. Finally, I saw it in my mind so clear I told Isiah and Joe Dumars, "Let me have him, I got him. Don't give me any help, I got Jordan now." And he got the ball and I stepped in and they called the charge—just like I imagined it! That was one of the most exciting moments in my life. I said, "I *got* it!" And I cried, too, because I couldn't believe I did it. I *still* can't.

Winning two world championships was special, but I take more pride in my two Defensive Player of the Year awards. That's important to me because it's the role I play on the team and I wanted to prove to everybody that scoring isn't everything. In the NBA, everyone wants to score 20 or 30 points a game. But the reason the Pistons won back-to-back championships in '89 and '90 was because of our defense. And I played a big role in that. The Bulls depend on Michael Jordan so much to score, and the Pistons depend on me so much for defense. So I like to play that tough defense to fire the team up.

But I have pride in my ability to score on offense, too. I can shoot, but you wouldn't know it because they don't let me do it. My biggest disappointment in the '90–'91 season—even though we beat Portland for our second championship—was that I wasn't in the offense as much as I wanted to be that year. They didn't hardly pass me the ball in the paint the whole Chicago series—seven games. I mean, when we get on a fast break, three-on-two, I can make a lay-up. I took some three-pointers in the playoffs at the end just to let people know I wanted to be involved in the offense. I knew the Pistons depended on me for my defense, and I liked that, and I worked hard on it. But I also wanted to be an all-around player, because I know that's what I am.

One thing I enjoyed, especially in the championship years, was the Pistons being called "The Bad Boys." I liked our style of play: rough, tough, don't take anything from anybody. I always needed a little spark to get me going and that's how we played—we created sparks. But I don't think we were "dirty" like people said. It's just that we tried to frustrate people and take 'em out of their offense by intimidation. If we had to play rough to win, that's what we did. You have to play rough in the NBA; this isn't college ball—we're paid to win. And I don't think I'm a dirty player. I never go out to hurt someone on purpose. I just think I'm emotional—I get charged up and I play like it's gonna be my last game because it *might* be. You never know.

But the press likes to create controversy. Plus, you only see the rough-type plays on the sports shows so people think, "These guys are *dirty.*" But just watching TV or reading the papers doesn't tell you how things *really* are. Take the Scottie Pippen incident from the '92 playoffs. When everybody saw me shove him out-of-bounds on TV, they said, "Rodman's playing dirty again." I admit I was frustrated, because

Chicago was flat kickin' our butts. They finally toughened up and played Detroit's type of game and beat us at our own game. Now that it's over I can say I admire 'em for that. But when it was happening, I just wanted to beat 'em. We had already won two championships in a row and that was about to be spoiled, so we were frustrated. But it wasn't as big a deal as everybody made it out to be. It's a physical game and it was just a hard foul. Scottie knew that, too. It's part of playin' in the NBA. In fact, we always say, "No blood, no foul."

Meantime, it got all this blown-up press in Chicago, and it was like I killed the mayor. But there was a lot goin' on that people didn't know about. Like flagrant fouls the refs didn't call on the Bulls; and all the trash Pippen was talkin' at me the whole game. That's just NBA; it's the *championship*. And anyway, Pippen and me have been talkin' trash back and forth for years. It's no big deal. Even Jordan was talkin' trash that series—and that wasn't like him. Though I think it's more like him now. But he's not trying to knock anybody when he says somethin', he's just motivating himself to play at another level. Like when he scored on Gerald Wilkins this year in the Bulls' first playoff game against Cleveland, and then he turned to the crowd and said, "He can't guard me! He can't guard me!" You see that on TV and you think, "Boy, Jordan's a hotdog. He's trying to humiliate Gerald Wilkins. Why does he need to do that?"

But he wasn't trying to humiliate him. He was just showing Cleveland the *reality*. Because when they won their last regular-season game against the Bulls, they started boasting, "Well, we got the Bulls solved, we can beat 'em in the playoffs now." So I think Jordan took that as a personal challenge to show 'em, "You better think again. You didn't solve anything. We're still your biggest nightmare." That's what got him pumped up to win. And you *need* to get pumped up in these big games because it's a long season and you can't always play at your peak. So sometimes when you motivate yourself inside it can look like somethin' else outside—and people who don't play don't understand that. But the *players* understand it. They know the truth.

Like that shove I gave Pippen. A lot of the public thought I was a dirty player, and I was out to hurt him, and I pushed him down on purpose. But everyone knows that's not the kind of player I am. I *never* try to hurt someone in a game. So after I read all that and heard what people said, I decided to apologize to Pippen. I wanted everyone to know that I felt bad about it and I didn't try to hurt him, and that I was just frustrated at getting beat. But I learned that if people wanna think somethin' about you, they're gonna think it no matter what you do. Because after I wrote the apology, people said it sounded like someone else wrote it for me and I just read it because I had to. Or that it wasn't even my idea. It *was* my idea. Bryne Rich was with me when I talked to my agent about it, so he knows what happened. And I did write it myself. But I guess the team figured it would end up in the press anyway, so they revised it a little—because it was goin' out to the *world*. There's nothing wrong with that; it was still my apology. But people made such a big deal out of it because the press played it up big and TV kept showing the replay.

It's funny: in the first round of the playoffs against the Bullets one year, Darrell Walker spit in my face *twice*, and nobody said anything about that. He tried to kick me in the groin and nobody said anything about that. Nobody said anything when we played the Celtics from '88 to '90 and Larry Bird talked trash to me all the time, like, "Worm, you need to come to my basketball camp to learn how to shoot free throws." He talked all kinda noise at me that series, but it's part of the game. I talked trash right back. Sometimes it gets to you, sometimes it doesn't.

I can't hide my feelings like other players, so the press takes it and stretches it out. Like what I said about Larry Bird after Boston beat us in the seventh game of the conference finals, 117–114. I said, "Larry Bird is overrated in a lot of areas. I don't think he's the greatest player. He's way overrated. Why does he get so much publicity? Because he's white. You never hear about a black player bein' the greatest." It was somethin' I shouldn't've said and didn't mean, but the press blew it way up. That was my rookie year, and he was talking all that trash at me, and then he beat me and we lost in the last minute.

I was so disappointed in myself that I had let the team down, I just lost my cool and blamed *him*. But then the press went after me like I was a racist—which I'm not. I mean, that's gotta be the craziest thing you could think. It would've shocked people to know where I went right after that game. I drove thirteen straight hours to Oklahoma to be with the Riches—*white* folks—so how could I be racist? I was disappointed how people believed all that.

I was even more disappointed after losing to Chicago in the '92 playoffs. I don't think we played together as a team like we did the last few years. I don't think everybody was giving a hundred percent all the time. We had some run-ins behind the scenes that affected the team. Guys had contract problems through the year, and it had a lot to do with why our record wasn't as good as the last year. We won two titles in a row, and some guys were fighting over the money, wantin' better contracts than each other, like who can make the most money. I know some guys said, "If Rodman makes such-and-such, I think I should make more." And that's a big reason we didn't play together the way we did before.

Certain guys have big egos and they like to be on top. I don't need to always be on top, I just wanna play hard and win. I don't need to be the center of attraction, I just wanna be one of the guys that goes to work and does his job. I always put it in my mind that when I'm done with this game, no one is gonna remember me anyway. So I just take that frame of mind and say: "I'm goin' to work and do my job and then get outta here." I won't miss the limelight at all.

I wouldn't wanna live like this the rest of my life—bein' rich and famous. I'd rather have to work harder for what I get in order to survive; I think that's more exciting than just havin' it there right in front of you. The millions of dollars I make don't make *me*. Because when I'm on the floor, I don't think about the money. I don't think about anything but makin' people happy and winning. And it doesn't help when you have problems, either. Like when I had motivation problems in '90 and '91. One game in '90, I was sitting in my house watchin' TV with my daughter and I just didn't wanna go play the game against San Antonio. There wasn't anything wrong with me, I just felt like I didn't wanna go to work that day. My wife said, "You have a game, don't you?" And I said, "I might just stay here and paint the house." And to this day, I don't know what came over me. I just get in those moods sometimes. I lose my drive to play, my desire to be out on a basketball court.

At the last minute, I said, "I better go." I didn't have any desire to play, but I went, and I got there just as the game started and I told Coach Daly, "I don't really wanna play." So I sat. After the game, Coach Daly asked me, "What's wrong with you? Are you having personal problems?" I said, "Well, I just don't know if I should play anymore." He said, "You only go around one time. Just block out all the other stuff and do what you do best. And when you look back on it, you'll really appreciate all the things you've accomplished." I said, "Yeah, but is it all worth it? I could be workin' in Dallas for my own excavation company right now, and that might be more challenging than basketball now. And I could spend more time with my little daughter. I could keep on playin' here but it comes to a dead end. Boom, one day it's over." But I respected everything he said and decided to go back and finish the season.

I was going through a lot of turmoil about my marriage and bein' with my daughter and whether basketball was enough for me. All season I kept feeling like, "Should I keep playin' basketball? This is pretty much the same old thing." And I was goin' great, too. I could've had 30 rebounds a game if I wanted to. There was one game against Charlotte I knew I could've had 40 rebounds, easy. I had 27 with nine minutes to go and I wanted to get 40, but Coach Daly took me out because we were winning and he didn't wanna burn me out. To be honest, I think if I could have everything goin' right for me in my personal life, I might break every rebound record there is.

But there's always a part of every season where I start to feel like things are coming too easy. Like I would only play thirty minutes and

I'd have 28 rebounds and then my desire would leave me. I'd be throwing off 20 rebounds a night, or 23, 25. And people got so accustomed to me getting 20 every game that when I'd get 16: "Oh, sixteen, somethin's wrong with him." I don't wanna be held to any standard. That's why I shake things up. Those things are no accidents. I like to keep people guessing: "What's with with that guy? How is Rodman? Is he down-to-earth, or what's with him?" And people have to say, "I don't know." If they believe what they read, they think I'm the mad scientist around here, they think, "He's crazy." But I'm not. I'm just like anyone else; I'm just in the public eye and that's when everyone wants somethin' from you.

As to whether Dennis Rodman took a gun and tried to commit suicide at the Palace in Auburn Hills in 1993, that was total bull. I was down about my wife not letting me see my daughter after our divorce, and I told a friend of mine that I was real down, and then I went to the gym to work out at five in the morning. I do that a lot and I work out and come back and go to sleep. It helps me—I don't like to sleep sometimes, and then if I sit home and look at the walls I have to go do somethin' to throw off my feelings.

I had a rifle with me that night—I have two .22s and I like to shoot across the lake behind my house to let off steam. This time I left my friend a note that said I was really feeling bad, and he panicked and called the police because I had the guns. So I was in the parking lot of the Palace, listening to music in my pickup at five in the morning with the gun beside me on the seat, and the police came over and said, "We just got word that you were trying to kill yourself." I figured they looked in the parking lot because they'd seen me there before, but it turned out they had every county in the State of Michigan out looking for my truck—even the Highway Patrol. It wasn't what they thought; I was just chilling out, nothing more than that.

I have never really known how good I am. I'm not trying to understand the things I do; I just keep doin' 'em and things keep falling into place.

I don't voice my opinions or feelings too much. I'm quiet; I like being in the background. Whatever people say about me doesn't matter. For three years at college, I did everything people wanted me to do and now I live mostly by my own rules because I was *there* already. I told myself: "I'll pay my dues and do whatever they want me to do. But when that's over, I'm doin' what *I* wanna do."

If you understand that about me, then you understand Dennis Rodman pretty good.

A Cup

in the Kiln

PAT RICH: One of the first art classes I took at Southeastern was a figure-drawing course.

We had models posing in leotards so we could draw their bodies, and my art teacher came around to us one by one and encouraged everybody, "You're doin' fine." When he looked at my drawing he complimented it, at first, but then he saw something was wrong. For some reason, the model was posing with her hand raised—like she was wavin' at us—and I ended up drawing her hand so it was wavin' *backwards*. So my teacher told me I needed to turn it around. It was embarrassing, but we laughed at it because we both knew it was the first picture I ever drew.

Many years after Dennis had come to stay with us and then left for the pros, I got to remembering those days before we met, and I thought: "You know, maybe that first picture I drew with the hand facing backwards was really a message to me that I needed to start turnin' my values around, too. Especially about black people." Because that's exactly what happened. And in a lot of ways, even though he still don't know it, Dennis Rodman was my teacher on that.

■   ■   ■

I'm a Christian woman; I believe everything happens for a purpose. And I believe God had a purpose when he sent us Worm. He
knew that Bryne was hurtin', and our family was hurtin', and Worm
was hurtin'. And He knew Bryne wanted a brother and Worm wanted
a brother. So he sent Dennis to our house to make us laugh again and
to help Bryne grow and help himself grow and help us grow, too.
Spiritually, I believed that from the start and I still believe it today.
Because look at how everything turned out.

Sometimes, it seems almost magical. After Dennis was on the
Pistons, for example, Bryne spent a year at Tarleton State University
in Texas. He made the basketball team and ended up playing for Lonn
Reisman in his first head coaching job. And of course, Dennis showed
up to watch Bryne play whenever he could, and he stuck around and
helped the coach impress some recruits. Coach Reisman used to always
tell us, "Dennis Rodman made me a helluva good coach, didn't he?"
The story kept goin': the same two years when Dennis's team won
back-to-back NBA championships, Bryne's team at Tarleton State
won conference championships, too. So here they were, coming back
for the summer to our home where they had all their struggles, and
they were both champions, and both wearin' championship rings too
big for their fingers, and both drivin' identical GT Mustangs side-by-
side all around town, proud and happy as they could ever be.

And Dennis has had an amazing pro career ever since. Out of
nothing came so much success. He never even dreamed of playin' pro
and yet he's already been called the greatest rebounder of all time. He
helped the Pistons to win two NBA championships; he was named
Defensive Player of the Year twice; and he led the NBA in rebounding
the last two years. It's all so overwhelming, he still tells us, "I can't
believe all this happened. I don't feel like anyone special. I feel like
I'm just the same old me." But he's not; he's gettin' shined and polished
more into a diamond every day. And he and Bryne just keep on growin'
as people and friends.

I think the most touching example happened a few years ago,
when Dennis received his first NBA Defensive Player of the Year

award, and got so emotional he couldn't hardly speak. He started cryin'
and then he finally announced, "If it hadn't been for Bryne Rich, I
wouldn't be here today." And there was Bryne in the corner, embarrassed and cryin' right along with Worm. And Dennis told us the same
thing when Southeastern retired his basketball jersey and hung it on
the wall beside those others. Boy, that was another big emotional
moment for him . . . *and* for Bryne.

And now the biggest irony of all: eleven years ago Worm came
into Bryne's life at the time of his greatest need and helped him get
back to being himself and enjoying his life again. Then comes 1993,
and it's Worm's toughest year ever, emotionally. Because he's had to
be separated so much from his daughter, and then losing another father
figure in Coach Daly when he took the New Jersey Nets job, and also
his friend John Salley when he went to play in Miami—he had no
one he really trusted to talk to. So what does Bryne do? He leaves a
real good job workin' for Earl Campbell in Texas and he moves to
Detroit to live with Dennis and help him with *his* life. Sort of returning
the favor.

Back around March, Bryne got interviewed for a *New York News-
day* story, and he told the reporter, "Dennis was there for me when I
needed him. I wanted to be there for him. I had to come here and
take care of him." And he *has* helped; Dennis said if it wasn't for Bryne
bein' with him this year, he might not have made it through the season
with his sanity. So the story just keeps goin' on and on.

If I look at it real close, I realize it was really me who had the most to
learn from Worm. Because I had all these cobwebs about things from
the way I was raised. He helped me clear away the cobwebs by teaching
me to stand up on my own two feet and think more for myself and
feel the way I want to feel about somethin', not just the way I was
taught to feel. It was like he was saying "You don't have to agree with
someone, even if it's your mom and dad, if they say things that you
don't think are right. You can go find out for yourself." And that's

somethin' I've learned to do a lot more than before. I used to think I was one of the little ducks and that I had to walk like everyone else, but now I'm more independent.

The most important lesson I've learned is the difference between bein' ignorant about somethin' and bein' prejudiced. Like, you can be ignorant about black people but not necessarily be prejudiced. Because that's the way I was: I have never hated another person based on the color of their skin, or their religion, or who their parents were, or anything like that. My problem was just that I didn't know better. As an adult, I had no real-life experience with black people at all. And the only thing I knew about 'em as a child was what my parents taught me.

Now, since I was around blacks like Chester and Reesa, I should've known for myself what kind of people they were. But I was only a kid; I had all kinds of funny notions floatin' around in my head that somebody else put there. And a lot of it was negative, like, "Stay away from blacks. They're not like us." No one ever said, "Hey, so what? People from California are different from us, too. It doesn't mean a thing!" That's because where I grew up, nobody ever said, "What do we really know about blacks anyway? Maybe we shouldn't be judging anyone else until we clean up our own house first." Including me, with all my cobwebs.

Look at how I had to get educated about "the N-word." Back then, whenever I said that word it was through ignorance. I didn't even know what I was sayin'—it didn't mean to me what it meant to a black person. It was just a word I'd always heard and never thought about. I could've been sayin' "Christian" or "Protestant." I had no idea how that word affected a black person until Dennis explained it to me. And even then I had to get the dictionary out and look it up to see what it meant. It took me a while to realize I didn't need a dictionary, because Dennis was there. Having him in my home was like goin' to college. I guess you could say I went to Worm University. I got my master's degree in bein' a better person, I can tell you that. But hey, I'm still workin' on my Ph.D.

Because of Dennis Rodman, I've been able to become more sensitive to black people in ways I never would've known about. For example, one day a few years after he turned pro, I was working as a youth counselor in Durant. And we had this black girl named Jenny working for us, and we got along fine. Well, on my birthday James sent flowers to me at the office, and everybody was back in the kitchen area, so I took the flowers back there. I said to another lady, "Melissa, can you tell me what the name of this flower is?" And she said, "It looks like a mum to me." And I looked at another flower and said, "I know what this one is. This one's a nigger toe." And I looked over to this guy we worked with who always kidded us about sayin' things like that, and I thought he would start laughing and teasing me. But he was making faces because Jenny was sittin' right there.

So I hid behind those flowers and started walkin' backwards out of the room because I was so embarrassed and ashamed. And then I set the flowers down and I said, "Oh no. Jenny, I am so sorry. I did not mean anything by that. I just said it to be funny because Carlton's always teasing us about things like that and I thought he would laugh." She knew me well enough to know it wasn't a slur. But I felt so terrible I went on and on defending myself. I said, "You know, I had Dennis Rodman at my house for three years. So you know I didn't mean anything by that." And she did, but I was squirming anyway. It just showed me how hard it is to throw off language I learned as a kid that I considered normal. You have to almost relearn how to think about those things until they become a part of you. Which is the way I am now.

I can measure it in my daily life, even though I still live in Bokchito. For years now I've been working in Durant as a supervisor at a youth detention center. My job is to supervise these kids who've commited felonies while they're waiting on their court dates. Sometimes, social workers ask me about placements—like to foster homes or group homes or maybe a stricter environment a step short of prison—because they've learned to respect the way I communicate with these kids. One reason is because I feel real compassion for them in my heart and

I want to help them straighten out their lives. Another is because knowing Dennis Rodman has helped me reach more of these kids so I *can* help them with their lives. Especially the black kids that I never could've reached before.

A lot of the black kids have been deprived in life and I'm sensitive to that now in different ways. Like I'll try to cut their hair to get them to realize I care about 'em as people. I learned this by cutting Dennis's hair and talking to him and laughing with him and treating him like a human being. But these kids don't believe a white person would know how, so I say, "Just try me. I used to cut Dennis Rodman's hair." And I show them Dennis's picture on the wall and they recognize him and they get all excited. They say, "Can you put those little parts in it like he has?" I say, "Hey, I can do it all. There's nothin' I don't know about black people's hair." So I shave their hair and put little diagonal parts down the side, if they want, and they go out of there feelin' like a million dollars. And they stop giving me a hard time and start bein' more receptive.

I treat them that way because I saw how hurt Dennis was a lot of times when people threw their slurs at him, and even the ways I hurt him myself by bein' ignorant. My motto became: "I will not be ignorant anymore. Everyone's the same. We're all human beings." We had this fifteen-year-old black kid named Robert in there one time and I had to drop him a level in the ratings for his behavior, and he claimed I did it because he was black. Well, if this had been before I knew Worm, I'd've probably gotten really ticked off. But I didn't; I realized he'd probably heard this stuff all his life and maybe been treated that way by a lot of whites. So I said, "Robert, it really hurts me that you think that. Do you see that picture on the wall?" And I showed him Dennis's picture and said, "I was like that young man's foster mom." And I told a little bit of the story and then I said, "Just to show you that you're wrong and I'm not favoring whites over blacks, I'm gonna give you your level back. So what do you think *now?*" He thanked me and looked at that picture again and looked back at me and said, "I actually met a white person that ain't prejudiced!" He admitted he'd been wrong and said I'd just helped him to look at white people a little differently. I got all teary-eyed over that.

So I am actually passing on what I learned all the time at work. I use Dennis's picture every time they start saying they're bein' treated unfair just because they're black. I say, "I never treated him unfair. Why would I treat you like that?" And they start feeling like: "Hey, Dennis Rodman stayed at her house! The basketball player! She must be okay." They will look at that picture and think: "He was in trouble once and he made somethin' out of his life." And they even ask me if they can come and live with me because they think we can turn them pro, too. I've been hit up for that by about fifty kids the last five years.

One night when I'd first started working at the detention center, I was getting ready to leave for the night when this one black kid, Willie—he was a big 6-4 kid who played basketball real well—called out to me, "My name is Willie *Rich!*" I couldn't believe it; it reminded me so much of when Worm called himself Dennis Rich. So I came home and I was all emotional and I said, "James, could we possibly take this boy into our home like we did Dennis?" And he said "No! One experience like that is enough!" And we laughed about it then, but that kid was like so many of 'em over there. Color isn't the issue; it's having someone to love them and show them care and support.

I don't tell those kids about the times I failed Dennis, of course, because I overcame that and I'm not that way anymore. I don't think I'm one bit better than anyone else, white or black, and they can sense that. They look at his picture and they consider me the good Christian woman I am now. Because I don't look at color, I look at the heart. And when I counsel with them, I think of Dennis. I say, "All you need is a goal in life that you want to reach. You get your priorities straight and go for your goal and the color of your skin won't matter. You can't let anyone intimidate you and call you names and defeat your purpose. You have to be strong-minded, like Dennis Rodman was, and strong-willed and you can overcome all that. You just remember who you are and what you stand for and what you want out of life."

And I teach them to have their own self-identity rather than what someone else says about them: "Just because some ignorant person calls you a name, that doesn't mean you have to listen. You are a human being with a heart and soul like everyone else on God's earth, and you can reach for your dreams and fulfill your purpose in life, if you try." And that is definitely somethin' I learned from Dennis, and I have probably touched a lot of lives with that at the detention center.

Like I say, I have grown, I'm a better person for knowing Dennis Rodman. He forced me to grow as a person, so I found out more about who I am and what I stand for. I feel the need to help other people more than ever before. But I still have a long way to go—I know that. The truth is, you don't know how good a Christian you are until you're tested in real life. I can stay home in Bokchito and go to church on Sunday, but then when I'm tested and someone gets right in my face and says all these things to me about, "Well, you shouldn't use that word. Don't you know what that means?" I can't just sit there and pretend I'm the good little Christian anymore. I mean, I was put to the test and, in some ways, I failed. And I realized: "Hey, I am just not quite the person I thought I was. I'm not that purely good little Christian woman who goes to church every week and prays and comes back home and then does everything right. I'm in the *real* world now. I was so upset about that, I cussed out loud and used God's name in vain—things Christians aren't supposed to do. And I scolded myself: "You're not as strong as you thought." And, boy, that opened my eyes to who I really was, and it told me I needed to change my thinking.

That's what Dennis did for me; it took *him* to cause me to start really digging deep into my problem. I can remember when this business of interracial dating was causing me all kinds of trouble, I finally said: "I've gotta find out the truth." I never told this to anyone but I went and asked my minister if there were scriptures in the Bible that condoned racial marriage, and if it was wrong to marry a black, and if people in the Bible days married blacks. He said there was nothing pertaining to that in the scriptures, except that Moses might've married an Ethiopian. He said, "But I do know it causes other people pain.

As good Christians, we should be careful not to inflict pain on others. And we must realize that we don't have the right to judge others just because they're different from us."

That helped me a lot. I decided that I should let each person do what they feel is right and let God be the judge. I told myself: "Don't try to judge it—you are not God. You just take care of your own business. Whatever Worm wants to do, that's his business. God can be the judge, not you." And ever since then, I've stayed out of the judging business.

The best part of that is instead of feeling angry and bitter toward the people that gossiped about me and made my life miserable when Dennis was at my home, I can see the beauty in them again. I realized that you have to consider *their* background and what *their* lives have been like to know why they said what they did. I can see both sides of the story now, I can be objective about it. I realized people were being truly who they were and, through stupidity or ignorance, they didn't know any other way to be. I learned not only how to deal with prejudiced, narrow-minded people, but also that you have to over-look the hurt and try to help *them* become better people, too. That's what life is all about, isn't it? Reaching out to others and trying to help them?

There's a scripture that says, "God chastizes those He loves." Meaning He molds you into what He wants you to be. And I think He's molding me, too. I compare myself to the china cup that you have to keep on baking to smooth out all its imperfections. Well, I really think God's watching what's goin' on with me and He's saying, "*That* cup's getting real close. But, you know what? I think it still needs a little more baking."

Index